# Tying the Autocrat's Hands
## *The Rise of the Rule of Law in China*

Under what conditions would authoritarian rulers be interested in the rule of law? What type of rule of law exists in authoritarian regimes? How do authoritarian rulers promote the rule of law without threatening their grip on power? *Tying the Autocrat's Hands* answers these questions by examining legal reforms in China. Yuhua Wang develops a demand-side theory arguing that authoritarian rulers will respect the rule of law when they need the cooperation of organized interest groups that control valuable and mobile assets but are not politically connected. He also defines the rule of law that exists in authoritarian regimes as a partial form of the rule of law, in which judicial fairness is respected in the commercial realm but not in the political realm. *Tying the Autocrat's Hands* demonstrates that the rule of law is better enforced in regions with a large number of foreign investors but less so in regions heavily invested in by Chinese investors.

YUHUA WANG is an assistant professor of political science at the University of Pennsylvania. His articles have appeared in the *China Journal*, the *China Review*, the *China Quarterly*, *Communist and Post-Communist Studies*, the *Journal of Peking University* (Beijing Daxue Xuebao), and *Studies in Comparative International Development*. He is a frequent commentator on political developments in China and has been featured in the *New York Times*, *Reuters*, and *South China Morning Post*, as well as on CNN and DR (the Danish Broadcasting Corporation).

# Cambridge Studies in Comparative Politics

*(continued after Index)*

# Tying the Autocrat's Hands

## *The Rise of the Rule of Law in China*

YUHUA WANG

*University of Pennsylvania*

CAMBRIDGE
UNIVERSITY PRESS

# CAMBRIDGE
## UNIVERSITY PRESS

32 Avenue of the Americas, New York NY 10013-2473, USA

Cambridge University Press is part of the University of Cambridge.

It furthers the University's mission by disseminating knowledge in the pursuit of
education, learning and research at the highest international levels of excellence.

www.cambridge.org
Information on this title: www.cambridge.org/9781107417748

First published 2015
First paperback edition 2016

*A catalogue record for this publication is available from the British Library*

*Library of Congress Cataloguing in Publication data*
Wang, Yuhua, 1981–
Tying the autocrat's hands : the rise of the rule of law in China / Yuhua Wang.
    pages   cm
Includes bibliographical references and index.
ISBN 978-1-107-07174-2 (Hardback)   1. China–Politics and government–1976–2002.
2. China–Politics and government–2002–   3. Authoritarianism–China.   4. Political corruption–
China.   5. Rule of law–China.   I. Title.
JQ1510.W368 2014
340′.11–dc23   2014020707

ISBN 978-1-107-07174-2 Hardback
ISBN 978-1-107-41774-8 Paperback

*For my parents, Wang Yanli and Yin Shulan*

# Contents

# Figures

# Tables

# Acknowledgments

Writing a book is like embarking on a long journey; I cannot imagine arriving at the destination without the companionship of family, friends, teachers, and colleagues. Without them, the journey would have been a lonely one.

First and foremost, I want to thank the members of my dissertation committee at the University of Michigan: Mary Gallagher, Ken Lieberthal, Bill Clark, Rob Franzese, and Nico Howson. Their consistent support, encouragement, and scrutiny have transformed a simple idea of mine into a dissertation, and now a book.

I would not have started an academic career if I had not met Shen Mingming in my sophomore year at Peking University. Shen *laoshi* showed me how fun political science could be, and he taught me to use scientific methods to generate interesting observations about the real world.

It would be shameful to claim that this is my work alone, as many people have contributed ideas. John Ferejohn, Susan Whiting, and Bruce Dickson read the whole manuscript and provided constructive comments. Avery Goldstein, Ed Mansfield, Jacques deLisle, Rogers Smith, Ian Lustick, Brendan O'Leary, Rudy Sil, Devesh Kapur, Julia Lynch, Tulia Falleti, Matt Levendusky, Jeff Green, Julia Gray, Alex Weisiger, Marc Meredith, Daniel Gillion, Guy Grossman, Eileen Doherty-Sil, Guobin Yang, Seung-Youn Oh, Neysun Mahboubi, Wang Xixin, Lin Yan, Tom Ginsburg, Randy Peerenboom, Susan Shirk, Kevin O'Brien, Pierre Landry, Melanie Manion, Andy Mertha, Carl Minzner, Danie Stockmann, Mayling Birney, and Yuen Yuen Ang offered helpful suggestions at various stages of the project.

My teachers and friends at the University of Michigan provided the most academically stimulating environment you can imagine for a graduate student, especially Ron Inglehart, Chuck Shipan, Anna Grzymala-Busse, Nancy Burns, Allen Hicken, Rob Mickey, Gina Brandolino, Kharis Templeman, Huong Trieu, Spencer Piston, Cassie Grafström, and Dominic Nardi. Over the last three years, I have also benefited enormously from the friendly intellectual community at the University of Pennsylvania. My colleagues in the Political Science Department, the Center for the Study of Contemporary China, and the Center for East Asian Studies have given me a cheerful place to work.

The research is based on a yearlong fieldwork. My friends and *tongxue* helped me arrange visits and interviews and entertained me with the best local wine and food. I especially want to thank Cheng Xiao, Mu Zhiping, Deng Xuan, Zhang Jiabing, Qian Yong, Xiong Lei, Li Jiangtao, Yu Jing, Hou Jingli, Song Jing, and Teng Shihua.

Special thanks are due to Shen Mingming, Yang Ming, Pierre Landry, Tang Wenfang, Tong Yanqi, Yan Jie, Chai Jingjing, and my colleagues at the Research Center for Contemporary China at Peking University for designing and implementing the survey "Institutionalization of Legal Reforms in China." And I want to thank Colin Lixin Xu for sharing the World Bank survey data.

For financial support I am grateful to the Center for Chinese Studies and the Department of Political Science at the University of Michigan, the National Science Foundation (SES-0921614), and the Department of Political Science at the University of Pennsylvania.

At Cambridge University Press, I would like to extend my sincere thanks to Robert Dreesen for his enthusiastic support of the project, three anonymous reviewers for providing constructive reviews, and Liz Janetschek for editorial assistance.

My many thanks to Margaret Levi for her encouraging comments on the manuscript and including my work in the prestigious Cambridge Studies in Comparative Politics series.

Finally, and above all, I am indebted to my family. I have spent much more time in my office than at home. My wife, Boyang Chai, and my daughter, Yushi Wang, have given me much-needed distraction and relaxation after work. My parents, Wang Yanli and Yin Shulan, deserve my deepest apologies and appreciation. As the only child of the family, I should have spent more time with them over the past eight years. Their support and sacrifice make everything possible. This book is dedicated to them.

I

# Introduction

Before the law sits a gatekeeper.

Franz Kafka

In 1982, six years after the turmoil of the Mao era, the Chinese Communist Party (CCP), under the leadership of Deng Xiaoping, amended the radical 1978 constitution and embraced the basic principles of the rule of law: "No organization or individual may enjoy the privilege of being above the Constitution and the law."[1] Fifteen years later, in his report to the Fifteenth Party Congress, Deng's successor, Jiang Zemin, declared that "governing the country according to law and making it a socialist country ruled by law" was the state's "basic strategy."[2]

Chinese leaders are not unique among authoritarian rulers in welcoming the rule of law. On September 22, 1972, after seizing control of the government, Philippine dictator Ferdinand Marcos proclaimed martial law, shut down the mass media, and closed all schools and universities. However, in a speech delivered on nationwide radio and television a day later, Marcos said, "The judiciary shall continue to function," and he stated that his new government would have effective "checks and balances" that would be enforced by the Supreme Court in a new framework of "constitutional authoritarianism" (Carmen 1973). Anwar Sadat, an Egyptian ruler, explicitly pinned his regime's

[1] Constitution of the People's Republic of China (1982), Article 5.
[2] "Jiang Zemin's Report at the 15th National Congress of the Communist Party of China," available at http://www.fas.org/news/china/1997/970912-prc.htm, accessed June 4, 2013.

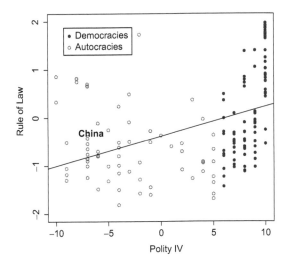

FIGURE 1.1 The Rule of Law versus Democracy (2008)
*Sources*: Kaufmann, Kraay, and Mastruzzi (2009) and Marshall and Jaggers (2009).

legitimacy to the rule of law and used rule-of-law rhetoric hundreds of times throughout his eleven years at the head of Egypt's authoritarian state (Moustafa 2007). Vladimir Putin, the all-powerful Russian leader, stepped down from his role as president in 2008 to become prime minister to adhere to the term limits stipulated in Russia's constitution. The list of authoritarian regimes embracing the rule of law continues. Consider Augusto Pinochet's Chile (1973–90), Lee Kuan Yew's Singapore (1959–90), Mohammad Reza Pahlavi's Iran (1941–79), and Chiang Ching-kuo's Taiwan (1978–88).

Figure 1.1 shows a scatterplot of 157 countries' rule-of-law scores (Kaufmann, Kraay, and Mastruzzi 2009) and their *Polity* scores, which measure the degree of democracy in 2008. There is clearly no linear relationship between the measures of rule of law and democracy. While democracies tend to have stronger rule of law, there is a large variation in the rule of law among authoritarian regimes.

This book addresses the following puzzles: Under what conditions would authoritarian rulers be interested in the rule of law? What type of rule of law exists in authoritarian regimes? How do authoritarian rulers promote the rule of law without threatening their grip on power?

There has been a long-standing presumption among many social scientists that authoritarian rulers who come to power by force and have unconstrained political power refuse to be ruled by the law. The Washington Consensus in the 1990s also believed that democracy, markets, and the rule of law would all develop in unison. However, empirical studies on the correlation between democracy and the rule of law are inconclusive. While some scholars have indeed found that democracies are more likely to support the rule of law (Leblang 1996, 22; Rigobon and Rodrik 2005), others have found no relationship. Barro (2000) argues that the rule of law occurs in both democracies and dictatorships.

I answer the aforementioned questions by examining legal reforms in China. The history of the People's Republic of China (PRC) reflects a transformation from a rule-of-man regime to a *partial* rule-of-law regime. Mao Zedong turned the judicial system into a tool for consolidating socialism after establishing the PRC in 1949. The new regime used courts to penalize counterrevolutionaries who were associated with the previous Kuomintang regime, to sentence landlords who were deprived of property and rights in the land reforms, and (during the "Anti-Rightist Campaign") to legitimize the punishment of "rightists" who criticized the party and the government. The *rule of man* in China reached its peak during the Great Proletarian Cultural Revolution, in which Mao's own words were held to be superior to any laws. The whole legal system was almost completely abolished during the Cultural Revolution, except that some courts still functioned to adjudicate cases involving "class enemies." Law schools were shut down, bar examinations terminated, and lawyers sent to the countryside.

In the late 1970s China resumed its state-building process, of which the institutionalization of a formal legal system was a crucial component. The post-Mao leadership believed that installing a reliable legal system in which there are constitutional checks on individual power would prevent political disasters such as the Cultural Revolution from happening again. More systematic legal reforms, in which building a professional, efficient, and fair legal system was the essential goal, started in the 1990s as market reforms deepened.

Despite the national progress, the development of the rule of law has been quite uneven across the country. Figure 1.2 graphs a measure of judicial corruption against per capita gross domestic product (GDP) in 102 Chinese counties. While wealthy counties have a lower level of judicial corruption, there is large variation among underdeveloped counties. This variation cannot be explained simply by modernization theory, which posits that economic development brings improved institutional performance. The variation is even more puzzling, given that China is a unitary state in which institutions are identical across the country.

My overarching argument for these cross-national and subnational outcomes is that authoritarian rulers will respect the rule of law when they need the cooperation of *organized* interest groups that control *valuable* and *mobile* assets but are *not politically connected.*

I define the rule of law that exists in authoritarian regimes as a *partial* form of the rule of law in which judicial fairness is usually respected in the commercial realm but not in the political realm. Authoritarian rulers have no interest in implementing the rule of law in full, which would imply both fairness and efficiency; most authoritarian rulers are unwilling to respect judicial fairness,

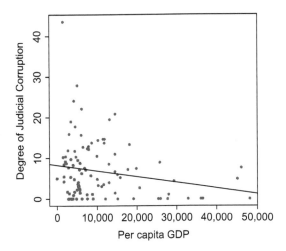

FIGURE 1.2 Judicial Corruption across Chinese Counties in 2003
*Source:* ILRC 2003.[3]

especially when they are in front of the court themselves. Authoritarian rulers therefore face a dilemma. On the one hand, they must respect the rule of law to make a credible commitment to investors, whose assets are urgently needed; on the other hand, a strong judiciary might open new avenues for political activists to challenge the state. The solution to this dilemma is for authoritarian rulers to build the rule of law in a partial form: they sequence the legal reforms such that they "tie their hands" in commercial cases yet extend their discretionary power in the political realm. Through increasing costs, raising the bar, manipulating the procedure, lowering the benefits, and distorting the law, authoritarian rulers discourage citizens from utilizing the judiciary to sue the government.

## A DEMAND-SIDE THEORY OF AUTHORITARIAN RULE OF LAW

Existing literature on the rule of law has focused on the *supply side*.[4] Realizing that the judiciary has neither the power of the purse nor the ability to take up arms, many argue that the empowerment of the judiciary must come from the delegation of powerful politicians. Some suggest that legislators have an interest in creating an independent judiciary that can enforce the deals struck by enacting legislatures, thereby increasing the value of campaign contributions that legislators can extract from contributors on whose behalf they made those

---

[3] The Institutionalization of Legal Reforms in China (ILRC) survey is described in Chapter 6.
[4] For a good review of the literature, please see Helmke and Rosenbluth (2009).

deals (Landes and Posner 1975). Some point to politicians' desire to avoid blame for unpopular policies (Graber 1993; Salzberger 1993; Whittington 2009). McCubbins and Schwartz (1984) suggest that an independent judiciary can help the legislature encourage executive agencies to adhere to legislative intent. Some contend that an incumbent legislative majority might willingly transfer some of its power to the judiciary as political insurance against being dominated by a future majority (Ramseyer and Rasmusen 1997; Finkel 2008).

Supply-side theories, while useful in explaining the rule of law in democracies, fall short in autocratic settings. Since politicians can delegate power to the judiciary under certain conditions, they can also withdraw their support under other conditions. This *time inconsistency* problem is particularly acute in authoritarian regimes, where the rulers are not bound by strong rules.

I offer a *demand-side* theory of the authoritarian rule of law. According to this theory, interest groups are constituencies of the rule of law. The theory is based on the premise that authoritarian rulers cannot solely rely on force to stay in power; they need cooperation as well – especially from interest groups that control valuable assets. Authoritarian regimes, like all states, need to collect revenues from their citizens in the form of either tax or rents. Authoritarian rulers consume part of the revenues themselves, distribute some to their loyalists, and spend the rest on providing public goods to maintain a minimum level of public support. Without adequate revenues, authoritarian rulers are unable to stay in power, satisfy their supporters (whose loyalty can be bought by a challenger), or pacify the masses (whose grievances might escalate into a fatal revolt). Therefore, to survive, authoritarian rulers need the cooperation of asset holders, whose valuable assets can be taxed or confiscated.

The exchange between the ruler and asset holders, however, is a bargaining process. Asset holders exchange their assets for policies. By granting asset holders' preferred policies, the ruler can secure their compliance. Otherwise, asset holders can hide, destroy, or move their assets. In this bargaining process, the ruler's *power* is determined by how urgently she needs the assets. In situations in which revenues are necessary for the ruler's survival – such as during war, crises of legitimacy, and the consolidation of power – the ruler is willing to sacrifice some of her benefits to seek the cooperation of asset holders. In addition, the ruler's *preference* in the bargain is determined by the costs of policies. Some policies, such as building a fair and efficient legal system, are costly for the ruler, because the ruler has to treat everyone equally, which means taking privileges away from the politically connected. This will decrease the amount of rent that the ruler can extract from privileged social groups.

On the other side of the bargain, asset holders' *power* is determined by how organized they are, and by the value and mobility of their assets. Organized interest groups have stronger bargaining power than unorganized groups. Asset holders can organize themselves via associations, clubs, or unions. A centralized hierarchy can help them overcome collective action problems. Furthermore, asset holders with large assets that can significantly contribute to the ruler's revenues have more power than those with few assets. Therefore, economic elites who control abundant wealth have a stronger voice at the bargaining table than the "have-nots." Finally, the mobility of assets gives asset holders more leverage vis-à-vis the ruler. Interest groups with mobile assets can credibly threaten to exit by moving their assets away from the ruler's jurisdiction. Mobile assets also make it easier for asset holders to hide from taxation or confiscation. In summary, organization and valuable and mobile assets empower interest groups by enabling them to withdraw (or threaten to withdraw) urgently needed cooperation from the ruler.

Asset holders' policy *preference* is a function of their existing or potential political connections with the ruler. Each asset holder as an individual would naturally prefer privilege to a level playing field, because the former grants one a monopolistic position in the market where rent can be generated, whereas everyone must compete fairly in the latter. However, privilege, by definition, cannot be granted to everyone. Interest groups must compete for it. In the competition for privileges, some are disadvantaged by their skills, prior political connections, and ability to build new connections. Therefore the advantaged will hold on to their privileges, while the disadvantaged will seek a level playing field. Politically connected groups and individuals do not favor the rule of law, which creates a level playing field for all asset holders. Interest groups with political connections seek to maintain their privileges, whereas those who are not politically connected will advocate the rule of law, under which everyone is treated equally. A strong judiciary protects contract and property rights, makes dispute resolution predictable, and speeds up the litigation process. The privileged interest groups will block the leveling of the playing field to eliminate competition, whereas the disadvantaged groups will push for judicial empowerment to create a fair competition environment.

## THE SUBJECT: WHY CHINA?

I illustrate the demand-side theory based on an empirical study of contemporary China, which offers several advantages in testing such a theory. First, China is one of the most durable authoritarian regimes in the world; single-party rule has lasted for over sixty years. The regime has remained resilient in the face of the "third wave" of democratization and the "Arab Spring" in which many closed autocracies have collapsed. Second, China has made significant progress in its domestic legal reforms. Many scholars and pundits believe that it has transitioned away from a rule-of-man regime, in which Mao Zedong ruled by his personal will, and started a "long march toward the rule of law" (Peerenboom 2002). Finally, China offers considerable heterogeneity across regions. The large number of subnational units offers an ideal laboratory in which to test theoretically driven hypotheses in a large-N context while controlling for institutional factors.

## AUTHORITARIAN RULE OF LAW WITH CHINESE CHARACTERISTICS

To apply the theory in China, I ask the following question: under *what* conditions would the Chinese state make *what* policy concessions, and to *whom*? My answer, in brief, is that the Chinese authoritarian state, under the leadership of the CCP, is a revenue maximizer. To increase its revenues, the state cooperates with economic elites who pay taxes and generate rent. Interest groups, represented by state-owned enterprises (SOEs), domestic private enterprises, and enterprises owned by ethnic Chinese, have strong political connections in China, whereas those represented by foreign-invested enterprises (FIEs) do not. Politically connected interest groups monopolize privileges and therefore prevent the equalization of the playing field. Governments that rely on politically connected interest groups for revenues will block significant legal reforms that increase judicial fairness. In contrast, interest groups that are not politically connected will push for judicial empowerment to prevent favoritism and establish a fair commercial environment. Governments that rely on these interest groups will need to tie their hands, disentangle their ties with the privileged, and respect the rule of law in the economic realm. Specifically, we expect to observe better enforcement of the rule of law in regions with a large number of foreign investors but a higher level of judicial corruption and judicial inefficiency in regions heavily invested in by domestic and ethnic Chinese investors.

However, Chinese local governments have no incentive to strengthen courts in every respect. A fair and efficient court will not only protect investors whose assets are crucial for local officials' political advancement but also provide openings for discontented citizens and social groups to challenge the state, which undermines the officials' careers. Therefore, the best strategy for the government is to curb corruption in the commercial realm while imposing constraints on citizens' rights to sue the authoritarian state through legal channels. *Ex ante*, this is achieved through the Communist Party's power to selectively intervene in judicial decisions; as an *ex post* remedy, the Communist Party can manipulate the setup of anticorruption agencies to gain a "first-mover" advantage to protect corrupt party officials.

## CAUSALITY

This book describes China's journey from investment to the rule of law, rather than the other way around. Foreign companies entered China for reasons other than the rule of law: most of them were attracted by the big market, incredibly low labor costs, and access to the East Asian market. They were confident in their investment because of commitments made by individual Communist Party leaders rather than a sound legal system. Foreign corporations invested in China in the hope that they would be privileged; some indeed were, but most were not, and almost all of them lost their privileges as the number of foreign companies increased and the Chinese leadership changed. Foreign investors were frustrated. Their strategy then was to lobby the state to strengthen its formal legal institutions. The following cases help bring the theory to life.

In 1978, when Deng Xiaoping announced that China would open up, a "dream market" was created for Western corporations. This was an old dream that had beguiled Western companies since the Industrial Revolution. One British writer declared more than 170 years ago, "If we could only persuade every person in China to lengthen his shirttail by a foot, we could keep the mills of Lancashire working round the clock" (Mann 1989, 24).

American Motors Corporation (AMC), once the fourth-largest auto company after the Big Three (General Motors, Ford, and Chrysler), was sustained in the 1970s largely by a single, highly profitable product – the Jeep – yet AMC never grabbed more than 7.5 percent of the American car market.[5] Tod Clare, AMC's vice president of international operations, a Stanford graduate who majored in international relations with a special interest in the Far East, had been eyeing China ever since Nixon's visit in 1972. In 1978, Clare felt that it was time to drive AMC to China.

There were at least three attractions of doing business with China. One was the big market. Ralph A. Pfeiffer Jr., chairperson of the board of IBM's international division, said in an interview, "You never know what would happen if they really got going. Japan's got only one-seventh of China's population... If we would just sell one IBM PC for every 100 people in China, or every 1,000, or even every 10,000..." (Mann 1989, 54). By establishing a presence in China, AMC could gain some competitive advantages over its major global competitors. General Motors (GM), the world's largest automaker, was not very aggressive in the world market. Clare thought that GM "wanted to sit back in their offices at home and write orders" (Mann 1989, 39). Access to a market with a billion people would help AMC catch up with the Big Three. It would also help AMC compete with Japan: China could become a base from which AMC could export cars throughout the rest of East Asia, whose market was then dominated by Japan.

The second incentive was the incredibly low labor costs. In the early 1980s, American auto companies were paying wages of roughly $20 an hour, while their Japanese competitors were paying $12. Making cars in

---

[5] The Jeep case is largely borrowed from Mann (1989).

China, where workers were paid the equivalent of sixty cents an hour, might help even out the difference.

The third motivator was national interest. Starting in the late 1970s, the United States was eager to develop strong commercial ties with China to counterbalance the Soviet Union. "Our new ties with China are of fundamental importance to the United States, and to the prospects for a peaceful and prosperous world," Deputy Secretary of State Warren Christopher told the U.S. Congress in 1979 (Mann 1989, 54).

All the attractions created what the *Wall Street Journal* called "a gold rush aura"[6] or what the *Economist* dubbed "China fever"[7] in the 1980s to 1990s to invest in China. From 1979 to 2000, China absorbed a total of $346.2 billion in foreign direct investment (FDI) (Huang 2003, 6), which made it the second-most attractive destination for foreign investment after the United States.

However, systematic legal reforms in China did not start until the mid-1990s. Jiang Zemin, then the party general secretary, made "ruling the country in accordance with law" a "basic strategy" in 1997, and the phrase was incorporated into the Chinese constitution in 1999. Most scholars agree that meaningful legal reforms started only in the late 1990s (Peerenboom 2002, 58–59; Clarke, Murrell, and Whiting 2008, 399).

Without the rule of law, why did foreign companies rush to China? It was certainly not "drinking the Kool-Aid"; they went to China hoping they would be privileged. In 1979, when AMC executives sat down with their counterparts from the Beijing Automotive Works (BAW) to draft a contract for a joint venture, AMC insisted on an "exclusivity" clause guaranteeing that it would be the sole foreign manufacturer of four-wheel-drive vehicles in China. "If the company was going to start up operations in China, it wanted to be sure it had a preferred position there" (Mann 1989, 46). The Chinese refused to write this into the contract, but AMC did obtain "a preferred position" by building strong political connections in China.

AMC's intermediary, C. B. Sung, was a well-connected Chinese national who was a good friend of Zhu Rongji, who became the Chinese premier in 1997. Sung's wife, Beulah, was a family friend of Rong Yiren, a Shanghai millionaire who was later elected China's vice president.

In 1986, the one-year-old joint venture, named Beijing Jeep, was in trouble: it was short of foreign exchange to purchase auto parts from the United States. Don St. Pierre, the manager of the joint venture, tried to solve the issue by negotiating with his Chinese partner, but nothing worked. He finally decided to go to the top. He talked to Hulan Hawke, a Chinese-American woman working

[6] Frank Ching, "China's New Economic Zones on Trial: Special Areas Attract Billions in Investments," *Wall Street Journal*, August 12, 1982, p. 23.

[7] "Not Quite So Sparkling China," *Economist*, March 1, 1997, p. 38. http://search.proquest.com /docview/224102560?accountid=14707, accessed June 7, 2013.

in C. B. Sung's company and the daughter of an important Communist Party official. They decided to write to Zhao Ziyang, the Chinese premier, who was known as an open-minded reformer. Mrs. Hawke promised to put the letter into Zhao's hands.

After drafting the letter with St. Pierre in both English and Chinese, Hawke gave it to a Chinese friend, a woman who had access to China's top leaders. St. Pierre suspected that the woman might be Zhao's daughter. Several months later, St. Pierre was sitting in an office in AMC's headquarters in a suburb of Detroit when a telex arrived from Beijing. It was from Zhu Rongji, then the deputy head of China's State Economic Commission. Zhu said he had been entrusted by Premier Zhao to resolve the problems at Beijing Jeep. Beijing Jeep was subsequently guaranteed $120 million in foreign exchange.

Beijing Jeep's story had a happy ending, but it is far from a typical one. The company was privileged because it was the first big joint venture in China, and the Chinese government wanted to make it a "model joint venture." The Chinese did not want to extend the same deal to other Western companies, so the final section of the written agreement with Beijing Jeep swore both sides to secrecy.

Outside the "model," other foreign companies were not as lucky. In 1994, Beijing ordered McDonald's to vacate its 28,000-square-foot site so that an enormous commercial and residential development called Oriental Plaza could be built by Hong Kong tycoon Li Ka-shing, who was a close friend of Jiang Zemin, then the party general secretary. That administrative order violated the twenty-year contract signed between the company and the Beijing government in 1989.[8]

Even the politically favored Beijing Jeep faced uncertainties as China's political climate shifted. In 1987, the party's general secretary, Hu Yaobang, was ousted from power. In the following weeks, there were signs that some Chinese leaders favored a return to orthodoxy. "We must rely on our own efforts," said the *Workers' Daily*, a party paper. "Capitalists are capitalists. They will never be so generous as to assist a country like ours without benefiting themselves" (Mann 1989, 266). In a meeting with a delegation of French officials, China's then vice premier, Li Peng, said, "You must be psychologically prepared for some projects to be rejected or restudied" (Mann 1989, 266). A couple of years later, one day before the Tiananmen Square massacre, Beijing Jeep's highest patron, Zhao Ziyang, was ousted as well.

Political connections are costly to build and easy to lose. Very few investors, such as Li Ka-shing, are able to befriend China's top leaders; most seek connections with local officials, who are nonetheless constantly rotated across localities. The key, then, is the ability to build new connections. However,

---

[8] "After 2-Year Dispute, McDonald's to Move Showcase Beijing Site," *Bloomberg Business News*, December 2, 1996. http://community.seattletimes.nwsource.com/archive/?date=19961202&slug=2362871, accessed June 7, 2013.

foreign companies have a comparative disadvantage in building political connections due to language, cultural, and institutional barriers. Foreign corporations' strategies then shifted to demanding a level playing field.

Multinationals began to go to court. Some of them lost, but others won. In 2006, the Starbucks Corporation won a trademark infringement lawsuit against a Chinese company that used a similar name and logo. A Shanghai court ordered the Shanghai Xingbake Coffee Shop to pay Starbucks 500,000 *yuan* ($61,956) in damages, which is believed to be one of the largest awards against a Chinese company for trademark infringement. The court also said that Shanghai Xingbake must stop using the logo and name, which translates into "Starbucks" in English.[9] In 2010, Microsoft won a victory in its fight against piracy in China when a Shanghai court sentenced a regional insurer to pay the US software company 2.17 million *yuan* ($318,000) in damages. The Shanghai Pudong New Area district court found Dazhong Insurance, a Shanghai-based insurer backed by a number of Chinese state-owned and listed companies, guilty of infringing Microsoft's intellectual property by using illegal copies of its software.[10] The victors' list also includes famous brands such as Ferrero, Burberry, Chanel, Gucci, LVMH, and Prada.[11]

This book is based on the stories of Beijing Jeep, Starbucks, Microsoft, and thousands of other multinational corporations that got China fever but became frustrated and then demanded the leveling of the playing field.

## METHODS OF INQUIRY

I employ a *multilevel time-series and cross-section* research design. First, this study explains the rise of partial rule of law at the national, provincial, prefectural, and county levels in China. Unlike previous Chinese politics research that focuses on one level of government,[12] this study collects a wide range of data from the national level to the county level and shows how the theory is applied at various levels. In addition, I have collected time-series cross-sectional data sets to examine the variation in the rule of law both across space and over time.

---

[9] "Starbucks Wins Trademark Infringement Suit," *New York Times*, January 4, 2006. http://query.nytimes.com/gst/fullpage.html?res=9A07E5DB1130F937A35752C0A9609C8B63, accessed June 7, 2013.

[10] K. Hille, "Microsoft Wins in Court over China's Pirates," *Financial Times*, April 22, 2010. http://www.ft.com/intl/cms/s/2/66a1b906-4e09-11df-b437-00144feab49a.html#axzz2VXhpxSFj, accessed June 7, 2013.

[11] M. Dickie and R. Minder, "China's Real Progress against Sellers of Fakes," *Financial Times*, January 17, 2006. http://www.ft.com/intl/cms/s/0/a52aa822-8702-11da-8521-0000779e2340.html#axzz2VXhpxSFj, accessed June 7, 2013.

[12] Recent examples include Tsai's (2007b) research of public goods provision at the village level, Whiting's (2001) research on private enterprises at the county level, and Landry's (2008) research on mayors' promotion at the prefectural level.

Second, this book reports on *within-country comparative* research. It has several advantages. Rule of law is a complex phenomenon embedded in historical (for example, civil law system versus common law system), political (for example, two-party system versus multiparty system, or plurality system versus proportional representation system), and economic (for example, planned economy versus market economy) conditions. Cross-national research is likely to suffer from collinearity, which makes it difficult to tease out a clear causal mechanism from various confounding factors. Within-country comparative research in China can control for historical (locales share similar legal traditions) and political (institutions are identical across the country) factors and focus on variables of interest.

In addition, existing measures of the rule of law, such as Transparency International and Kaufmann et al.'s (2009) *Governance* scores, are based on surveys. It is difficult to judge whether respondents in the surveys used the same standard to evaluate the status of the rule of law in their own countries due to differences in their cultural and political backgrounds. For example, a corrupt activity that is considered a major crime in Germany might be seen as only a tolerable misdemeanor in China. Although survey methodologists have designed ways to compare answers in different cultures (for example, vignettes), consistent measures of the rule of law have not yet been developed. Within-country comparative research in China can utilize identical survey instruments to measure the rule of law, assuming that respondents share similar standards across the country. Finally, while many single-country studies suffer from low degrees of freedom and lack of variation in units, a large number of subnational units in China and considerable regional variation make it possible to carry out both fine-grained qualitative research and large-N quantitative analysis.

The data used in this book are both qualitative and quantitative.[13] On the qualitative side, I conducted over one hundred semistructured interviews with party and government officials, judges, investors, lawyers, scholars, litigants, and ordinary citizens in seven Chinese provinces in 2007 and 2010. On the quantitative side, I compiled and analyzed four data sets. The first data set includes survey data of ordinary citizens across mainland China's 102 counties in 2003 matched by yearbook statistics on the local political economy. The second data set is a large national survey of 12,400 firms that includes detailed information on firms' accounting records, business-government relations, and the local investment environment. The third combines business survey data in mainland China's 120 cities in 2005 and yearbook statistics for the local economy. The fourth is comprised of variables on provincial government budgets and other demographic and economic aspects of mainland China's thirty-one provinces from 1995 to 2006.

---

[13] Please see Appendix A for a note on research methods.

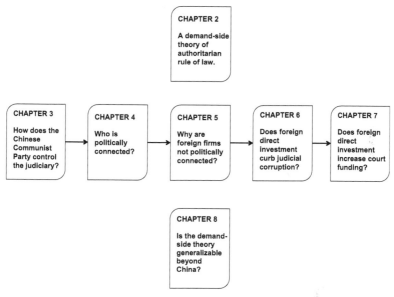

CHAPTER 2

A demand-side theory of authoritarian rule of law.

CHAPTER 3

How does the Chinese Communist Party control the judiciary?

CHAPTER 4

Who is politically connected?

CHAPTER 5

Why are foreign firms not politically connected?

CHAPTER 6

Does foreign direct investment curb judicial corruption?

CHAPTER 7

Does foreign direct investment increase court funding?

CHAPTER 8

Is the demand-side theory generalizable beyond China?

FIGURE 1.3 Road Map of the Book

## PLAN OF THE BOOK

In the chapters to come, I seek to establish the internal validity of my arguments by showing qualitative and quantitative evidence to support the empirical implications of the theoretical model while pursuing a research design geared toward maximizing the potential for external validity.

Figure 1.3 provides a road map of the book. Chapter 2 spells out a demand-side theory of authoritarian rule of law. I then answer one question in each chapter from Chapters 3 to 7. The questions and chapters are logically connected. Chapter 8 discusses the generalizability of my theory and its broader significance.

Chapter 2 describes a theory that explains the occurrence of the partial rule of law in authoritarian regimes and its application to China. I argue that authoritarian rule of law occurs when organized interest groups that control valuable and mobile assets (but are not politically connected) demand a level, legal playing field. Applying the theory to the Chinese context, I argue that Chinese local officials are more likely to promote judicial fairness when they rely on foreign capital from outside the "China circle" for tax revenues and economic growth. Conversely, Chinese local officials are less likely to promote judicial fairness when they depend on Chinese SOEs, domestic private enterprises, and foreign capital from within the China circle for revenues and growth. I also argue that the rule of law in authoritarian regimes is incomplete. Authoritarian rulers have incentives to build the rule of law only in the commercial realm, while imposing constraints on citizens' political and civil rights to use the court to challenge the state.

Chapter 3, drawing from qualitative data, provides an overview of China's judicial system. I show that the CCP and the Chinese government have used the personnel and financial system to control the judiciary to prevent the court from being used by ordinary citizens to challenge the state.

Chapter 4 examines state-business relations in China by addressing the following questions: How do different firms settle disputes? How do they perceive state-business relations in China? Who is subject to discrimination? Based on a quantitative analysis of a large national survey of 12,400 firms conducted jointly by the World Bank and the Enterprise Survey Organization of the National Bureau of Statistics (NBS) of China, I am able to draw three main conclusions. First, foreign firms are more likely to settle disputes through formal legal institutions than domestic and China circle firms. Second, foreign firms believe that their property rights are not as well protected as those of Chinese domestic enterprises and companies owned by ethnic Chinese. Third, foreign firms are not as confident in China's legal system as other firms. These findings suggest that there is a gap between foreign firms' demand for the rule of law and what the Chinese legal system has offered.

Chapter 5 examines how firms in China build political connections. Based on an analysis of the firm-level survey, this chapter empirically probes the question of who offers bribes. Firms' entertainment and travel costs (ETC) are used as a proxy for bribery among Chinese firms. ETC is a standard expenditure item that covers entertainment (such as food, beverages, gifts, karaoke, and sports club memberships) and travel expenditures. Since it is publicly reported in the accounting books of Chinese firms, it is not subject to the biases associated with subjective survey data. In addition to legitimate business travel and other expenses, Chinese firms commonly use the ETC accounting category to reimburse expenditures used to bribe government officials, entertain clients and suppliers, or accommodate managerial excess. As shown in this chapter, Chinese domestic private enterprises spend at a significantly higher level on ETC than FIEs. Constrained by anticorruption regulations instituted by their countries of origin, FIEs from outside the China circle have limited instruments to build political connections, while indigenous Chinese firms are not subject to similar regulatory constraints.

Chapter 6 examines the conditions under which local officials in China have an incentive to build clean and reliable courts. This is a quantitative chapter that tests the theory using survey measures of judicial corruption at the county and prefectural levels. The first data set is a cross-sectional data set of 102 Chinese counties. The measure of judicial corruption is drawn from a 2003 survey on the Institutionalization of Legal Reforms in China (ILRC). The explanatory variables are collected from government-released yearbooks. Statistical analysis shows that the weight of foreign capital in regional GDP has a significantly positive effect on judicial fairness across Chinese counties.

The analysis also finds that local governments' financial support is an important factor that contributes to judicial fairness. The findings are further confirmed by analyzing a cross-sectional data set of 120 Chinese cities. Drawing from the World Bank's Business Environment Survey, the analysis shows that the county-level findings also stand at the prefectural level. Finally, this chapter tests an empirical implication of the theoretical model: if FIEs do not rely on political connections to conduct business, then a strong foreign presence in the local economy should not increase government corruption. The empirical results support this claim.

Chapter 7 goes one step backward in the causal chain and asks when subnational governments invest in courts. Analyzing an original time-series cross-sectional data set of provincial court funding from 1995 to 2006, this chapter shows that the share of FDI from outside the China circle in the overall GDP has a significantly positive effect on how much money local governments are willing to spend on courts. In contrast, SOEs, domestic private enterprises, and ethnic Chinese enterprises exert negative pressure on provincial governments' financial assistance to courts.

Chapter 8 concludes with a discussion of the generalizability of the demand-side theory. While many scholars and policy makers believe that the rule of law is a panacea for all the world's problems, few have suggested how we can build and sustain it. Drawing from legal reform experiences in Latin America, Eastern Europe and Russia, Western Europe, Africa, and East Asia, I show that the demand-side theory is applicable in many contexts, including authoritarian regimes or even new democracies, and that my focus on interest groups as constituencies provides a more sustainable solution to supporting the rule of law.

## 2

# A demand-side theory of authoritarian rule of law

> You may object that it is not a trial at all; you are quite right, for it is only a trial
> if I recognize it as such.
>
> Franz Kafka

I address the following question in this book: why do authoritarian regimes promote a certain type of rule of law? I argue that *authoritarian rule of law* – a partial form of the rule of law – is likely to occur when *politically unconnected, organized* interest groups with *valuable and mobile assets* demand it. I call this a demand-side theory of authoritarian rule of law, because it takes into account not only authoritarian rulers' political calculations of implementing the rule of law in certain realms but also the conditions under which interest groups would prefer the rule of law to privileges. The demand-side component makes the theory differ from most existing theories of the rule of law, which tend to focus on the supply side.

The coexistence of authoritarianism and the rule of law is puzzling in the context of an overwhelming literature that links the rule of law to democratic accountability (North and Thomas 1973; North 1990; Olson 2000). The logic is that competitive elections in democratic regimes keep politicians accountable to voters and prevent them from engaging in predatory behavior. Authoritarian rulers, by definition, are "arbitrary" (Friedrich and Brzezinski 1965, 22), "rent seeking" (Wintrobe 2000, 145), and "territorial" (Olson 2000, 3–11). Since authoritarian rulers need only to maintain the loyalty of a small segment of the elites to stay in power, they have no incentive to treat every citizen equally (Bueno de Mesquita et al. 2003).

The rule of law is an enemy of authoritarianism. In its most classic version, the core spirit of the rule of law is the protection of individual liberty against the exercise of discretionary power by government officials. Dicey (1915, 183–191) defines it as "a characteristic of our country, not only that with us no man is above the law, but (what is a different thing) that here every man, whatever be his rank or condition, is subject to the ordinary law of the realm and amenable to the jurisdiction of the ordinary tribunals." In the same vein, Hayek saw a connection between "the growth of a measure of arbitrary administrative coercion" and the destruction of "the Rule of Law" (Hayek 1994, xliii).

However, we see ample examples of respect for the rule of law in authoritarian regimes. The Egyptian Supreme Constitutional Court has frequently struck down regime legislation since the 1980s (Moustafa 2007, 7). The Argentine Supreme Court justices have constantly ruled against the authoritarian government (Helmke 2002). In Russia, progovernment candidates have no advantage in courts in an electoral registration trial (Popova 2010). In 1990, authoritarian Taiwan's Council of Grand Justices forced the retirement of old members of the notorious National Assembly and then called for a new election in accordance with the "spirit of the constitution" (Ginsburg 2002, 770).

Why do some authoritarian rulers tie their hands to respect the rule of law? My demand-side theory starts with the premise that authoritarian rulers cannot solely rely on force to stay in power; they need cooperation, as well. Authoritarian rulers particularly need the cooperation of investors who control valuable assets. Authoritarian regimes, like any state, need to collect revenues from their citizens in the format of either tax or rents. Authoritarian rulers consume part of the revenues themselves, distribute some to their loyalists, and spend the rest on providing public goods to maintain a minimum level of public support. Without adequate revenues, authoritarian rulers are unable to stay in power, satisfy their supporters (whose loyalty can be bought by a challenger), or pacify the masses (whose grievances might escalate into a fatal revolt). Therefore, to survive, authoritarian rulers need the cooperation of asset holders, whose valuable assets can be taxed or confiscated.

The exchange between the ruler and asset holders, however, is a bargaining process. Asset holders exchange their assets for policies. By granting asset holders' preferred policies, the ruler is able to secure their compliance. Otherwise, asset holders can hide, destroy, or move their assets. In this bargaining process, the ruler's *power* is determined by how urgently she needs the assets. If revenues are necessary for the ruler's survival, such as during war, a crisis of legitimacy, and consolidation of power, the ruler is willing to sacrifice part of her benefits to seek the cooperation of asset holders. In addition, the ruler's *preference* in the bargain is determined by the costs of policies. Some policies, such as building a fair and efficient legal system, are costly for the ruler because the ruler must treat everyone equally, which means taking the privileges away from the politically connected. This will decrease the amount of rents the ruler can extract from privileged interest groups.

On the other side of the bargain, asset holders' *power* is determined by how organized they are and the value and mobility of their assets. Organized interest groups have stronger bargaining power than unorganized groups. Asset holders can organize themselves via associations, clubs, or unions. A centralized hierarchy can help them overcome collective action problems. Furthermore, those with large assets that can significantly contribute to the ruler's revenues have more power than those with few assets. Therefore, economic elites who control abundant wealth have a stronger voice at the bargaining table than the "have-nots." Finally, mobile assets increase the asset holders' leverage vis-à-vis the ruler. Investors with mobile assets can pose a credible exit threat by moving their assets away from the ruler's jurisdiction. Mobile assets also make it easier for asset holders to avoid taxation or confiscation. In summary, organization, size of assets, and mobility empower the asset holders by enabling them to withdraw urgently needed cooperation from the ruler.

Asset holders' policy *preference* is a function of their existing or potential political connections with the ruler. Each asset holder as an individual would naturally prefer privilege to a level playing field, because the former grants one a monopolistic position in the market where rents can be generated, whereas in the latter everyone must compete fairly. However privilege, by definition, cannot be granted to everyone. Interest groups must compete for it. In the competition for privileges, some are disadvantaged by their skills, prior political connections, and ability to build new connections. Therefore the advantaged strive to hold on to their privileges, while the disadvantaged seek a level playing field. The politically connected do not favor the rule of law, which serves as a level playing field for all asset holders. Interest groups with political connections seek to maintain their privileges, whereas those who are not politically connected will seek the rule of law, where everyone is treated equally. A strong judiciary protects contract and property rights, makes dispute resolution predictable, and speeds up the litigation process. Privileged interest groups would block the leveling of the playing field to eliminate competition, whereas disadvantaged groups would push for judicial empowerment to get a fair competing environment.

The theory is that authoritarian rulers are more likely to respect the rule of law when they need the cooperation of organized interest groups that control valuable and mobile assets but are not politically connected.

However, authoritarian rulers have no interest in implementing the rule of law in its full scale, which involves both fairness and efficiency. The rule of law that exists in some authoritarian regimes is a *partial form* of the rule of law. Most authoritarian rulers are unwilling to respect judicial fairness, especially when they are in front of the court themselves. Authoritarian rulers therefore face a dilemma. On the one hand, they must respect the rule of law to make a credible commitment to investors whose assets are urgently needed; on the other hand, a strong judiciary might open new avenues for political activists to challenge the state. The solution to this dilemma is for authoritarian rulers to implement a partial form of the rule of law; they sequence the legal reforms in such that judicial fairness is usually respected in the economic realm but not in the political realm. They achieve this by limiting their political interference in commercial cases while extending their discretionary power in the political realm. Through increasing costs, raising the bar, manipulating the procedure, lowering the benefits, and distorting the law, authoritarian rulers discourage citizens from utilizing the judiciary to sue the government.

The partial form of the rule of law in authoritarian regimes is different from a popular concept termed "rule *by* law" (Ginsburg and Moustafa 2008). Tamanaha (2004, 92) defines "rule by law" as "the notion that law is the means by which the state conducts its affairs." I do not use this terminology, because "rule by law" is a very fuzzy concept. As Tamanaha (2004, 92) argues, "understood in this way, the rule of law has no real meaning, for it collapses into the notion of rule by the government... Every modern state has the rule of law in this narrow sense." But not every modern state has the partial form of rule of law.

## INTELLECTUAL LINEAGES

The theory is informed by the following strands of literature. First, the theory of the state examines the preference and power of authoritarian rulers. The predatory view of the state, represented by Tilly (1990), Levi (1988), North (1981), and Olson (2000), sees the state as a revenue maximizer. Tilly (1990) shows that the rulers in early modern Europe emerged out of a period of lawlessness. After the decline of the Roman Empire, Europe was comprised of a hodgepodge of local lords who offered protection to peasants in exchange for rents paid either in kind or in service on the lord's land. Levi (1988) argues that rulers could extract the resources they needed through "quasi-voluntary compliance" – a situation in which the subject feels that he is getting policy concessions or limits on future state behavior in return for the tax dollars the state is extracting. North (1981) similarly defines the state as "an organization with a comparative advantage in violence, extending over a geographic area whose boundaries are determined by its power to tax constituents." Using the "criminal metaphor," Olson (2000, 3) makes the argument that the state acts like a Mafia family that has an encompassing interest in the society because there is more to steal in a rich society.

The works of Bates and Lien (1985), North and Weingast (1989), and Weingast (1997) discuss the bargaining between the state and citizens. Bates and Lien (1985, 53) contend that:

Revenue-seeking governments may well find it to their advantage to strike bargains with citizens whose assets they seek to tax. To induce a greater willingness to pay taxes, they may defer to the citizens' policy preferences. Such bargains may become more beneficial from the citizens' point of view the more mobile the assets the citizens hold.

North and Weingast (1989) and Weingast (1997) show that the emergence of parliamentary supremacy in England in the seventeenth century was a conse-quence of (1) organized capitalists, who controlled mobile assets, demanding veto powers against the Crown's discretion; and (2) institutional changes in Parliament that provided a credible commitment to the asset holders, whose cooperation was urgently needed, as the country was at war. Weingast (1997) also argues that citizens organized in a decentralized manner are often unable to impose costs when a ruler does not follow the law, so the foundation of the rule of law is often based on the bargaining of organized capitalists.

Next, the theory of collective action investigates the problems that citizens face in bargaining with the government. As Ostrom (1998, 1) bluntly argues, "the theory of collective action is *the* central subject of political science." Olson (1965) shows that an individual must sacrifice time and money to contribute to the public goods of an organization. The individual will at best succeed in advancing the cause to a small degree. Even if she can get favorable results, the benefits are shared with everyone in the group. So an individual in any large group will reap only a small share of benefit. Since any gain is distributed to everyone in the group, those who contribute nothing to the effort will get just as much as those who made the contribution. So, absent any special arrangement or circumstances in a large group, organizations have the free rider problem, in which people want to sit back and let others further the cause. The collective action problem helps us understand how asset holders as a group engage in collective bargaining with the government. This theory suggests that asset holders can influence government policies only when they are organized.

Various works consider the preference of interest groups regarding the rule of law. Schattschneider's (1960) classic work has pioneered the "group theories of politics" in which he famously argued, "the pressure system has an upper-class bias" (32). He shows that the outcome of a controversy is often determined by the success or failure of efforts to enlarge its scope, and that it is often the weaker side in the controversy that has an incentive to enlarge the scope to alter the power balance. Voigt (1998) challenges the conventional wisdom that interest groups would universally seek the rule of law. Instead, "they all seek privileges from the government which, if granted, would reduce the degree to which the rule of law is effectively enforced, and that the privileges sought by one group negatively affect another group" (Voigt 1998, 201–202). For example, granting an import tariff to one group means that an industry that has hitherto used imported goods as inputs would need to pay higher prices. If that industry is already organized as an interest group, it will oppose the privilege sought by the first interest group. The first interest group, on the other hand, will hold on to its privileges. The logic is similar to Hellman's (1998) "partial reform equilibrium," in which the interest groups that benefit from earlier reform policies will block further reforms to maintain their monopolistic position in the market. The implication is that interest groups with political connections will block the enforcement of the rule of law to prevent the equalization of the playing field. In contrast, interest groups on the weaker side would oppose the privilege and push for judicial fairness.

## THEORETICAL CONTRIBUTIONS

The demand-side theory of authoritarian rule of law is different from most existing theories of the determinants of the rule of law.[1] While the literature on what the rule of law could lead to is rich, there are fewer studies on what leads to the rule of law. It is well established theoretically and empirically that the rule of law is a precondition for the protection of human rights, property rights, and economic growth. Empirical studies often link credible rule-of-law institutions with elevated levels of foreign investment, external finance, and higher aggregate levels of economic growth (Keefer and Knack 1997; Feld and Voigt 2003; Oliva and Rivera-Batiz 2002; Barro 1997; La Porta et al. 1997). The mechanism is that a well-functioning legal system offers fair and efficient dispute settlement and contract enforcement, which increase investment confidence.

Most studies on the determinants of the rule of law are conducted in the context of liberal democracies, with a focus on judicial independence.[2] There are two types of institutional explanations for judicial independence.[3]

The first is focused on historical legacy. As La Porta et al. (1998) argue, judicial independence is more likely to occur in common-law countries, which also happen to be of Anglo lineage. Judges in common-law countries have the power to interpret and create laws, whereas judges in civil-law systems can enforce only existing bodies of law.

The second is focused on delegative models, in which politicians tie their hands vis-à-vis an independent judiciary. It is argued that legislators under certain conditions might find it in their interest to delegate judicial authority to courts, thus building intentional institutional walls against political intervention in judicial decisions (Landes and Posner 1975).

Another delegative explanation of judicial insulation is based on politicians' desire to avert blame for unpopular policies. For example, a legislative majority might want to delegate politically divisive issues to the court to avoid blame (Graber 1993; Salzberger 1993; Whittington 1999).

McCubbins and Schwartz (1984) provide a third delegative rationale: that an independent judiciary can serve as a "fire alarm" for the legislature to keep executive agencies from veering from legislative intent.

A fourth delegative explanation is political insurance against being dominated by a future majority. A political party expecting to lose the upcoming election or fall into minority status might want to establish an independent judiciary to prevent the "majority tyranny" of the future regime (Ramseyer and Rasmusen 1997; Finkel 2008).

---

[1] One exception is Hendley (2001), which examined demand for law in Russia.

[2] For theoretic models of judicial independence, please see Ferejohn and Weingast (1992) and Shipan (1997).

[3] This brief review is based on Helmke and Rosenbluth (2009).

One of the weaknesses of these delegative models, as Helmke and Rosenbluth (2009) argue, is their ignorance of the fact that courts, like legislators, are strategic actors. For example, in Landes and Posner's (1975) model, judges may try to achieve outcomes as close as possible to their own preferences by taking into account the possibility that the incumbent legislature can write new legislation if it is sufficiently unhappy with the court's ruling. Or in the blame-shifting model, strategic courts may have an interest in throwing the matter back rather than provoking public wrath themselves.

While the historical argument and the delegative models have gained some purchase in explaining the emergence of the rule of law in democracies, they fall short in autocratic settings. The legal-origins argument presents a very pessimistic picture of the rule of law in civil-law systems: the rule of law is difficult to establish no matter what people do or how hard they try, given their legal legacies. The delegative models' focus on the supply side loses its explanatory power in nondemocratic settings in which the rulers are unwilling to supply the rule of law or might pay lip service to the rule of law but can easily withdraw their support. This time inconsistency problem in autocracies makes the supply unsustainable.

The demand-side theory contends that interest groups need to serve as constituencies in order for the rule of law to last, and the interest groups should be able to secure a credible commitment from the ruler.

THE THEORY IN ACTION

To apply the theory in China, I ask the following question: under *what* conditions would the Chinese state make *what* policy concessions, and to *whom*? My answer is that the Chinese authoritarian state, under the leadership of the CCP, is a revenue maximizer. To increase its revenues, the state cooperates with economic elites who pay tax and generate rents. Economic elites represented by SOEs, domestic private enterprises, and enterprises owned by ethnic Chinese have strong political connections in China, whereas those represented by FIEs have no (or weak) connections. Politically connected elites monopolize privileges and therefore prevent the equalization of the playing field. Governments that rely on politically connected elites for revenues would block significant legal reforms that further judicial fairness. In contrast, elites who are not politically connected would push for judicial empowerment to oppose privilege and establish a fair commercial environment. Governments that rely on these elites would need to tie their hands, disentangle their ties with the privileged, and respect the rule of law in the economic realm. More specifically, we expect to observe better enforcement of the rule of law in regions with a large number of foreign investors but a higher level of judicial corruption and inefficiency in regions with heavy investments from domestic and ethnic Chinese investors.

## The Chinese State

I assume that the Chinese state, under the leadership of the CCP, is a revenue maximizer. The party's survival directly hinges on the amount of revenue it possesses. The party, first of all, distributes the revenue as rents to secure the loyalty of its own ruling elites by providing them with a luxury lifestyle with which no alternative club can compete. Party privileges include subsidized or free housing, vehicles and chauffeurs, bodyguards and servants, first-class flights, five-star hotels, VIP rooms in hospitals, and other exclusive goods and services. In addition, the party needs the revenue to provide public goods to defend the country from foreign invasion and maintain a minimum level of public support. This includes maintaining strong armed forces; building infrastructure; and providing education, health care and pensions, and clean air and water.

Despite its importance, the party does not possess its own assets. The CCP obtains revenue through "state capture," that is, extraction from the state (Grzymala-Busse 2008). This creates a "fusion of party and state" in China in which the party's fate is closely tied to the well-being of the state. The "encompassing interests" of the CCP in Chinese society incentivize the party to form institutions and implement policies that could generate growth and revenues from which the party can extract assets (Olson 2000, 9).

The party, however, faces the principal-agent problem of making its local agents accountable. To solve this problem, the party creates formal institutions to incentivize its local agents to comply with the central directives. In this incentive structure, the performance on revenue collection is tied to local officials' personal well-being.

Like its Soviet counterpart, the Communist Party of China uses the *nomenklatura* to regulate authority over party and state "main leading cadres" and other important individuals (Lieberthal 2004, 234). The Russian term *nomenklatura* generally refers to the lists of offices controlled by the various party committees (Manion 1985, 212). In this system, the appointment, promotion, transfer, and removal of leading cadres are based, in principle at least, on officials' qualifications and performance as assessed regularly in the cadre evaluation system (Whiting 2004).

I obtained a sample of the cadre evaluation form from the city of Guangzhou in Guangdong Province. This form was introduced in late 2008 by the Guangzhou Municipal Party Organization Department to evaluate the performance of major party and government officials at the county level. It reflects the spirit of the Scientific Concept of Development proposed by the then Chinese president and party general secretary Hu Jintao. The Scientific Concept of Development emphasizes the quality of development, social equality, environmental protection, and social harmony. The concept is believed to depart from previous party policies that prioritized speed of development at the expense of income disparity, environmental degradation, and social conflict.

Another innovation of the Guangzhou cadre evaluation system is that localities are differentiated by their stages of development and assigned different evaluation forms accordingly. The three categories include central urban districts (*zhongxin chengqu*), new urban districts (*xin chengqu*), and county-level cities (*xianjishi*). The key difference among the evaluation systems in the three types of localities is how measures of economic development are weighted. For example, for central urban districts, the index on economic development carries a weight of 30 percent, whereas new urban districts and county-level cities give 31 and 28 percent, respectively, to economic development. This reflects the developmental strategies of the Guangdong provincial government to encourage the economic development of new urban districts while placing more emphasis on social harmony and environmental protection in central urban districts and county-level cities.

Table 2.1 is a sample of the form used to evaluate central urban districts in Guangzhou City. The first set of indicators in the municipal version of the cadre evaluation forms assigns the highest priority (30 percent) to indicators of economic development, among which the most important indicators are GDP growth rate and growth rate of per capita fiscal revenue. The second set of indicators (22 percent) focuses on measures of social development, including social stability, family planning, and school enrollment rates. The third set of indicators covers people's livelihood (23 percent). The final index is the quality of ecological environment (25 percent). Compared to the cadre evaluation forms documented in Whiting (2004) and Landry (2008),[4] this version from Guangdong gave more weight to the quality of economic development, social development, and ecological environment. Other provinces, such as Zhejiang and Hunan, were also considering reconstructing their evaluation systems to assess performance on promoting "scientific development."

However, interviews with local officials sent a strong message that in practice, the enforcement of the evaluation using the new form is similar to that of the previous form. A Guangzhou Municipal Party Organization Department official told me that only four of the indicators are critical: GDP growth rate, growth rate of per capita fiscal revenue, social stability index, and fertility rate. The latter two are veto targets: that is, they only matter if officials fail on these two targets. For example, a large-scale collective protest or a fertility rate that is higher than the family planning threshold would deny the official the opportunity to be promoted the following year, but high social stability and a low fertility rate will not increase their chances of promotion. The official also told me that high rates of GDP growth and fiscal revenue increase an official's chances of promotion only when they are exceptional. An official is very likely

---

[4] Whiting (2004) documented a cadre evaluation form promulgated in 1989 by Jiangsu Province, and Landry (2008) collected a cadre evaluation form from the China Urban Development Research Committee in 2001. All of these forms were designed before Hu Jintao took office in 2002.

TABLE 2.1 *Sample Cadre Evaluation Form, Guangzhou City*

| Index | Variable | Direction | Weight |
|---|---|---|---|
| Economic Development | GDP growth rate | + | |
| | Per capita GDP growth rate/GDP growth rate | + | |
| | Growth rate of per capita fiscal revenue | + | |
| | Overhead/Fiscal expenditure | − | |
| | Growth rate of the private sector | + | 30 |
| | Output ratio per unit of land for construction | + | |
| | Added value of high-tech products/GDP | + | |
| | Research and development investment/GDP | + | |
| | Added value of modern service industry/Added value of the service industry | + | |
| Social Development | Social stability index | + | |
| | Fiscal expenditures on social programs and public service/Overall fiscal budget | + | |
| | Area of public cultural facilities per 10,000 people | + | |
| | Fertility rate permissible under the family planning policy | + | |
| | Occurrence of contagious diseases and food poisoning per 10,000 people | − | |
| | Index of social safety | + | 22 |
| | Index of democracy and the rule of law | + | |
| | Index of informationalization | + | |
| | College enrollment rate of high school graduates | + | |
| | Community health services | + | |
| | Completion rate of "Five-Ones" project* | + | |
| People's Livelihood | Unemployment rate | − | |
| | Social insurance coverage | + | |
| | Growth rate of per capita income/GDP growth rate | + | 23 |
| | Correction rate of city environmental management cases | + | |
| | Households with housing difficulties/All households | − | |

Table 2.1 *(cont.)*

| Index | Variable | Direction | Weight |
|---|---|---|---|
| Ecological Environment | Forestation rate | + | |
| | Expenditure on environmental protection/Overall fiscal budget | + | |
| | Area of farmland | + | |
| | Completion rate of major pollutants emission reduction | + | 25 |
| | Completion rate of separation of rain, sewage, and removing septic tanks | + | |
| | Completion rate of comprehensive management of rivers | + | |
| | Rate of underground wiring in newly constructed and reconstructed roads | + | |
| | Index of comprehensive evaluation of city appearance and environment | + | |

*Note:* This form is used by the Organization Department of the CCP Committee in Guangzhou to evaluate the performance of major party and government cadres in central urban districts in Guangzhou. It was obtained during the author's fieldwork in 2010.
* "Five-Ones" refer to having one public service center, one public park, one community activity center, one medical service center, and one surveillance camera center in charge of public security and urban management in one community.

to be promoted if her locality's GDP growth and fiscal revenue have been outperforming those of other localities for two or more consecutive years.[5]

Scholarly studies on factors that determine Chinese officials' promotion are inconclusive. Landry (2008) shows empirically that GDP growth rate is not a strong predictor of mayors' promotion. Shih, Adolph, and Liu (2012) show that educational qualifications, provincial revenue collection, and factional ties played substantial roles in elite ranking in the reform era, while provincial economic growth did not. Conversely, Guo (2009) finds that county officials strategically increase fiscal spending to stimulate economic growth before they are up for promotion. My findings during the field research portion of this study reconcile this debate. The general impression is that the determinants of political advancement vary across bureaucratic ranks. For county-level officials and below, due to their large number and lack of factional ties,[6] performance on economic development is critically important for advancement.

[5] Interview with a party official in Guangzhou, Guangdong Province, March 25, 2010.
[6] By "lack of factional ties," I mean only that they lack ties to the central leadership. Local officials are often embedded in dense networks with local families and factions.

On the contrary, for municipal- and provincial-level cadres, other factors such as factional ties carry more weight.[7]

The Guangzhou Party Organization Department official explained how promotions work. Each year, if there are vacancies, the Organization Department prepares a list of officials based on their rankings in the evaluation system for the municipal party secretary to review. But the party secretary often has her own list. If the officials are on both lists, then it is fine. The party secretary will pick some names from the list, and the names will include some of her own people and other officials who have exceptional performance. However, if the party secretary's preferred names are not on the Organization Department's list, the secretary will say: "People on this list do not have credentials; give me a new list." Then the Organization Department must figure out who should be added to the list. Only when the party secretary's people are included does the list become "valid."[8] This explanation demonstrates that China's cadre advancement is a mixture of meritocracy and factionalism. And, as other interviews indicate, there is more factionalism at higher ranks and more meritocracy at lower ranks.[9]

In addition to affecting advancement opportunities, performance on the criteria included in the evaluation form is also used to determine the bonuses of state cadres and the total salaries of collective cadres. Therefore, local officials, especially lower-ranking officials, seriously include these indicators in their calculus when they make and implement polices.

In summary, the CCP, through the state apparatus and the *nomenklatura*, incentivizes its local agents to maximize revenue extraction from society. These revenues are critical for the party's survival.

## Interest Groups with Valuable Assets

To survive, the CCP needs the cooperation of asset holders. In the war era, the party extracted resources from landlords and capitalists partly through confiscation. Examples include the land reforms in the 1930s and 1950s and the nationalization of private assets in the 1950s. In the reform era, as the ownership structure gradually diversified in the Chinese economy, the state accumulates resources primarily through taxation.

Asset holders, however, have divergent interests in policies. Their preferences are a function of their existing or potential political connections. Their ability to retain old connections and build new ones is determined, in turn, by the institutions that constrain and incentivize them. In China, SOEs, domestic

---

[7] Interview with a government official in Guangzhou, Guangdong Province, March 27, 2010. Interview with a government official in Dean County, Jiangxi Province, April 8, 2010.

[8] Interview with a party official, Guangdong Province, March 25, 2010.

[9] Interview with a government official, Guangdong Province, March 27, 2010. Interview with a government official, Jiangxi Province, April 8, 2010.

private enterprises, and enterprises invested in by ethnic Chinese are more competitive than FIEs in building and retaining political connections and, therefore, are less interested in the enforcement of the rule of law. As a consequence, the diversification of ownership structures in the reform era has led to a varying degree of judicial fairness and empowerment across regions in China.

The history of reforms in China is the history of diversification of ownership. In the mid-1950s, right after the establishment of the People's Republic, the communist government nationalized all private enterprises from the Kuomintang era. Throughout the Mao era, there were only two types of ownership in China: SOE and collective enterprise.

Traditional SOEs were integrated into the government bureaucracy under the planned economy before the reforms. The government finance department acted as the financial department of SOEs, administering their cash flows, revenues, and expenditures, and collecting taxes, fees, and profits (Wu 2005, 141). The SOE managers were government officials managed by the *nomenklatura* system at various levels of government (Burns 1989). The SOEs, as employees' "work units (*danwei*)," also carried the heavy burden of providing basic social welfare services such as health care, pension, day care, and housing (Walder 1986).

Facing increasing competition from township and village enterprises (TVEs) and domestic private enterprises, the Chinese government in the 1980s experimented with ways to improve incentives and management capabilities within the state sector (Naughton 2007, 95). The main theme of state sector reforms can be described as "power delegating and profit sharing (*fangquan rangli*)." The components of the reforms include transferring enterprises to governments at lower levels, expanding enterprise autonomy, and introducing the enterprise contracting system (Wu 2005, 142). The managerial reforms in the state sector are considered a more desirable alternative to privatization, which is more radical and hence more likely to encounter opposition (Qian 2003). The experimental process focused on a steady shift in emphasis away from plan fulfillment toward profitability as the most important indicator of enterprise performance (Naughton 2007, 95).

After the managerial reforms of the 1980s, SOEs' performance improved. But their inefficiency gradually manifested as the market reforms went deeper and as more FIEs and domestic private enterprises entered the competition. From the mid-1990s, the Chinese government began to restructure the state sector. The Third Plenary Session of the Fourteenth CCP Congress issued the Decision on Issues Regarding the Establishment of a Socialist Market Economic System, which stated that deepening state sector reform should "emphasize the institutional innovation of enterprises." This marked a shift in the state sector reform strategy from power delegating and profit sharing to enterprises' institutional innovation. One of the significant steps to corporatizing SOEs was the enactment of the Company Law of the People's Republic of China by the National People's Congress on December 29, 1993. In the Company Law,

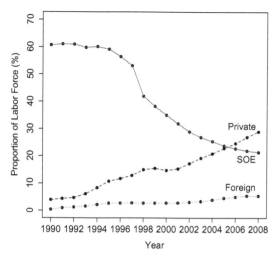

FIGURE 2.1 Share of Labor in Different Ownerships (1990-2008)
*Source*: National Bureau of Statistics of People's Republic of China (Various years)

clearly established property rights, well-defined powers and responsibilities, the separation of enterprises from the government, and scientific management became core goals of state sector corporatization (Wu 2005, 154–155).

At the same time, the central government decided to only selectively reform SOEs.[10] A policy called "grasping the large, letting the small go (*zhuada fangxiao*)" was announced at the CCP's Fifteenth Party Congress in 1997. "Grasping the large" means that the government should focus on maintaining state control over the largest SOEs, which are considered vital to the government's control of the economy. "Letting the small go" indicates that the central government should relinquish control over smaller SOEs through various means, including giving local governments the authority to restructure the firms, privatize firms, or close down unprofitable ones (Naughton 2007, 105–106). The latter policy resulted in a significant downsizing of the state sector. Figure 2.1 illustrates a remarkable drop in SOE employees from 1997 to 1998.

However, some of the goals of SOE corporatization were not achieved. For example, the original intention to separate the government's function as the administrator of society and economy from that of the owner of state assets by establishing the state assets management commissions was not really implemented (Wu 2005, 158). The remaining large SOEs are still under the firm control of the central and provincial governments. For example, as

---

[10] Steinfeld (1998) provided an excellent review of the SOE reforms.

FIGURE 2.2 Protection Pad *Translation*: "Enterprises' legal rights: Without the permission of the county party committee and government, no organization or individual is allowed to enter this factory to investigate or fine" (author's photograph).

Wu (2005, 159) observed, "To maintain control by the government, corporatization usually left listed companies dominated by state-owned shares."

As a consequence, SOEs become allies of the government: SOEs help governments at various levels create tax revenues, maintain social order by co-opting discontented labor, and provide the basic necessities of life (such as housing and health care) for state sector employees. SOEs receive big rewards in return from the government. Figure 2.2 is a photograph that I took in De An County in Jiangxi Province of a "Protection Pad" hung just outside the gate of a Jiangxi state-owned plastics enterprise. The pad, issued by the county party committee and government, reads: "Enterprises' legal rights: Without the permission of the county party committee and government, no organization or individual is allowed to enter this factory to investigate or fine." A judge in the county's court directed me to it. He told me that when he was trying to investigate a case in this enterprise, this pad blocked him and his colleagues.[11] This is just one of many examples in which local governments protect SOEs. A more systematic study by Wang, Wong, and Xia (2008) shows that compared to non-state-owned firms, Chinese SOEs controlled by various levels of government are more likely to hire small auditors within the same region. This auditor pattern is best explained by SOEs' collusion incentives.

In Kornai's (2008) typology of postsocialist economic transitions, there are two pure strategies. Strategy A, or the strategy of organic development, emphasizes the creation of favorable conditions for bottom-up development of the private sector. Strategy B, or the strategy of accelerated privatization, emphasizes the elimination of state ownership as quickly as possible through the speedy privatization of

[11] Interview with a judge in Jiangxi Province, April 8, 2010.

SOEs. As Wu (2005, xv) argues, "Since the beginning of the economic reform the Chinese leadership has been emphasizing SOE reform, which more or less fits Kornai's description of Strategy B; however, the transition itself has followed another path, similar to Kornai's Strategy A." Parallel to the SOE reform in China, the private sector also went through structural changes during the reform era.

The Chinese economy before 1949 was dominated by the private sector. Private businesses accounted for two-thirds of total industrial output and more than 85 percent of total retail sales (Wu 2005, 179). In 1955 and 1956, China appropriated all private enterprises to consolidate the socialist regime. The dominance of the state sector continued until the late 1970s. After the Cultural Revolution, it became urgent to find employment for a large number of educated urban youths who had been dispatched to work in rural areas and then returned to cities. The August 1980 Circular of the CCP Congress on Transmitting the Documents of the National Conference on Labor and Employment stipulated that "the development of the urban individual business sector be encouraged and fostered" (Wu 2005, 181–182).

The private sector in China includes two types of entities: self-employed household businesses (*getihu*) and privately run enterprises (*siying qiye*). The regulatory definition of the former is an entity with seven or fewer employees; the latter has more than seven employees (Huang 2008, 22). The private sector developed rapidly in the early 1980s after the state gave the green light. In April 1988, the Seventh National People's Congress passed an amendment to the Constitution of the People's Republic of China, which stated in Article 11, "The State permits the private sector to exist and develop within the limits prescribed by law. The private sector is a supplement to the socialist public sectors. The State protects the lawful rights and interests of the private sector, and exercises guidance, supervision, and control over the private sector." The Fifteenth CCP Congress in 1997 finally confirmed the legalization of the private sector. "Keeping public ownership as the mainstay of the economy and allowing diverse forms of ownership to develop side by side" was established as China's basic economic system for the primary stage of socialism. Nonpublic sectors were acknowledged as "important components of a socialist market economy" (Wu 2005, 188–189). The private sector then experienced faster growth in the late 1990s and has continued to grow in the twenty-first century.[12] As Figure 2.1 shows, the share of private sector employees kept growing and surpassed that of state sector employees in 2006.

Although the private sector has received de jure status in law, private enterprises in practice have a lower political status than SOEs and FIEs. As Huang (2008) argues, in the 1990s the Chinese state systematically favored foreign firms at the expense of indigenous private-sector firms. Small private

---

[12] The Chinese government implemented a crackdown against the private sector after the 1989 Student Movement (Naughton 2007, 98–100; Huang 2008, 110).

businesses – for example, food and vegetable stalls operated by peasants just outside city boundaries – are considered "backward" and therefore contradict the goal of major Chinese cities to become world-class cities. According to Huang's (2008, chapter 4) case study of Shanghai, the government imposes many policy restrictions on private businesses. For example, the Shanghai government imposed onerous restrictions on who could start a second job as a private entrepreneur. The government also imposed a registration capital obligation and required entrepreneurs to register the entire amount of their capital requirement on the day of registration. Thus, a potential entrepreneur would have to show proof of the requisite capital rather than being able to pay the registered capital by installment. Facing the formal constraints imposed by the state, private entrepreneurs have to rely on political connections to survive and prosper. An informal way to make political connections is to build clientelist ties with local officials. As Wank (1999, 68) argues, "Much exchange conducted by private companies is embedded in clientelist ties with various administrative, policing, distributive, and manufacturing organs of the local state." A more formal way is for private entrepreneurs to join the CCP. It is well documented that the CCP is increasingly integrating itself with the private sector, both by co-opting entrepreneurs into the party and by encouraging current party members to go into business (Dickson 2003; Tsai 2007a). Private entrepreneurs with party membership are called "red capitalists." In a systematic study of "red capitalists," Li et al. (2008) show that the party membership of private entrepreneurs has a positive effect on the performance of their firms when human capital and other relevant variables are controlled. They further find that party membership helps private entrepreneurs obtain loans from banks or other state institutions.

In addition to liberalizing domestic ownership, the post-Mao leadership realized that the nation had been drained of capital and entrepreneurial expertise after the Cultural Revolution and decided to open up to attract foreign investors. The National People's Congress passed the first law on foreign investors in 1979.[13] The law, though groundbreaking, still reflected the leadership's caution in the sense that it allowed only equity joint ventures (EJVs). Forming a joint venture with a domestic Chinese firm offered foreign investors a sort of protection, since their Chinese partners at this time were mainly state-owned or collective enterprises with close ties to the Chinese government.[14]

Special economic zones were then established to attract foreign investors. Uncertain of China's political and economic environment, investors in the early 1980s were mainly from the China circle – Hong Kong, Macao, and Taiwan. Before the Asian Financial Crisis in 1997, over half of China's FDI inflows had been from the China circle. This generation of "foreign" investors is ethnic

---

[13] For a detailed discussion of the evolution of the FDI regulatory framework, please see Fu (2000).
[14] Pearson (1991) provided a comprehensive review of the joint ventures.

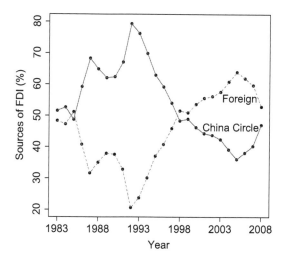

FIGURE 2.3 Sources of FDI Inflows in China (1983-2008)
*Source:* National Bureau of Statistics of People's Republic of China (Various years)

Chinese. They primarily relied on kinship connections to select places for investment, because the common language and customs made doing business on the mainland easy and cheap (Naughton 2007, 416–417). Another feature of FDI from within the China circle is that many of them are "round-tripping" FDI, whereby Chinese nationals first invest domestic capital into a foreign destination before repackaging it and reintroducing it to China as registered foreign capital. For example, Lenovo, arguably the most successful IT company operating in mainland China, is a wholly foreign owned company – it is 100 percent owned by Hong Kong Lenovo (Huang 2008, 2). All these features make investors from within the China circle very different from foreign investors from the outside.

Meanwhile, investors from the United States, the European Union, Japan, and other countries were attracted by China's big market and low labor costs. Firms from outside the China circle often have technological advantages over Hong Kong and Taiwanese firms. This characteristic of foreign firms became very attractive to Chinese government officials and entrepreneurs, who were searching for advanced technologies and know-how in the 1990s. Throughout the 1990s, especially after the Asian Financial Crisis, FDI from outside the China circle surged. Figure 2.3 shows the sources of FDI inflows from 1983 to 2008.

I argue that investors who came from outside the China circle have different preferences regarding the legal institutions than those from within the China circle. Foreign investors from outside the China circle have a stronger preference for judicial empowerment for two reasons. First, when foreign investors arrived in China, domestic and ethnic Chinese investors, who have language and network advantages, had already built strong connections with the Chinese government and occupied the market in the coastal areas. To have a fair competing environment, foreign investors were more likely to demand that local governments act according to the law when they have disputes with their domestic counterparts.

Second, foreign investors are often subject to stricter internal auditing rules and anticorruption rules imposed by their mother countries. One recent example is the 2002 US Sarbanes-Oxley Act, which set new or enhanced standards for all US public company boards, management, and public accounting firms. A recent study by Arping and Sautner (2010) indicates that, relative to a control sample of comparable firms that are not subject to Sarbanes-Oxley, cross-listed firms became significantly more transparent following the enactment of this legislation.

Another earlier example is the Foreign Corrupt Practices Act (FCPA) of 1977. Two key sets of provisions in the FCPA are the antibribery and record-keeping provisions. The FCPA's antibribery provisions make it unlawful for US persons, US companies, and certain foreign issuers listed on the US securities exchange to make payments to foreign officials for the purpose of obtaining or retaining business for or with, or directing business to, any person. A simple offer, promise, or authorization of a bribe triggers an FCPA violation (Pedersen 2008). The Act's record-keeping and accounting provisions require US corporations to keep their books, records, and accounts in reasonable detail, in a way that fairly reflects their transactions and the dispositions of their assets. The purpose of these provisions is to prevent issuers from concealing bribes and, more specifically, to discourage fraudulent accounting and reporting practices (Pedersen 2008). Violations of either the bribery or accounting provisions of the FCPA can subject individuals and/or corporations to both criminal and civil penalties.

Recent years have seen a spike in enforcement of the FCPA, from five actions in 2004 to seventy-four in 2010.[15] I interviewed a lawyer who has been practicing law with multinational corporations operating in China who remarked that the scope of the Act is "expansive" and the punishment "extreme."[16] For example, in 2005 DPC Tianjin, the Chinese subsidiary of a Californian company that makes medical equipment, admitted to paying bribes to doctors and laboratory personnel. American prosecutors asserted that this fell under the scope of the FCPA because health care in China is government run. And although the US company paid the bribe through its Chinese agency, this fell within the scope of the Act. Another recent example is that AGA Medical Corporation of Minnesota pled guilty to bribing doctors to purchase medical devices and bribing officials in China's Intellectual Property Office to push

---

[15] "A Tale of Two Laws: America's Anti-Corruption Law Deters Foreign Investment," *Economist*, September 17, 2011. http://www.economist.com/node/21529103, accessed October 10, 2011.

[16] Interview with a lawyer, February 10, 2012.

patent approvals. Even though a distributor made the payments, the courts still held the manufacturer responsible. The fines imposed on firms are also increasing. In February 2009, American courts fined KBR, a construction firm, and Halliburton, its former parent, $579 million over bribes paid to obtain contracts in Nigeria. Last year they imposed an $800 million fine on Siemens, a German conglomerate. The German authorities also fined Siemens a similar amount.[17] These cases make an important point about the anticorruption laws: even when companies bribe through a third party, for example a Chinese agency or individual, this still falls under the scope of the FCPA.

Members of the Organization for Economic Cooperation and Development (OECD) are also required to implement laws criminalizing the bribery of foreign officials (Pedersen 2008). The OECD Convention on Combating Bribery of Foreign Public Officials in International Business Transactions was enacted in 1997. All OECD member countries are expected to comply with this convention.

This does not imply that FIEs have completely clean hands. FIEs in China have adapted quickly to an environment in which bribery is often expected and political connections are critical in business success. The establishment of government relations offices in FIEs is a sign that foreign investors are learning the Chinese way. Many FIEs also hired Chinese nationals to take care of "public relations" with the government. However, what matters is whether foreign enterprises are *as competitive as* other firms in securing political connections. The answer is no. China's recent stimulus package of over 40 billion *yuan* (about $6 billion) in 2009–10 was invested in infrastructure building, of which SOEs are major beneficiaries.

A vice president of a French firm invested in Shanghai expressed his concerns:

Government policies are beneficial for central state-owned enterprises. For example, monetary policies and loan policies don't favor private and foreign enterprises. In terms of tax collection, nominally foreign enterprises pay the same tax rates with other enterprises, but state-owned enterprises can evade their taxes; private enterprises can do too if they are connected with the government; only foreign enterprises pay the full amount. There is a prevalent concern among foreign enterprises that the government starts to discriminate against foreign firms.[18]

As a result, the politically disadvantaged foreign investors strongly demand judicial empowerment. This proposition is consistent with some recent studies on foreign enterprises in China, which find that interaction between foreign and Chinese firms increases the use of meritocratic hiring and

---

[17] For more details of these examples, please see "Ungreasing the Wheels: Governments around the World Are Making Life Difficult for Corrupt Firms," *Economist*, November 19, 2009. http://www.economist.com/node/14931567/print, accessed February 10, 2012.

[18] Interview with a company manager, Shanghai, April 27, 2010.

promotion practices and enhances respect for the rule of law (Rosen 1999; Guthrie 1999; Santoro 2000).

A legal scholar who is also a practicing lawyer summarized the situation very clearly:

Usually, multinational corporations have to report their financial statements to their mother companies. So multinational corporations are constrained by two standards: one in the hosting country, the other in their countries of origin. The latter is often stricter than the former. As a consequence, multinational corporations hope that the hosting country's standard should also go higher. Otherwise, the competition between them and native companies would be unfair.[19]

Attracting new foreign investors and the incentive to retain existing foreign investors provide a strong impetus for Chinese officials to respect the rule of law. The Chinese legislatures at both the central and local levels have enacted many laws facilitating foreign investment and trade (Clarke 2007). My interviews also show that local officials in China often consider a fair and efficient legal system very important in servicing the foreign investors in their jurisdictions. Some local governments regularly send "legal service" teams to foreign companies to help solve their legal issues,[20] and some strengthen the local courts via staffing and funding to provide a higher quality of legal services to foreign companies.[21]

Meanwhile, FIEs owned by ethnic Chinese, which resemble domestic private enterprises, are not exposed to similar constraints. Ethnic Chinese investors have language, network, institutional, and geographical advantages in conducting business in China. Many of them are descendants of an older generation that migrated to Taiwan, Macao, and Hong Kong in 1949 or earlier. They still have strong family ties in mainland China. They speak the local dialect, and they understand local cultures and rules. More important, they also have institutional advantages, that is, they are not constrained by any anticorruption regulations. As a lawyer bluntly put, "Domestic private firms are very flexible in using their money. They are not susceptible to any auditing: it is the boss's own money. So they can use it in whichever way they want."[22] Commenting on companies from Taiwan investing in his county, an official said, "Most Taiwanese firms do not play by the rules."[23]

With strong political connections, domestic indigenous investors and ethnic Chinese investors have a strong incentive to prevent the leveling of the playing field to maintain their privileged status and eliminate competition from the foreign side. As Gallagher (2002) argues, the infusion of foreign capital into China's economy changed the nature of the economic debate. A typical

---

[19] Interview with a legal scholar, Shanghai, April 26, 2010.
[20] Interview with a court official, Jiangxi Province, April 2, 2010.
[21] Interview with the chairman of the County People's Congress, Jiangxi Province, April 8, 2010.
[22] Interview with a lawyer, Guangdong Province, March 31, 2010.
[23] Interview with the chairman of the County People's Congress, Jiangxi Province, April 8, 2010.

transitional economy debate over public versus private industry shifted to a debate that pits Chinese national industry against foreign competition in particular and globalization more generally. As Wank (1999, 81–83) shows, domestic investors often rely on clientelist ties to demand the lax enforcement of laws.

The European Chamber Business Confidence Survey shows that most European investors (70 percent in 2008, 66 percent in 2009, and 60 percent in 2010) believed that the enforcement of environmental laws and regulations on Chinese domestic firms was weak, whereas around half of the interviewees in each survey believed that the enforcement on foreign firms was strong.[24] To compete fairly, foreign investors prefer a strong legal system to protect their properties and contracts.

In summary, I argue that Chinese SOEs, domestic private enterprises, and enterprises owned by ethnic Chinese have political connections in China and, therefore, prefer privilege to a level playing field. In contrast, foreign investors from outside the China circle lack the competitive advantage gained from building political connections with Chinese officials. They therefore have a strong preference for judicial impartiality.

## Bargaining with the Government

To obtain policy concessions from the state, interest groups must be well organized and possess mobile assets that enable them to have strong bargaining power vis-à-vis the government. For this reason, well-organized economic elites are in a much better position than unorganized citizens to obtain preferred policies from the government.

Scholarly work has documented the rise of lobbying and its effect on public policy in China. Kennedy (2009) observes that the marketization of China's economy, and the attendant need for a supporting regulatory framework, have resulted in extensive lobbying by Chinese and foreign industry. He argues that on the one hand, the government has encouraged the development of industry associations, public hearings, and comment-and-response periods for draft laws and regulations to routinize public policy consultations. On the other hand, the central party state continues to constrain the maturation of these formal institutions and processes. As a consequence, informal lobbying practices, such as direct lobbying and manipulation of the media, have become more prominent vehicles for industry involvement in the policy process (Kennedy 2009).

SOEs have a "privileged position" at the policy table because they are practically part of the government (Lindblom 1977, 170–188). Managers and core leaders of large SOEs are managed as "state cadres" in the *nomenklatura*

---

[24] European Chamber, *European Chamber Business Confidence Survey 2010*, 2010. http://www .europeanchamber.com.cn/view/static?sid=7370, accessed January 12, 2011.

system (Burns 1989). Their party organization department determines their appointments, promotions, and dismissals. Many of the managers were government officials before they were appointed to an enterprise, and a transfer from a position in the state sector to the government is not uncommon. This gives SOE managers many opportunities to approach government officials. SOEs also have close business relations with the government. For example, SOEs are the major suppliers of government procurement and are also the primary taxpayers. The tax rate for SOEs is the highest of all types of enterprises. According to a 2010 report by the State-Owned Assets Supervision and Administration Commission of the State Council – the government ministry responsible for managing centrally owned companies – in 2002–09 the average tax rate for SOEs was 27.3 percent, which was five times the rate for domestic private enterprises.[25] Their political connections, business ties, and tax revenues give SOEs strong leverage in bargaining with the government.

SOEs organize themselves around industry-specific associations. As Kennedy (2009, 201) shows, for example, China's steel industry is led by a core group of large SOEs. The China Iron and Steel Industry Association was created in 1999 as a consequence of the planned elimination of the government's metallurgy bureaucracy. The association's offices are in the old ministry compound, and most of the association's leaders are former ministry officials. The members coordinate prices, pressing the Ministry of Commerce to defend Chinese steel companies more aggressively against foreign competition and to become involved in China's negotiations over iron ore imports.

SOEs take advantage of this leverage to maintain their monopolistic position in the market. The consequence is a trend termed "the state advances, the private retreats" (*guojin mintui*), a situation in which the state-backed conglomerates are expanding and consolidating their territories in critical industries while the private sector is shrinking. For example, the twenty-two Chinese companies that are listed in Forbes's Fortune 500 are unanimously state owned. The Chinese state is the biggest shareholder in the country's 150 biggest companies. State companies make up 80 percent of the value of the stock market in China.[26]

Chinese domestic private enterprises are polarized. There is a small number of large companies that are well connected and organized, while many small companies are constantly exposed to state expropriation hazards. For the small number of large companies, they are the major tax contributors to the government, their managers are CCP members ("red capitalists") and/or People's Congress representatives, they employ a large number of

---

[25] The State-Owned Assets Supervision and Administration Commission of the State Council, *Reflection of the State-Owned Assets Supervision and Administration Commission of the State Council*, 2010. http://www.sasac.gov.cn/2010rdzt/yjj/2009hg.pdf, accessed April 20, 2012.

[26] "The Visible Hand," *Economist*, January 21, 2012. http://www.economist.com/node /21542931, accessed May 23, 2012.

workers, and their patrons are high-ranking political officials. These companies have very strong bargaining power. They organize themselves via associations such as the All China Federation of Industry and Commerce, the All China Private Enterprises Federation, the China Enterprise Confederation, and the China Enterprise Directors Association. The All China Federation of Industry and Commerce is the most influential chamber of commerce in China. As Kennedy (2009, 200) shows, at the end of 2007 the federation had almost 2.2 million corporate and individual members and 3,130 branches at and above the county level around the country. The federation, despite its lack of independence,[27] advocates the interests of private business. It annually submits hundreds of proposals to different parts of the national and local bureaucracy and People's Congresses. For example, it advocated amending the constitution to add an article expressly protecting private property, which was adopted in 2004. It was also involved in pushing through a full-fledged Property Rights Law, passed by the National People's Congress in 2007. However, small private enterprises usually have no say in government policy making and are facing regulatory uncertainties, adverse discrimination in obtaining bank loans, and constant harassment by law enforcement officers.

Hong Kong and Taiwanese firms are often clustered regionally; for example, Hong Kong firms are in Guangdong and Taiwanese firms are in Fujian. They have family ties and language, networking, and cultural advantages in these regions. They are also well organized. Hong Kong firms have the Hong Kong Chinese Enterprises Association and Hong Kong Small and Medium Enterprises Association, while Taiwanese firms have the Association of Taiwan Investment Enterprises on the Mainland and Taiwan Federation of Industry and Commerce. My interviews show that ethnic Chinese investors, especially Taiwanese investors, are very united. They are often engaged in collective bargaining with the local government through their associations. The complex cross-strait relations further strengthened this solidarity because Taiwanese investors who got "mainland fever" were blamed domestically. It was reported that the economic ties stretching across the Taiwan Strait in the early 1990s worried both President Lee Teng-hui and Premier Hau Pei-tsun. An adviser to both men on China policy commented, "All of the time, we have to convince our people that we have to be cautious... Yet most businessmen are pursuing their individual, private interests at the expense of national interests."[28] When the pro-independence party – the Democratic Progressive Party (DPP) – was in power in Taiwan in 2000–08,

---

[27] Kennedy (2009, 200) shows that the federation's leaders, particularly at the national level, are formally elected, but the CCP's United Front Department has some say over who is nominated and holds office.

[28] Jeremy Mark, "Taiwan Struggles With 'Mainland Fever.'" *Wall Street Journal*, August 21, 1992, p. A4.

Taiwanese who had investments in mainland China were considered traitors by some DPP elites.[29]

Foreign investors in China primarily rely on two mechanisms to influence policies: voice and exit (Hirschman 1970). Foreign investors are frequently engaged in lobbying at every level of government and legislature to influence domestic policy making. Kennedy (2009, 204) argues that "any large multi-national that you can name – Microsoft, Fedex, IBM, Panasonic – interacts with the national government and local authorities on a regular basis." Major business associations that represent foreign investors include the American Chamber of Commerce in the People's Republic of China (AmCham-China), the European Union Chamber of Commerce in China (EUCCC), the Japanese Chamber of Commerce and Industry in China, and hundreds of country-specific, industry-specific associations and their local branches. These business associations have a strong voice in China's policy-making process.

Lobbying is an old practice in which firms try to influence government policies in the United States and Europe. When multinationals invested in China, they brought this practice to China, where corporate lobbying was not as common and public. American firms were in the vanguard. In 1986, American business executives and US government commercial officers wrote an unusual document that circulated in Beijing. The document called for establishing a model joint venture, a kind of utopian enterprise that would allow the Chinese and foreigners to see how foreign investment development might be done right, as opposed to how it was being done at the time. Some companies wanted to pull out, according to a survey of their representatives, if the Chinese government did not hear their cry. The document reached the top: then vice premiers Li Peng and Yao Yilin saw it.[30]

A recent example is the enactment of the Labor Contract Law in 2008. AmCham-China and the EUCCC both raised strong concerns about the potential impact of the new law to increase labor costs (Gallagher 2010). In response, the National People's Congress decided to revise the Labor Contract Law in 2012. Multinational corporations have also introduced a specialized government affairs staff to China, and Chinese domestic companies have followed suit. Many of these employees are former government and party officials themselves. As Kennedy (2009, 204) argues, they may be hired to lobby their former colleagues, but they are just as likely to be valued for their in-depth knowledge of how to navigate China's bureaucratic maze and interact with officials.

Because foreign investors are mobile, they also exert a credible exit threat when their voice is not heard. A recent example is Google's exit from the mainland market due to its dissatisfaction with China's Internet

---

[29] Interview with a scholar, Guangdong Province, March 27, 2010.

[30] James P. Sterba, "U.S. Firms Urge China to Make Changes or Risk the Loss of Foreign Investment," *Wall Street Journal*, June 6, 1986, p. 28.

censorship. However, many companies choose to stay in China to take advantage of the emerging market, and "a peculiar corporate mentality is at work: Nobody wants to be the first to go. Many are here only because their competitors are."[31]

Those companies, though, move within China. My interviews in a southern Chinese city suggest that multinational corporations frequently use the threat of exit to obtain bargaining leverage with the local government. A lawyer whose clients are mostly multinational corporations remarked that Procter and Gamble (P&G, an America-based multinational) has a strong influence on the city's policy-making process because of its significant weight in the city's economy: "The company usually threatens that they would move to Shanghai if the city government cannot satisfy them."[32]

Foreign enterprises have other ways besides advocating judicial empowerment to defend themselves against expropriation hazards. Delios and Henisz (2003) show that Japanese firms often sequence their entry into countries with uncertain legal contexts, so that the investment does not happen in full until they are satisfied that the venture is safe. Another strategy for multinational corporations is to partner with indigenous firms that have a comparative advantage in interactions with the host country government. However, as Henisz (2000) shows, as contractual hazards increase, the potential benefit to the joint venture partner of manipulating the political system for its own benefit at the expense of the multinational increases as well, thereby diminishing the hazard-mitigating benefit of forming a joint venture. This is exactly what happened in China. Because of frequent contractual frictions, infringement of intellectual property rights, and different management styles, the number of joint ventures started to decrease in the late 1980s. Since 2000, the number of wholly foreign-owned enterprises has surpassed that of joint ventures (Naughton 2007, 412). Figure 2.4 shows the growth of wholly foreign-owned enterprises compared to the decline of equity joint ventures.

## Policy Concessions

The state trades policies with revenues. Both domestic and ethnic Chinese investors seek policies that help them consolidate their privileged positions in the Chinese market. Facing competition from foreign companies that have a comparative advantage in capital, management, and technology, Chinese companies particularly need policy leverage (particularly related to entry, tariff, tax, land, and labor) to remain resilient.

---

[31] Ibid.
[32] Interview with a lawyer who has been working with P&G for many years, Guangdong Province, March 20, 2010.

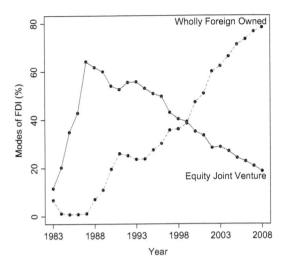

FIGURE 2.4 Forms of FDI Inflows in China (1979-2008)
*Source:* National Bureau of Statistics of People's Republic of China (Various years)


Foreign companies particularly care about whether they are in a level playing field with the indigenous firms. Given their disadvantages in language, networking, and entry time, they demand a fair competing environment. An important guarantor of fair competition is the legal system. FIEs are accustomed to signing a contract while forming business relations and filing a court case if a contract violation occurs, so they are especially looking for a functional, fair, efficient, and effective court system while operating in China.

Yet the early supply of legal institutions and services was inadequate to meet foreign firms' demands. Erik Guyot from the *Wall Street Journal* wrote in 1994:

In many alliances in China between Chinese and foreign companies, for instance, the Chinese partners prefer not to prespecify explicit conflict resolution terms, especially judiciary or arbitration resolution, in an alliance contract. From their perspective, leaving these terms ambiguous may nourish interpartner cooperation in the long term. When they form partnerships with Western firms, however, this ambiguity can lead to the exit of alliances. For example, Lehman Brothers sued Sinochem and Sinopec, the two giant state-owned Chinese firms, in 1994, for failing to honor their obligations in swap transactions. This accusation, however, was rejected by the Chinese partners, which argued that there was no explicit stipulation on these transactions in the agreement. As a result of this open confrontation, the partnership between Lehman Brothers and the two Chinese giants was ended.[33]

[33] Erik Guyot, "Contract Disputes Imperil China's Bid to Raise Foreign Capital, S&P Warns," *Wall Street Journal*, December 15, 1994.

To attract and retain foreign investors, Chinese local governments have taken deliberate actions to strengthen legal organizations. These include establishing more law schools, producing more professional lawyers and judges, enacting better laws to regulate the market economy, increasing court funding, and providing legal services to business.

Creating a fair and effective court system means minimizing or eliminating the favors extended to politically connected indigenous firms, which will certainly produce opposition from the domestic side. Therefore the policy outcome hinges on the balance of power between the domestic and foreign sides. In regions where the local economy is dominated by SOEs, domestic private enterprises, and enterprises owned by ethnic Chinese, local governments have no real interest in strengthening the legal organizations, whereas in regions where FIEs carry a significant weight in the economy, local governments must tie their hands and build a strong court system.

However, local governments have no incentive to strengthen courts in every respect. A fair and efficient court will not only protect investors, whose assets are crucial for local officials' political advancement, but also allow discontented citizens and social groups to challenge the state, which could undermine officials' careers. Therefore, the best strategy for the government is to curb corruption in the commercial realm while imposing constraints on citizens' rights to sue the authoritarian state through legal channels. *Ex ante*, this is achieved through the Communist Party's agenda-setting power to selectively intervene in judicial decisions. Or, as an *ex post* remedy, the party can manipulate the setup of the anticorruption agencies to gain a first-mover advantage to protect corrupt party officials (Manion 2004).

First, the CCP employs the *nomenklatura* and fiscal systems to control the courts. Although the formal law stipulates that presidents of People's Courts in China should be elected by the People's Congress at the same administrative level, most presidents, who are also court Communist Party secretaries, are nominated by the party committees. The election just confirms the nomination. Also, the government funds the courts at every level. Courts depend on local governments for basic necessities, including judges' salaries and bonuses, office supplies, vehicles, and buildings. By controlling the "head" and "purse" of the court, the party can exert a strong influence on court decisions.

In addition, the Communist Party has established ad hoc organizations to supervise the judicial system. In China, the political and legal committees (*zhengfa wei*) (which are set up at every level of government and are part of party committees) supervise the courts. The secretary of the political and legal committee is a member of the party standing committee. The political and legal committee's work is to coordinate all formal legal organizations in its jurisdiction, including the public security department, court, procuratorate, and legal bureau. A concrete mechanism to manipulate judicial cases is the "three-heads meeting" (*sanzhang huiyi*) in which the political and legal committee secretary convenes the court president, procuratorate president, and police chief to discuss politically sensitive cases.[34]

Another institution established by the party to influence judicial decisions is the adjudication committee (*shenpan weiyuanhui*) within each court. Most cases in China are adjudicated by a collegial panel of judges (*heyi ting*). Only simple civil cases and minor criminal cases are tried by a single judge. There is a presiding judge (*heyiting shenpanzhang*) in each collegial panel. In addition, as the Organic Law of People's Courts (Article 11) requires, each court also establishes an adjudication committee to discuss important (*zhongda*) and difficult (*yinan*) cases. The adjudication committee members are usually Communist Party members, and the president is always the party secretary of the court. The Organic Law stipulates that the presidents of the People's Courts preside over meetings of adjudication committees. All cases can enter the adjudication committee. However, as Su (2000, 104–105) observes, very few civil cases enter the adjudication committee, 10–15 percent of criminal cases enter the adjudication committee, and most administrative cases enter the adjudication committee.

The CCP, through the political and legal committees outside the court and adjudication committees within the court, manages to influence court cases that involve contention between citizens and the state.

In addition to these *ex ante* mechanisms, the Communist Party also has *ex post* mechanisms to prevent corrupt party members from being punished. Manion (2004) shows that the design of China's anticorruption enforcement routinely protects corrupt officials from criminal punishment by granting party agencies a first-mover advantage over procuratorates in information gathering and sequencing of investigations and punishments.

To summarize, although the inflows of foreign investors are expected to curb corruption in the judicial system, their impact is limited to the commercial realm. The political realm is still under the strict control of the CCP.

## CAUSALITY

The demand-side theory tells a story of moving from investment to the rule of law, rather than the other way around. Therefore, the theory is different from North and Weingast's (1989) account of the Glorious Revolution, in which the Crown first established parliamentary supremacy and then borrowed from the capitalists, who were guaranteed future repayment. However, Western investors decided to pour money into China not because they were "drinking the Kool-Aid"; they were guaranteed that their investments would be safe not by a strong legal system but by individual party leaders. Western companies were attracted to China not because it had good rule of

---

[34] Interview with a county political and legal committee secretary, Hainan Province, March 15, 2010.

law – China had very weak rule of law in the 1980s – but because it was a big market that nobody could afford to ignore.

China has been a dream market for Westerners since the Industrial Revolution. When the Europeans and Americans began producing goods at an astonishing rate, they began searching for a market to absorb their ever-expanding production, and China – which has the world's largest population – became an obvious target. In 1898 US Secretary of State William R. Day told Congress that American factories were producing a "large excess over home consumption," which required "an enlargement of foreign markets." The most favorable markets for American exports were in underdeveloped areas of the world, Day said, and "nowhere is this consideration of more interest than in its relation to the Chinese Empire"(Mann 1989, 30).

However, this dream was unfulfilled until eighty years later due to the interruption of the Chinese revolution, the Sino-Japanese War, the civil war, and the seclusion of the Mao era. When Deng Xiaoping announced that China would open its door to foreigners in 1978, Western companies were eager to pursue their old dream of doing business in China.

China's attractions for foreign companies were at least threefold. First, the sheer size of its market made China a magnet for factories that were struggling with the almost-saturated consumer appetite in the West.

The second attraction was the incredibly low price of labor, land, and taxes. In the late 1970s and early 1980s, land prices were astronomical and wages soared in most developed economies. "We are paying less for land in a year than we would for two weeks in Hong Kong," says Eddie Lo, managing director of the LMK Group, which invested $30 million in 1982 in a dyeing factory in Shenzhen, China's first special economic zone. "To put up a factory of this type in Hong Kong isn't worthwhile. Actually a lot are closing down."[35] As for taxes, foreign investors in the special economic zones and coastal open cities would pay 15 percent income tax, compared to 30–50 percent elsewhere in China. Among other incentives, they were also allowed to establish wholly owned enterprises and remit earnings outside China tax free.[36]

The third attraction was access to the Asian market, which included over half of the world's population. This was especially appealing to European and American investors, who faced stiff competition from Japan, which was dominant in Asia.

Good legal protection was not on this list of attractions in the 1980s, and it still is not now. In a document issued in 2009 by the Anqing municipal government in Anhui Province, the city government listed benefits that they thought would attract foreign investment: tax exemption within the first three years of investment, a 10 percent tax return after the first three years, a

---

[35] Frank Ching, "China's New Economic Zones on Trial: Special Areas Attract Billions in Investments," *Wall Street Journal*, August 12, 1982.

[36] Vigor Fung, "China Opens 14 Cities to Investment," *Wall Street Journal*, June 27, 1984.

300 million *yuan* reward if the company goes public, green cards that grant foreigners citizen treatment, and day care and public school access for their children.[37] Legal protection, however, is not on this list. And this is not unique in Anhui; similar lists are provided in Hubei,[38] Jiangxi,[39] and Liaoning.[40] This does not imply that foreign firms do not care about legal protection. Rather, it suggests that these other concerns about costs and markets trump legal concerns when they decide where to invest.

Without the guarantee of a strong legal infrastructure, how did foreign investors convince themselves that their investments would be safe and that they could take their earnings back home? In most cases, individual Chinese leaders made the commitment. Leaders at various levels of government frequently made commitments to protect foreign businesses. In 1986, sitting among American executives in a meeting room of the Great Hall of the People, Beijing's then mayor, Chen Xitong, said, "I promise you that I will let you make money and benefit." As a translator rendered Mr. Chen's words into English, the executives broke into applause.[41] Obviously, the strongest commitment was made by the most powerful leader: Deng Xiaoping. In his Southern Tour in 1992, Deng reassured foreign investors that China would reverse its conservative policies after the 1989 democratic movement and resumed reforms. "Reforms and greater openness (to foreign trade and investment) are China's only way out," Deng was quoted as saying by the pro-Beijing *Ta Kung Pao* newspaper in Hong Kong. "No reform is a dead end."[42]

The question, then, is whether these commitments were credible. The answer is that they *were* credible, at least temporarily. In a now-declassified speech, then vice premier Zhu Rongji in September 1992 told officials in Guangdong:

I especially felt that Guangdong has developed very fast since this year. This is obviously because comrade Deng Xiaoping's Southern Tour has ignited people's enthusiasm and stimulated foreign investors' passion. Big bosses from Hong Kong used to give me the impression that they would donate hundreds of millions but would not invest several millions... However, since this year foreign and Hong Kong investors have come in large numbers, not only to Guangdong, but also to Beijing, Shanghai, and the inland. They have a strong passion for investment... This is because comrade Deng Xiaoping's Southern Tour reassured the success of reforms and opening up and revealed the determination of the party to continue the basic policies, hence the tide of investment. (Zhu 2011, 224)

---

[37] Please see http://www.chinalawedu.com/new/1200_22016__/2009_3_23_li6091126351323900027 329.shtml, accessed June 19, 2013.

[38] Please see http://www.law-lib.com/law/law_view.asp?id=204462, accessed June 19, 2013.

[39] Please see http://www.law-lib.com/law/law_view.asp?id=263656, accessed June 19, 2013.

[40] Please see http://www.chinalawedu.com/falvfagui/fg22016/244440.shtml, accessed June 19, 2013.

[41] James R. Schiffman, "Chinese Regulations Seek to Mollify Foreign Investors," *Wall Street Journal*, December 24, 1986.

[42] "Deng Presses Chinese to Return to the Path of Economic Reform," *Wall Street Journal*, January 29, 1992.

However, leaders' commitments were inadequate to sustain long-term confidence, because not all leaders committed to protecting foreign business. Chinese politics, especially in the 1980s, was characterized by disagreement, instability, and what Baum (1994) dubbed *"Fang Shou* cycles," when the reformers and conservatives would alternate in power, all of which created uncertainties of economic policies. In 1988, during one of the retrenchments, China decided to "cool down" its economy. In a meeting, Wang Zhaoguo, then governor of the east coast province of Fujian, said, "With regard to Sino-foreign joint ventures on which contracts have been signed, we must honor the contracts – with the exception of a few."[43] In an earlier retrenchment in 1981, a Sino-Japanese joint project – Baoshan Iron and Steel – was canceled after Japanese-led groups had held an estimated $1.5 billion of the contract.[44]

The biggest blow to foreign companies was the 1989 Tiananmen Square massacre, which also led to the downfall of a generation of liberal reformers such as Zhao Ziyang, who was considered by many foreigners as "the nation's leading champion of the importance of attracting foreign investment"(Mann 1989, 304).

Foreigners were frustrated but well aware of the risks associated with political uncertainties. Amanda Bennett reported in the *Wall Street Journal*, "They are aware of Peking's long history of on-again-off-again policies. One lawyer with nearly a decade of China experience says he has seldom been busier but adds, 'This can't last. I am already preparing for the next downturn.'"[45]

The frustration shifted Western firms' focus from building connections with individual leaders to demanding institutional changes. This shift was further accelerated by foreign firms', and their Chinese partners', increasing reliance on contracts in the 1990s as an increasing number of large multinational corporations formed wholly foreign-owned enterprises rather than equity joint ventures in China. And although a significant proportion of foreign firms still resort to international arbitration centers for a fair third-party settlement for their disputes with their Chinese clients, they realize that Chinese local courts must enforce all arbitration awards. Legal institutions have become relevant.

In 2002, the Guangzhou Intermediate People's Court implemented a reform that changed their case-allocation system. Before the reform, when the court accepted a case, the president and several vice presidents would assign the case to the appropriate judges. While in most occasions the

---

[43] Adi Ignatius, "China's Effort to Curb Economic Growth Is Likely to Damp Foreign Investment," *Wall Street Journal*, October 26, 1988.

[44] Frank Ching, "China, Despite Retrenchment, Proceeds on Two Projects with Foreign Concerns," *Wall Street Journal*, March 11, 1981.

[45] Amanda Bennett, "China's Free-Market Tilt: Good News and Bad News for Foreign Companies," *Wall Street Journal*, November 8, 1984.

case-judge match was based on expertise and workload considerations, there were several instances in which a case was intentionally assigned to a judge who had a connection with one of the parties: usually a domestic private company. In those lawsuits, the connected firms unanimously won or received favorable mediation. However, the losing side included some foreign firms invested in Guangzhou. After a series of failed litigations, the foreign firms organized themselves and lobbied the Guangzhou government and courts through the local chamber of commerce to reform the case-assignment system. Thanks to their heavy weight in the local economy, the foreigners' lobby succeeded. In 2002, the previous case-assignment procedure was abolished and replaced with a new computer-based random allocation procedure. The new system significantly minimized opportunities for judicial corruption.[46]

The Guangzhou court is not a singular case. Starting in the mid-1990s, China began a systematic reform to strengthen its legal institutions and build a "socialist rule of law state." The state started to staff young, professional judges to courts at every level; court funding has been dramatically increased to enable judges to afford better offices and equipment; internal rules have been altered to better incentivize judges.

Around the same time, more stories emerged of foreign firms winning Chinese domestic firms. In 2006, Starbucks, the large US coffee shop chain, won a trademark infringement lawsuit against its Chinese rival, the Shanghai Xingbake Coffee Shop.[47] In 2009, Nike, another American multinational, won a lawsuit against five private Chinese companies.[48] In 2010, Microsoft won a victory in its fight against piracy in China when a Shanghai court sentenced a regional insurer to pay the US software company 2.17 million *yuan* ($318,000) in damages. The Shanghai Pudong New Area district court found Dazhong Insurance, a Shanghai-based insurer backed by a number of Chinese state-owned and listed companies, guilty of infringing Microsoft's intellectual property by using illegal copies of its software.[49]

## CONCLUDING REMARKS

I develop a demand-side theory to explain the puzzle of why some authoritarian regimes promote a certain type of rule of law. Authoritarian rule of law – a

---

[46] Interview with a senior judge at Guangzhou's Intermediate People's Court, March 31, 2010.

[47] "Starbucks Wins Trademark Infringement Suit," *New York Times*, January 4, 2006. http://query.nytimes.com/gst/fullpage.html?res=9A07E5DB1130F937A35752C0A9609C8B63, accessed June 7, 2013.

[48] "Nike Wins Lawsuits over Fake Chinese Shoes," *CBS News*, February 11, 2009. http://www.cbsnews.com/2100-500395_162-3188266.html, accessed June 19, 2013.

[49] K. Hille, "Microsoft Wins in Court over China's Pirates," *Financial Times*, April 22, 2010. http://www.ft.com/intl/cms/s/2/66a1b906-4e09-11df-b437-00144feab49a.html#axzz2VXhpxSFj, accessed June 7, 2013.

partial form of the rule of law – arises when authoritarian rulers need the cooperation of organized interest groups that control valuable and mobile assets and are not politically connected. This theory is distinctive compared to most existing theories.

I then apply the theory in China showing that the Chinese state – a revenue maximizer – would make policy concessions by strengthening the legal system for economic elites who are not politically connected. Specifically, the rule of law is expected to be better enforced in regions where there is relatively more foreign capital than domestic and ethnic Chinese capital. Yet the rule of law in China is not in its full scale. The Chinese government is interested only in promoting judicial fairness in the commercial realm while constraining citizens' rights to challenge the state.

The demand-side theory posits that the causal arrow is from investment to the rule of law. Foreign investors entered the Chinese market because China offered a large market, low costs of labor and land, and access to other Asian markets. Western companies went to China hoping that they would be favored. Some of them indeed were, but most were not. And this political favor granted by individual leaders soon evaporated as political struggle among the elites intensified and China's political climate changed. Foreign firms' strategies then shifted to pushing for more sustainable protective mechanisms such as legal reforms. As a consequence, FDI inflows have contributed to the rise of the partial rule of law in China.

# 3

# Authoritarian judiciary: How the party-state limits the rule of law

> The law should always be accessible for everyone, he thinks, but as he now looks more closely at the gatekeeper in his fur coat, at his large pointed nose and his long, thin, black Tartar's beard, he decides that it would be better to wait until he gets permission to go inside.
>
> Franz Kafka

## INTRODUCTION: MOTIVATION, FINDINGS, AND A ROAD MAP

Authoritarian rulers have no interest in implementing the rule of law in every respect; the rulers tie their hands in some instances but not in others. How does the CCP limit the rule of law? This chapter uses a descriptive quantitative analysis and in-depth qualitative interviews to address this question. It also provides a brief overview of China's legal system and legal development for readers who are not familiar with the subject.[1]

Since the start of the reforms in the late 1970s, China's legal development has made significant progress in lawmaking, the professionalization of judges and lawyers, and building the capacity of courts to deal with various cases. However, the development is rather uneven across regions, which begs an explanation, given that China is a unitary state with similar institutions across the country. I then investigate the court system and show that it is very decentralized and fragmented. Through the *nomenklatura* power and the fiscal muscle, the Communist Party and the government have exerted a strong influence on courts, especially when the state is threatened.

---

[1] Readers who are well versed in the Chinese legal system can skip this chapter without missing the main argument of the book.

Chinese judges are managed and incentivized internally by a mixture of formal and informal institutions. In practice, the informal institutions often subvert the formal institutions in personnel affairs. Externally, the courts are in a weak position in a nexus of political organizations including the party organizations, the police, the procuratorates, and People's Congresses. However, the courts are pressured to serve the goals of the Communist Party and the government, including developing the economy and maintaining social order. All of these jeopardize the judiciary's independence in the Chinese authoritarian state.

The chapter is organized as follows: the next two sections give an overview of China's legal development in the reform era and the basic setup of the judiciary, then I introduce the internal structure of a Basic People's Court. The subsequent two sections investigate the internal and external environments of Chinese judges and courts. Next I examine the role played by courts in economic development and keeping social order, followed by a summary of the findings and a discussion of their broader implications.

## AN OVERVIEW OF CHINA'S LEGAL DEVELOPMENT

The PRC's history in the past six decades reflects a transformation from a rule-of-man regime to a partial rule-of-law regime. Mao Zedong turned the judicial system into a tool of consolidating socialism after establishing the People's Republic in 1949. Courts were employed by the new regime to penalize counterrevolutionaries who were associated with the previous Kuomintang regime, to sentence landlords who were deprived of property and rights in the land reforms, and – during the Anti-Rightist Campaign – to legitimize the punishment of rightists who criticized the party and the government. The rule-of-man regime in China reached its peak during the Great Proletarian Cultural Revolution, during which Mao's words proved superior to any laws. The whole legal system was almost completely abolished during the Cultural Revolution except that some courts still functioned to adjudicate cases involving "class enemies." Law schools were shut down, bar examinations terminated, and lawyers sent to the countryside.

In the late 1970s, China resumed its state-building process, of which institutionalization of the formal legal system was a crucial component. The post-Mao leadership believed that installing a reliable legal system with constitutional checks on individual power would prevent political disasters such as the Cultural Revolution from happening again. More systematic legal reforms, which had the goal of building a professional, efficient, and fair legal system, started in the 1990s as market reforms deepened. A market economy in which contract rights need to be enforced by a fair third party and disputes need to be settled efficiently increasingly calls for a well-functioning legal system.

As the first step of moving toward a socialist legal system, China began to legislate. A market economy especially requires "rules of the game" to be put

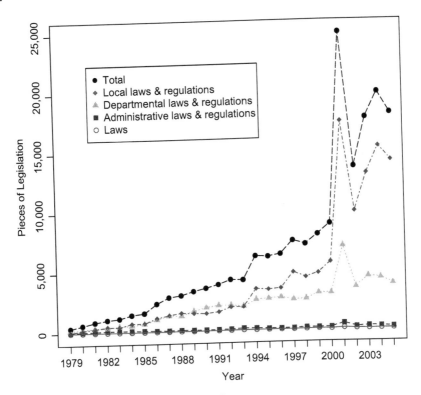

FIGURE 3.1 Pieces of Legislation (1979–2005)
*Source:* Zhu (2007)

into place to regulate the behavior of rational actors whose only incentive is to maximize profits. Figure 3.1 shows the number of various kinds of legislation enacted from 1979 to 2005. Although the National People's Congress is the highest lawmaking authority, most laws and regulations have been made by local People's Congresses, governments at various levels, and functional departments. As a consequence of "departmental legislation" (*bumen lifa*), laws and regulations have become tools for government organs to expand their powers.[2]

Meanwhile, more and more disputes have been brought to the courts. Figure 3.2 shows the trend of first-instance cases of various kinds accepted by courts at all levels in China from 1950 to 2008. As shown, there are some spikes in the 1950s around the years of the Campaign to Suppress Counter-revolutionaries, Land Reforms, and the Anti-Rightist Campaign. And then the numbers remained very low during the Cultural Revolution of 1966–76.

---

[2] Interview with a government official, Guangdong Province, March 29, 2010.

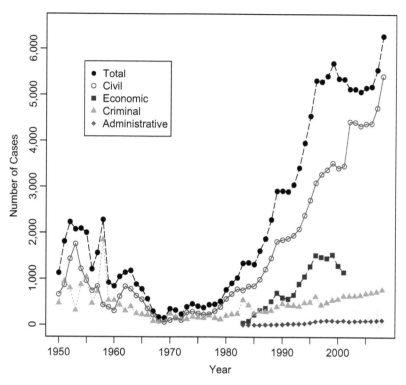

FIGURE 3.2 Number of First-Instance Court Cases in China (1950–2008)
*Source:* Zhu (2007) and National Bureau of Statistics of People's Republic of China
(Various years)

The numbers began to surge in the late 1970s when the reforms started. The
number of civil cases has experienced the highest growth rate, followed by
economic cases. In addition, since the passage of the Administrative Litigation
Law in 1989, citizens began to use the law to sue the government. However, the
number of administrative disputes has remained very low, likely due to the low
probability of winning a case against the government.

Adjusted by population size, Figure 3.3 shows the litigation rate of three
kinds of disputes from 1979 to 2008. *Litigation rate* is defined as the number of
first-instance cases brought to courts per 100,000 people. Unlike the conventional claim that Chinese culture is against litigation (Fei 1998), in the reform
era, the Chinese are increasingly litigious.

At the same time, as China opened its doors, investors from outside the
mainland started to conduct business in China. Figure 3.4 shows the numbers
of civil and economic disputes involving investors from Hong Kong, Macao,
and Taiwan (the China circle) and investors from other foreign countries.

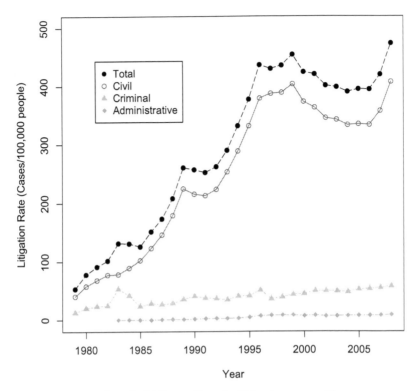

FIGURE 3.3 Litigation Rate in Different Cases in China (1979–2008)
*Source:* Zhu (2007) and National Bureau of Statistics of People's Republic of China
(Various years)

Consistent with the trend of FDI inflows discussed in Chapter 2, disputes involving foreign investors started to increase steadily in the 1990s. And disputes involving investors from within the China circle almost always outnumber those involving other foreign investors. This is possibly due to two reasons. First, the number of investors from within the China circle was larger than that of other foreign investors in this period (1983–98). Second, because of differences in management style, corporate culture, and organizational structure, FIEs from within the China circle are more likely to have disputes than those from outside the China circle.

Another trend in the reform era is the decline of alternative dispute resolution (ADR), especially mediation. Figure 3.5 shows the numbers of disputes mediated by people's mediators (*renmin tiaojieyuan*) and disputes adjudicated by judges. Figure 3.6 shows the number of first-instance court cases that were settled through mediation rather than adjudication in courts. In both cases, the proportion of mediated cases has decreased over the years among all

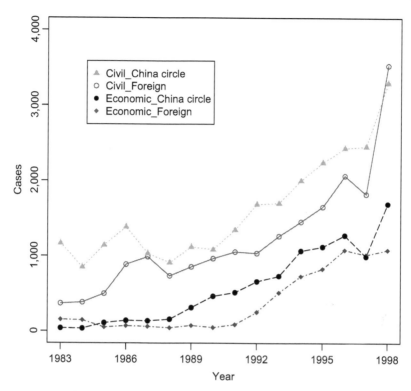

FIGURE 3.4 Number of Cases Involving Foreign Investors (1983–98)
*Source:* The Research Department of the Supreme People's Court (2000)

cases. Substantively, mediation requires compromise between the two parties, and the resolution is not necessarily in accordance with the law. The decline of mediation further reflects the rise of rule of law in Chinese society.[3]

ADR is more relevant for foreign companies; these mechanisms are specified in bilateral investment treaties (BITs) signed by China and other countries. The most popular method is through international arbitration. In theory, the arbitration centers are located outside the country where the dispute occurs, which guarantees neutrality.[4] Studies show that BITs increase investors' confidence in their investments in developing countries (Neumayer and Spess 2005; Elkins, Guzman, and Simmons 2006; Kerner 2009). Some famous centers include the International Chamber of Commerce, JAMS International, the

---

[3] Minzner (2011) has noticed a recent trend since 2005 to "turn against law," which emphasizes mediation over litigation. I do not find empirical evidence to support or challenge this argument.
[4] This is stipulated in the "New York Convention," see http://www.uncitral.org/uncitral/en/uncitral_texts/arbitration/NYConvention.html, accessed January 10, 2011.

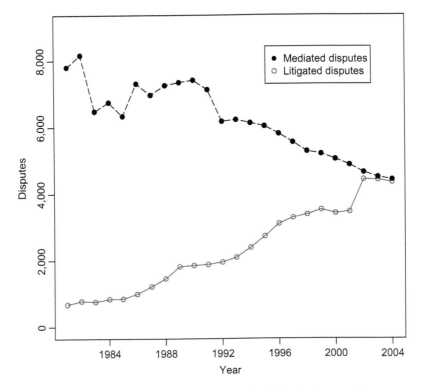

FIGURE 3.5 Number of Mediations and Litigations in China (1981–2004)
*Source:* Zhu (2007)

International Centre for Dispute Resolution, the international branch of the American Arbitration Association, the London Court of International Arbitration, the Hong Kong International Arbitration Centre, and the Singapore International Arbitration Centre. However, this does not mean that local courts are irrelevant for foreign investors. BITs often serve as complements of, rather than substitutes for, domestic institutions in protecting property and contract rights (Neumayer and Spess 2005; Desbordes and Vicard 2009). Local courts are still crucial, because they need to enforce all of the arbitration awards.[5]

---

[5] The following case illustrates this point. GRD Minproc (an Australia-based multinational corporation) signed a contract with Shanghai Flying Wheel Company (a domestic Chinese company) in 1994. In the contract, GRD agreed to sell equipment and materials for battery recycling to Flying Wheel. In 1999, GRD installed the equipment in Shanghai. However, Flying Wheel claimed that the equipment was not consistent with what was specified in the contract. As stipulated in the contract, the two companies resorted to the Arbitration Institute of the Stockholm Chamber of Commerce for settlement. The Stockholm Institute decided that GRD did not violate the contract,

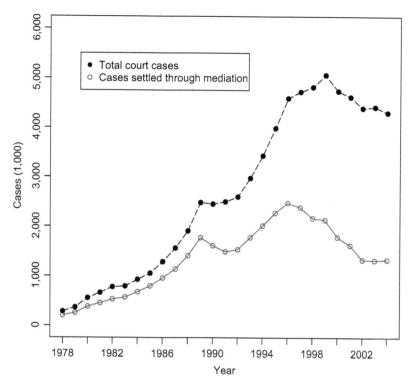

FIGURE 3.6 Number of Cases Mediated in Chinese Courts (1978–2004)
*Source:* Zhu (2007)

As societal demand for the legal system has increased, so has the state's supply. The number of judges has increased from 60,439 in 1981 to 190,627 in 2004. In 1981, there were only 6.08 judges for every 100,000 people, whereas the number was 14.69 in 2004. The number of lawyers has grown from 8,571 in 1981 to 107,841 in 2004. For every 100,000 people, there were 0.86 lawyers in 1981 and 8.3 in 2004. Figure 3.7 shows the numbers of judges and lawyers per 100,000 people from 1981 to 2005. The quality of judges has also improved over the years. In 1987, only 17.1 percent of newly appointed judges

because Flying Wheel's claims were based on an earlier version, rather than the final version, of the contract. Flying Wheel appealed the decision in Shanghai's First Intermediate People's Court, and the Shanghai Court ruled in favor of Flying Wheel. GRD then appealed to Shanghai's Higher People's Court to enforce the Stockholm Arbitration Institute's decision. After consulting with the Supreme People Court, Shanghai's Higher People's Court decided to uphold Stockholm's original decision and enforce the decision made by the Stockholm Arbitration institute. This case illustrates the importance of the domestic legal system even when foreign companies frequently resort to international arbitration institutes.

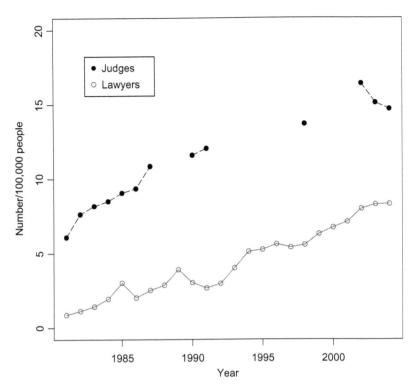

FIGURE 3.7 Judges and Lawyers per 100,000 People in China (1981–2004)
*Source:* Zhu (2007)

had junior college (*dazhuan*) degrees; this number increased to 66.6 percent in 1992, 84.1 percent in 1995, and 100 percent in 2000.

Despite the national progress, the development of the rule of law is quite uneven across regions and issue areas. Studies have found significant variation in the evaluation of the legal system (Gallagher and Wang 2011), people's preferences for courts (Shen and Wang 2009), trust in the courts (Landry 2011), implementation of laws and regulations (O'Brien and Li 1999), and the effectiveness of law (Lu and Yao 2009) in different regions and issue areas in China.

Figure 3.8 shows the number of legislation pieces by province in 2005. As shown, while Guangdong, Beijing, and other prosperous provinces had enacted thousands of laws and regulations by 2005, Tibet had made only 350.

Similarly, Figure 3.9 shows the litigation rate (number of first-instance court cases per 100,000 people) by province in 2004. While there were 1,307.9 cases brought to court per 100,000 people in Beijing, the national average was 390.2, and merely 177.5 in Tibet.

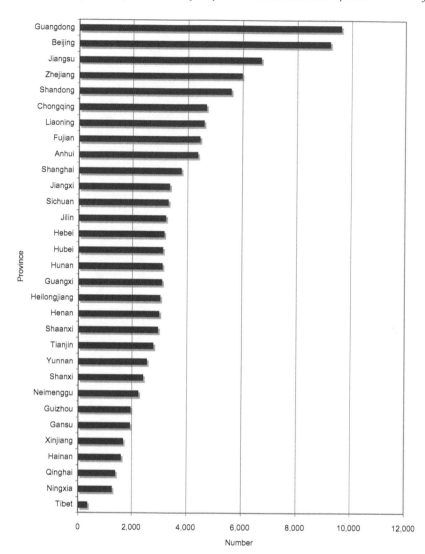

FIGURE 3.8 Pieces of Legislation by Province in China (2005)
*Source:* Zhu (2007)

The same pattern appears on the supply side, too. Figure 3.10 shows the number of lawyers per 100,000 people across thirty-one provinces. Beijing is at the top with 54.3 lawyers per 100,000 people, whereas Tibet only has 1.3 lawyers per 100,000 people.

These regional variations beg explanation, given that China is a unitary state with almost identical institutions across the country.

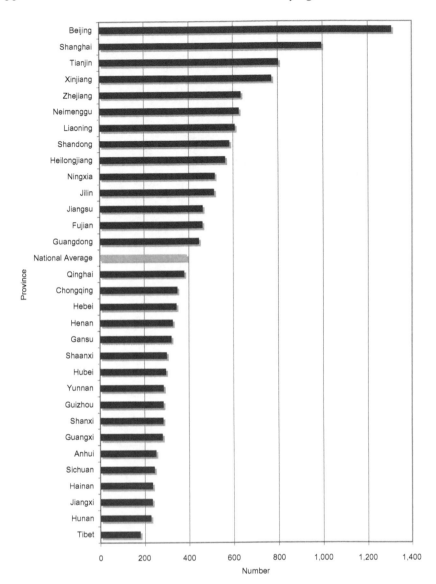

FIGURE 3.9 Litigation Rate by Province in China (2004)
*Source:* Zhu (2007)

## THE CHINESE JUDICIARY: A SNAPSHOT

As stipulated in Article 123 of the Constitution of the People's Republic of China, "The people's courts of the People's Republic of China are the judicial organs of the state." The PRC establishes the Supreme People's Court and People's Courts at various local levels, as well as military courts and other special People's Courts.

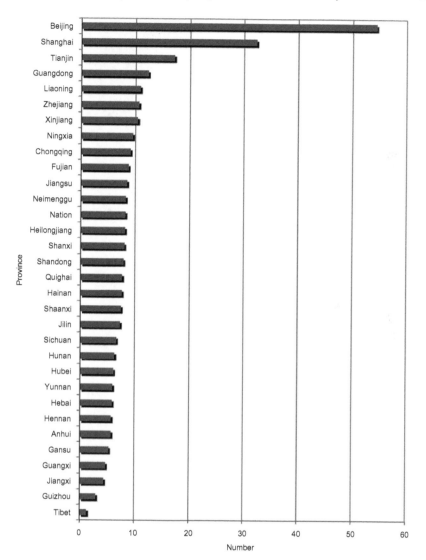

FIGURE 3.10 Lawyers per 100,000 People across Thirty-One Provinces in China (2003)
*Source:* Zhu (2007)

China has a four-level judicial system, as shown in Figure 3.11. The system includes the Supreme People's Court and local People's Courts. The local People's Courts at various levels are divided into Basic People's Courts, Intermediate People's Courts, and Higher People's Courts. Military courts, railway transport courts, and maritime courts are special courts, which are in independent judicial systems separate from the mainstream judicial system.

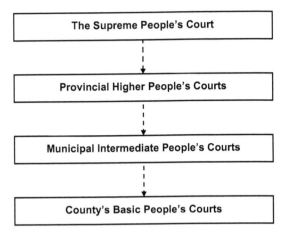

FIGURE 3.11 Hierarchy of China's Judicial System
*Source:* Graph made by the author

Basic People's Courts are county-level courts, which include (1) county People's Courts and municipal People's Courts, (2) People's Courts of autonomous counties, and (3) People's Courts of municipal districts. A Basic People's Court adjudicates criminal and civil cases of first instance. When a Basic People's Court decides that a criminal or civil case it is handling is of major importance and requires trial by the People's Court at a higher level, it may request that the case is transferred to that court for trial. As stipulated by Article 20 of the Organic Law of People's Courts of the People's Republic of China (the Organic Law hereafter), a Basic People's Court may set up a number of People's Tribunals according to the conditions of the locality, population, and cases. A People's Tribunal is a component of the Basic People's Court, and its judgments and orders are judgments and orders of the Basic People's Courts.

Intermediate People's Courts are prefectural-level courts, which include (1) Intermediate People's Courts established in prefectures of a province or autonomous region, (2) Intermediate People's Courts established in municipalities directly under the central government, (3) Intermediate People's Courts of municipalities directly under the jurisdiction of a province or an autonomous region, and (4) Intermediate People's Courts of autonomous prefectures. As stipulated by Article 25 of the Organic Law, an Intermediate People's Court handles the following cases: (1) cases of first instance assigned by laws and decrees to their jurisdiction, (2) cases of first instance transferred from the Basic People's Courts, (3) cases of appeals and protests lodged against judgments and orders of the Basic People's Courts, and (4) cases of protests lodged by the People's Procuratorates in accordance with the procedures of judicial supervision. Organic Law Article 25 also stipulates that when an Intermediate People's Court decides that a criminal or civil case it is handling is of major importance and requires trial by a People's Court at a higher level, it may request that the case is transferred to that court for trial.

Higher People's Courts are provincial-level courts, which include (1) Higher People's Courts of provinces, (2) Higher People's Courts of autonomous regions, and (3) Higher People's Courts of municipalities directly under the central government. A Higher People's Court handles the following cases: (1) cases of first instance assigned by laws and decrees to their jurisdiction, (2) cases of first instance transferred from People's Courts at lower levels, (3) cases of appeals and protests lodged against judgments and orders of People's Courts at lower levels, and (4) cases of protests lodged by People's Procuratorates in accordance with the procedures of judicial supervision.

The Supreme People's Court is the highest judicial organ of the state. It supervises the administration of justice by the local People's Courts at various levels and by the special People's Courts. The Supreme People's Court handles the following cases: (1) cases of first instance assigned by laws and decrees to its jurisdiction and that it decides it should try itself, (2) cases of appeals and protests lodged against judgments and orders of Higher People's Courts and special People's Courts, and (3) cases of protests lodged by the Supreme People's Procuratorate in accordance with the procedures of judicial supervision. As stipulated by Article 33 of the Organic Law, the Supreme People's Court also interprets questions concerning the specific application of laws and decrees in judicial proceedings.

In the People's Courts system, the second instance is the last instance: from a judgment or orders of first instance of a local people's court, a party may bring an appeal to the People's Court at the next highest level in accordance with the procedure prescribed by law, and the people's procuratorate may present a protest to the People's Court at the next highest level in accordance with the procedure prescribed by law. Judgments and orders of first instance of the local People's Courts at various levels become legally effective judgments and orders if, within the period of appeal, none of the parties has appealed and the procuratorate has not protested. The Organic Law also stipulates that judgments and orders of second instance of intermediate courts, Higher People's Courts, and the Supreme People's Court, and judgments and orders of first instance of the Supreme People's Court are all judgments and orders of last instance – that is, legally effective judgments and orders (Article 12).

As of 2012, China had 32 Higher People's Courts (including one military court), 409 Intermediate People's Courts, and 3,117 Basic People's Courts. There are over 190,000 judges, of which 7,000 are in Higher People's Courts, 36,000 in Intermediate People's Courts, and 146,000 in Basic People's Courts.

## THE INTERNAL STRUCTURE OF A BASIC PEOPLE'S COURT

Most Basic People's Courts were established around 1949, when the People's Republic was founded. Some of them date back to 1934, when the Nationalist

Party was still in power, whereas some were established as late as 1961 (Landry 2011). Basic People's Courts are on the lowest rung of the judicial system, but they handle the majority of cases. According to a study, in 2008 courts at various levels in Jiangsu Province accepted 882,352 cases, of which the Higher People's Courts accepted 8,135 cases (1.0 percent); Intermediate People's Courts, 66,826 cases (7.5 percent); and Basic People's Courts, 807,391 cases (91.5 percent).[6]

As Su (2000) argues, a Chinese court has two functions: legal adjudication and administrative management. It is, therefore, both a legal organization and a bureaucratic organization. As a legal organization, a basic court has a very clear division of labor. As required by the Organic Law, a Basic People's Court is composed of a president, vice presidents, and judges. In law, the president, vice presidents, division chief judges, division associate judges, and ordinary judges all have the same duties and responsibilities. So as a legal organization, a court is a flat organization in which all judges have equal powers.

A Basic People's Court may set up a criminal division, a civil division, and an economic division, each of which has a chief judge and associate chief judges. In practice, some basic courts combine the civic and economic divisions. In developed areas, some courts have more than one civil division to meet high societal demands. For example, the first Basic People's Courts in Dongguan City has four civic divisions. A typical basic court has one criminal division, one or two civil divisions, at most one economic division, and one administrative division. Another important function of basic courts is the enforcement of court judgments. Every basic court has an enforcement bureau (*zhixing ju*).[7] The enforcement bureau is not a designated organization in the Organic Law, so its legal status is unspecified by law. In some places, there is an enforcement division under an enforcement bureau. The rank of an enforcement bureau head is often higher than that of a division head.

Most cases are adjudicated by a collegial panel of judges (*heyi ting*). Only simple civil cases and minor criminal cases are tried by a single judge. There is a presiding judge (*heyiting shenpanzhang*) in each collegial panel. The responsibility of the presiding judge is not specified in the Organic Law.

An important means for the party-state to control the courts is the adjudication committee. As the Organic Law (Article 11) requires, each court establishes an adjudication committee (*shenpan weiyuanhui*) to discuss important (*zhongda*) and difficult (*yinan*) cases. A basic court adjudication committee – which has nine to eleven members – is usually composed of the president, vice presidents, and chief judges of major divisions. The Organic Law stipulates that

---

[6] Zhenguo Yin, "Jiceng fayuan anduo renshao de kunjing yu chulu" [Too Many Cases, Too Few Judges: Problems of and Solutions to Basic Courts], http://www.law-lib.com/lw/lw_view.asp ?no=9986, accessed June 21, 2013.

[7] Enforcement bureaus were established after the National People's Congress Standing Committee issued a decision on revising the Civil Procedure Law in 2007.

the presidents of the People's Courts preside over meetings of adjudication committees. All cases can enter the adjudication committee. As Su (2000, 104–105) observes, very few civil cases enter the adjudication committee, 10–15 percent of criminal cases enter the adjudication committee, and most administrative cases enter the adjudication committee. Su (2000, 104–105) also argues that only "difficult" cases are discussed in the adjudication committee, which include (1) cases with significant social influences and reactions; (2) cases interfered with by People's Congresses, government, or other government organizations; and (3) cases difficult to define in law. By determining what cases enter the adjudication committee, the party exercises its agenda-setting power in judicial decisions. While the party ties its hands in most civil (including economic) cases, its discretionary power is extended to administrative cases where the party-state is directly affected.

As Su (2000, 103) summarizes, the procedure of cases entering the adjudication committee works as follows: If the case is adjudicated by a single judge, and the judge is not certain about the nature of the case or what law to apply, the judge should report the case to the chief judge of her division. If the chief judge agrees with the judge's original opinion, a verdict can be decided; if there is a disagreement, the chief judge should report to a vice president. If the vice president cannot make a decision, he or she should report the case to the president, and then the case enters the adjudication committee. If the case is adjudicated by a collegial panel, and the panel's opinion contradicts that of the division chief judge, the chief judge reports the case to a vice president. The vice president proposes her opinion, and the panel discusses the case again. If there is still a disagreement, the vice president reports the case to the president, and then the case enters the adjudication committee. Figure 3.12 summarizes the structure of a basic court as a legal organization.

At the same time, a basic court is also a bureaucratic organization. As such, it is a hierarchical organization in which judges and staff members have different ranks and levels of power. In addition to those functional departments in a basic court, there are also several administrative organs. Among them, the most important is the Communist Party committee. According to Article 29 of the Constitution of the CCP, "Primary party organizations are formed in…basic units, where there are at least three full party members." Every court in China has a party committee. And in most cases, the president is also the party secretary of the court, and vice presidents are also party committee members.[8]

A typical Basic People's Court also has an administrative office (*bangong shi*), a political work department (*zhenggong ke*), a disciplinary department (*jijian shi*), a research department (*yanjiu shi*), and a legal police department (*fajing dadui*). They are at the same rank as a division.

---

[8] Interview with a basic court president, Hainan Province, March 15, 2010.

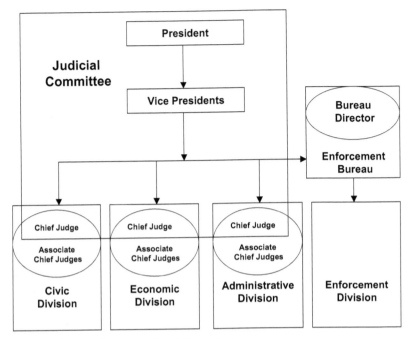

FIGURE 3.12 A Basic Court as a Legal Organization
*Source:* Graph made by the author

This hierarchy operates according to certain rules that keep the court running. The foremost rule is that the power of a court lies in the party committee; and the power of the party committee lies in the party secretary.[9] The party committee is composed of the president (also the party secretary), vice presidents, and sometimes heads of the political work department and disciplinary departments. The party committee meets frequently to discuss major issues in the court and decides on major administrative issues, such as personnel decisions (for example, appointments, promotions, and dismissals of judges and staff members) and monetary decisions (for example, salary structure and budget). Below are the major rules for the party committee meetings in a basic court:[10]

---

[9] It is difficult to distinguish whether this is a formal rule or an informal rule. According to the Constitution of the PRC, the basic tasks of the nation should be achieved "under the leadership of the Communist Party of China," and one of the tasks is to "improve the socialist legal system" (Preamble). In this sense, the party leadership in courts is a formal rule. But none of the other laws, including the Organic Law and procedural laws, is explicit in the party's leadership. In this sense, this is also an informal rule.

[10] These are informal rules that were printed on a framed piece of paper that hangs on the wall of a meeting room of a basic court that I visited. These rules are not stipulated in any formal laws and may vary in different courts.

1. The party committee meets twice a month. Additional meetings will be convened if necessary.
2. The party secretary sets the agenda of the meetings. Committee members can make proposals for the party secretary to deliberate.
3. Party committee meetings are convened by the party secretary. If the party secretary is absent, the party secretary designates a committee member to preside.
4. Representatives from other government departments can sit in committee meetings if necessary.
5. More than half of the committee members should be present to run the meetings. For meetings on personnel decisions, more than two-thirds of committee members should be present.
6. Party committee members should have adequate discussions before making a personnel decision. If the committee cannot reach a consensus, the decision should be postponed. But once the committee makes a decision, the committee must comply.
7. In emergent situations, the party secretary or committee members can make decisions without convening a committee meeting. But the committee should hear the report afterward.
8. Any documents issued in the name of the party committee should be signed by the party secretary or a committee member designated by the party secretary.

There are also written rules for party committee members to follow:

1. Party committee members are assistants to, are in charge of certain issues under the leadership of, and report to the party secretary.
2. Party committee members should report major issues to and seek suggestions from the party secretary.
3. Party committee members can suggest or keep disagreements to the party secretary's decisions; party committee members can also report disagreements to a higher-ranking official. But committee members must comply with the party secretary's orders.
4. Party committee members should frequently communicate with and support the party secretary.

As a consequence, the hierarchical nature often triumphs the egalitarian nature. Judges hold different levels of power according to their administrative posts. The most powerful person in a basic court is the president, who is also the party secretary. According to Article 11 of the Organic Law, the president presides over meetings of adjudication committees. As Su (2000, 105) observes, during adjudication committee meetings, the president does not usually reveal her opinion in the beginning. After listening to other committee members, the president will conclude and announce her own opinion. In this way, the president can assure that her opinion is always the right one. But sometimes,

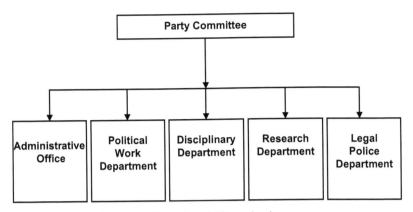

FIGURE 3.13 A Basic Court as a Bureaucratic Organization
*Source:* Graph made by the author

if the president really wants to influence a case, she will reveal her opinion first and impose it on other members.[11]

Division chief judges are also more powerful than ordinary judges. Article 10 of the Organic Law stipulates that the chief judge of a division can appoint one of the judges to act as the presiding judge of the collegial panel. And when the chief judge of a division participates in the judicial proceedings, she acts as the presiding judge. By selecting the presiding judge, a chief judge can largely influence the decision of a case. Another way chief judges influence judicial decisions is through division affairs meetings (*tingwu hui*). Su (2000, 79) observes that division chief judges sometimes convene division affairs meetings to discuss difficult and complicated cases. All judges in the division should participate. The chief judge's opinion often influences other judges.

Figure 3.13 summarizes the structure of a basic court as a bureaucratic organization.

## APPOINTMENT, REMOVAL, DISMISSAL, AND EVALUATION OF JUDGES

The Judges Law is the formal rule that regulates the appointment and removal of judges. However, in practice, the informal rules subvert the formal rules in personnel affairs. The key difference between the formal and informal rules is who has the power to appoint and remove judges. For the formal rules, the power lies in the legislative body, whereas party organizations have the power according to the informal rules. The following paragraphs specify the appointment and removal procedures of major posts in a basic court: the president, vice

[11] Interview with a judge, Guangdong Province, March 23, 2010.

presidents, adjudication committee members, division chief judges, division associate judges, and ordinary judges.

## Appointment

Article 11 of the Judges Law stipulates: "The presidents of the local People's Courts at various levels shall be elected or removed by the local People's Congresses at various levels. The vice presidents, members of the adjudication committees, chief judges and associate chief judges of divisions and judges shall be appointed or removed by the standing committees of the corresponding levels upon the suggestions of the presidents of those courts." The term of the presidency post is five years. A president can be reelected only once.

However, in practice, People's Congresses have the power only to confirm nominations. The elections in congresses are not competitive, hence, not meaningful, since congresses rarely veto a nomination.[12] The appointment procedures for the major posts work as follows:[13]

The party committee and court at a higher territorial level jointly nominate the candidate of the president of a basic court, and this nomination is finalized in consultation with the county party committee. If there is agreement, the nomination will be passed by the county People's Congress. For example, if the county is directly under a municipal city, the municipal party committee and the city intermediate court will jointly nominate a candidate. Then the county party committee will discuss the nomination. If there is agreement, the county People's Congress will pass this nomination. If there is disagreement, the municipal party committee and the intermediate court should nominate a new candidate, or the county party committee can make a recommendation. The rule of thumb is that there should be a consensus among all three organizations: the municipal party committee, the intermediate court, and the county party committee.

The Judges Law and the Organic Law are both very vague in describing the qualifications for court presidents. Article 12 of the Judges Law stipulates: "Persons to be appointed presidents or vice presidents of People's Courts shall be selected from among the best judges and other people who are best qualified for the post." Article 34 of the Organic Law says: "Citizens who have the right to vote and to stand for election and have reached the age of 23 are eligible to be elected presidents of People's Courts...; but persons who have ever been deprived of political rights are excluded. Judicial personnel of People's Courts must have an adequate knowledge of the law." It is difficult to define what constitutes an "adequate knowledge of the law." There are no systematic data

---

[12] Interview with a police school chancellor, Hainan Province, March 8, 2010.
[13] Interviews with a basic court president in Hainan Province and a political work department director in a basic court in Guangdong Province.

on the qualifications of basic court presidents; among the courts that I visited, at least half of the court presidents did not have professional legal training, for example, degrees from law schools. According to a media report, fourteen of the thirty Higher People's Court presidents do not have any legal training and have never worked in a law-related profession.[14]

Appointing court presidents with no legal training has its advantages and disadvantages. Since courts in China are not independent, a court president who previously had a political career outside the legal system can help the court secure funding from the government, communicate with the party committee, and coordinate with other government organs.[15] But because the court party committee also makes judicial decisions, a president without legal training usually politicizes cases.

The candidates for vice president of a basic court are nominated by the county CCP standing committee and then passed by the county People's Congress standing committee. There is no term limit for vice presidents. According to my observation, vice presidents are mostly professional judges. Because vice presidents are also adjudication committee members, the professionalization of vice presidents helps mitigate the weaknesses of the president.

Adjudication committee members, chief judges, and associate judges of divisions are nominated by the court party committee, approved by the county party committee standing committee, and then passed by the county people's congress standing committee.

Ordinary judges are appointed by the court president, but this appointment must be approved by a higher-level court. As for the qualifications of judges to be appointed for the first time (*churen faguan*), Article 12 of the Judges Law stipulates: "Persons to be appointed judges for the first time shall be selected, through strict examination and appraisal, from those who have passed the uniform national judicial examination and who are the best qualified for the post, in conformity with the standards of having both ability and political integrity." However, in practice, as He (1998) observes, a large number of first-time-appointed judges are retired military officers who have basically no legal training or experience in the legal profession. My impression during the fieldwork stage of my research was that the situation is now much better than what He observed in the late 1990s. The bar for becoming a judge is set higher, and judges in local courts are much more professionalized. To become a judge, one must go through the following three steps: (1) take the civil service examination (*gongwuyuan kaoshi*) and obtain a qualification, (2) pass the national judicial examination (*guojia sifa kaoshi*), and (3) participate in a training session in the Supreme People's Court and receive a certificate.

---

[14] Guo Guangdong, "Fayuan yuanzhang weihe feiyao zai dangzheng guanyuan litiao?" [Why Choosing Court Presidents from Party and Government Officials?], *Southern Weekend* (*Nanfang zhoumo*), July 23, 2009, http://www.infzm.com/content/31840, accessed January 23, 2010.

[15] Interview with a division chief judge, Jiangxi Province, April 8, 2010.

It is noteworthy that all judges in China are also civil servants. So they all need to take the civil service examination and obtain a qualification. As civil servants, all judges are also managed by the personnel bureaus at the same territorial level.

## Removal and Dismissal

Chinese judges do not have tenure; they can be removed or dismissed. Removal (*lizhi*) means leaving the current position, and dismissal (*citui*) means being discharged from the current position. Therefore dismissal is a form of removal. The Judges Law has different stipulations on who should be removed or dismissed.

Article 13 stipulates:

If a judge is found to be in any of the following circumstances, a suggestion shall be submitted according to law for his or her removal from the post: (1) having forfeited the nationality of the People's Republic of China; (2) having been transferred out of a court; (3) having no need to maintain his or her original post after a change of post; (4) being determined to be incompetent in the post through appraisal; (5) being unable to perform the functions and duties of a judge for a long period of time due to poor health; (6) having retired from the post; (7) having resigned the post, or having been dismissed; or (8) being disqualified from continuing to hold the post because of violation of discipline or law or commission of a crime.

Article 40 stipulates:

A judge shall be dismissed if he or she is found to be in any of the following circumstances: (1) to be confirmed by annual appraisal as being incompetent for two successive years; (2) to be unqualified for the present post and decline to accept other assignments; (3) to refuse to accept reasonable transfer, which is necessitated by restructuring of the judicial organ or reduction of the size of the staff; (4) to have stayed away from work without leave or to have overstayed his or her leave without good reason for 15 days or more in succession, or for 30 days or more in a year aggregated; or (5) to fail to perform a judge's duty, and make no rectification after criticism.

There is no systematic data on how many judges are removed or dismissed every year. A judge told me that it is very rare for a basic court judge to be promoted to a higher-level court – for example, an intermediate court. The vertical mobility within the judicial system is very limited.[16]

## Evaluation

There are two evaluation systems for judges: one in the judicial system, the other in the bureaucratic system. The judicial evaluation assesses judges'

[16] Interview with a judge, Guangdong Province, March 31, 2010.

TABLE 3.1 *External Judicial Evaluation Form (Adjudication Category)*

| Indicator | Direction |
|---|---|
| Total number of cases (*zong anjian*) | + |
| Total number of complete cases (*zong jiean*) | + |
| Number of mediated cases (*tiaojie*) | + |
| Number of withdrawn cases (*chesu*) | + |
| Number of mediated and withdrawn cases (*tiaoche zongshu*) | + |
| Number of appeals (*shangsu*) | − |
| Quality of adjudication (*zhiliang*) | + |
| Completion rate (*jiean lu*) | + |
| Mediation and withdrawal rate (*tiaoche lu*) | + |
| Appeal rate (*shangsu lu*) | − |
| Correction rate (*gaipan lu*) | − |
| Complaint rate (*shensu lu*) | − |

*Note:* This is the judicial evaluation form used by an Intermediate People's Court to evaluate the performance of judges in the adjudication divisions in a Basic People's Court.
*Source:* Author's fieldwork in 2010

performance as judges, whereas the bureaucratic evaluation assesses judges' performance as civil servants. This section examines the judge evaluation system in a basic court in the city of Water Grass in Guangdong Province.[17]

There are external and internal judicial evaluations. The external judicial evaluation is carried out by a higher-level court. For example, judges in a basic court are evaluated annually by an intermediate court.

The external judicial evaluation has two categories of indicators: adjudication and enforcement. The adjudication category includes indicators in Table 3.1.

A first glance at the indicators shows that the evaluation form emphasizes quantity rather than quality. This emphasis has some unintended consequences on judges' incentives. For example, complete cases are those that have been adjudicated. And the completion rate is calculated by the number of complete cases divided by all accepted cases by the end of the year. This indicator was designed to increase the efficiency of judges; however, in practice, to decrease the denominator, courts are often reluctant to accept cases toward the end of the year. The bottom line of completion rate is 91 percent for basic courts and 88 percent for intermediate courts. But most basic courts cannot achieve this goal. The average completion rate of basic courts in a city

[17] The judge evaluation system is informed by a political work department director in a basic court, Guangdong Province, March 23, 2010.

in 2008 was 87.86 percent, and 89.32 percent in 2009.[18] Another way to increase the completion rate is to encourage plaintiffs to withdraw their cases, because withdrawn cases are not included in the denominator. The number of withdrawn cases and the withdrawal rate are other indicators on which judges are evaluated. It is in judges' strong interest to pressure plaintiffs to withdraw.

The indicators that directly or indirectly measure the quality of adjudications include the number of appeals, quality of adjudication, appeal rate, correction rate, and complaint rate. To some extent, these indicators play important roles in incentivizing judges to make a fair judgment. But judges have ways to circumvent them. For example, to avoid appeals, judges are inclined to mediate a case rather than adjudicate. The result is a compromise between the two parties, so either side is less likely to appeal to a higher-level court. In addition, corrections to verdicts of first-instance cases are made by a higher-level court. For example, an intermediate court can change the verdict of a basic court if either side appeals. However, intermediate courts rarely change basic court verdicts. As an intermediate court judge told me, "We do our best to respect basic courts' decisions. We do not correct if it is a borderline case unless there is a fatal mistake."[19]

In addition to adjudication, judges in the enforcement bureau are also evaluated on their performance on enforcing court judgments. The enforcement category includes the indicators in Table 3.2.

Enforcing judicial decisions has long been a headache for Chinese courts. In addition to some obvious reasons such as the costly process and limited resources, government intervention has been the most important obstacle. When asked why enforcement is so difficult, a judge who works in the enforcement bureau in a basic court responded:

The foremost reason is government intervention. For example, enterprises are attracted by the county government. If the court enforces a judgment that harms the enterprise, the county government will say this is like "killing chickens for eggs." To attract investors is already hard; investors who are already here need to be protected. To enforce according to the law will set a bad example for other enterprises that are thinking about moving here... Here in this place, there is a saying: "No matter if it is a black firm or a white firm; as long as it pays taxes, it is a good firm."[20]

The judge told me that the actual completion rate for his court is only around 50 percent but that they have alternative ways to calculate. For example, they can claim that the enforcement process is terminated for inevitable reasons, such as the death of a party or one side applying for an adjournment. Although

[18] Yang Jianmin, "Renmin fayuan jieanlu zhibiao de juxian yu gaige" [The Limitations and Reforms of People's Court Case Completion Rate], *Guangming Web* (*Guangming wang*), January 5, 2011, http://court.gmw.cn/html/article/201101/05/484.shtml, accessed February 3, 2011.

[19] Interview with a judge, Guangdong Province, March 31, 2010.

[20] Interview with a judge, Jiangxi Province, April 8, 2010.

TABLE 3.2 *External Judicial Evaluation Form (Enforcement Category)*

| Indicator | Direction |
| --- | --- |
| Total number of cases (*zong anjian*) | + |
| Total number of complete cases (*zong jiean*) | + |
| Number of compromised cases (*hejie anjian*) | + |
| Number of documented cases (*yiguidang anjian*) | + |
| Average days of the enforcement process (*pingjun zhixing tianshu*) | − |
| Completion rate (*jiean lu*) | + |
| Compromise rate (*hejie lu*) | + |
| Appeal rate (*shangsu lu*) | − |
| Documentation rate (*guidang lu*) | + |
| Rate of disbursement (*zijin daowei lu*) | + |
| Ranking of completion rate (*jieanshu paiming*) | + |
| Ranking of disbursement rate (*zijin daowei lu paiming*) | + |
| Ranking of enforcing termination rate (*zhongzhi zhixing lu*) | − |

*Note:* This is the judicial evaluation form used by an Intermediate People's Court to evaluate the performance of judges in the enforcement division in a Basic People's Court.
*Source:* Author's fieldwork in 2010

this increases the enforcement termination rate, the completion rate will be higher.[21] Another way to increase the completion rate is for judges to encourage the two parties to agree to a compromise, which is less costly and is considered a complete case.

In addition to the external evaluation conducted by a higher authority, political work departments within courts also conduct internal judicial evaluations, which include the indicators in Table 3.3.

As shown in Table 3.3, the internal evaluation has more specific indicators. However, because courts conduct their own internal evaluations, they are often biased.

Although the judge evaluation system can be easily manipulated, the results are important for a judge's career and financial well-being. As Article 24 of the Judges Law stipulates: "The results of the annual appraisal shall fall into three grades: excellent, competent, and incompetent. The results of appraisal shall be taken as the basis for award, punishment, training, removal or dismissal of a judge, and for readjustment of his or her grade and salary." Article 37 of the Judges Law states: "The salary of a judge who has been confirmed through appraisal as being excellent or competent may be raised in accordance with regulations." And as discussed previously, a judge will be dismissed if she is assessed as incompetent for two successive years.

[21] Ibid.

TABLE 3.3  *Internal Judicial Evaluation Form*

| Indicator | Direction |
| --- | --- |
| Rate of change of registration category (*lian biangeng lu*) | − |
| Rate of first-instance cases with juries (*yishen anjian peishen lu*) | + |
| Rate of correction in appeals (*shangsu gaipan lu*) | − |
| Rate of remand for new trial after appeal (*shangsu fahui chongshen lu*) | − |
| Quality of written report of judgment (*panjue wenshu zhiliang*) | + |
| Completion rate (*jiean lu*) | + |
| Number of complete cases (*jiean lu*) | + |
| Stability of completion rates throughout the year (*jiean junheng du*) | + |
| Mediation rate of first-instance civil cases (*minshi yishen anjian tiaojie lu*) | + |
| Withdraw rate of first-instance civil cases (*minshi yishen anjian chesu lu*) | + |
| Appeal rate (*shangsu lu*) | − |
| Rate of complaints through petitions (*xinfang tousu lu*) | − |
| Rate of second trial (*zaishen lu*) | − |
| Rate of cases actually enforced (*shiji zhijie lu*) | + |
| Rate of disbursement of enforced cases (*zhixing biaodi daowei lu*) | + |

*Note:* This is the judicial evaluation form used by a Basic People's Court to evaluate the performance of its own judges.
*Source:* Author's fieldwork in 2010

As civil servants, judges are also subject to a bureaucratic evaluation, which is conducted by the party organization department at the same territorial level. The indicators in this evaluation are more general and difficult to operationalize. It evaluates judges on four major dimensions: virtue (*de*), ability (*neng*), diligence (*qin*), and performance (*ji*). This evaluation is less important than the judicial evaluation and is used only as a reference to assess a judge.

The judge evaluation system has become an effective instrument for higher authorities to incentivize judges for some desirable outcomes. My fieldwork revealed that mediation rates carry a heavy weight in the evaluation system, because the then CCP general secretary Hu Jintao advocates a "harmonious society" idea that emphasizes avoiding litigation and minimizing the possibility of social conflicts. This party principle is realized in the judge evaluation system by emphasizing mediation rather than adjudication – which gives judges an incentive to falsify the statistics for their mediation rate.[22]

It is important to note that not every basic court has a quantitative evaluation system, since the evaluation process consumes human and technical resources. The president of a basic court in Hainan Province told me that his court had not

---

[22] Interview with a judge, Jiangxi Province, April 7, 2010.

yet implemented an evaluation system but was considering doing so, which he claimed would be the first basic court in the province to have such a system.[23]

## THE EXTERNAL ENVIRONMENT OF THE JUDICIARY

Article 126 of the current (2004) version of the constitution guarantees judicial independence: "The People's courts exercise judicial power independently, in accordance with the provisions of the law, and are not subject to interference by any administrative organ, public organization or individual." However, this is not always the case. During the Cultural Revolution (1966–1976), the 1975 constitution did not respect the independence of the judiciary; Article 25 stipulated that the "masses" should be involved in the judicial process: "The mass line must be applied in procuratorial work and in trying cases. In major counterrevolutionary criminal cases the masses should be mobilized for discussion and criticism." This article remained in the 1978 constitution, with minor revisions. The 1982 constitution deleted this article and reemphasized judicial independence. However, as shown in the following discussion, this principle has never been realized.

The Chinese judiciary is not an independent branch. Chinese courts are embedded in – and constrained by – various party and government organizations. This section examines the external environment in which a Chinese basic court is embedded. The external environment is comprised of the party committee, the political and legal committee, the government, the local congress, the intermediate court, and the procuratorate.

According to the constitution, the Basic People's Court is at the same rank as the county government, since they are all elected by the county People's Congress. However, in reality, because of the courts' fiscal dependence on the government, the court is considered a functional department of the government.

The county party committee is the principal of the county basic court. As discussed in the previous section, the nomination of the court president needs to be approved by the county party committee, which micromanages the county basic court through the court party committee. As a basic court president (also party secretary) commented:

The leadership of the Communist Party is realized through the party committee in the court. The court party committee is an agency of the county party committee and, therefore, is under the leadership of the county party committee. The court party committee needs to understand and implement the decisions of the county party committee.[24]

The county party committee only provides guidelines for the basic court and rarely intervenes in individual cases unless they are especially politically

---

[23] Interview with a basic court president, Hainan Province, March 15, 2010.     [24] Ibid.

sensitive, such as corruption cases or those that could potentially provoke social unrest. It is worth noting that the basic court president rarely sits on the county party committee standing committee. This means that the court president is not in the core decision-making organ of the county and is usually not informed of party committee decisions in advance.

The county political and legal committee (*zhengfa wei*) is the supervisor of the basic court. This committee is first a branch of the county party committee. The secretary of the political and legal committee is a member of the county party committee standing committee. He or she is also usually the director of the county police department.[25] The county political and legal committee's work is to coordinate all formal legal organizations in the county, including the police department, court, procuratorate, and legal bureau (*sifa ju*). A concrete example is the three-heads meeting (*sanzhang huiyi*). The political and legal committee secretary convenes the court president, the procuratorate president, and the police chief for three-heads meetings if a case meets one of the following four conditions: (1) the case could potentially provoke collective protests, (2) the case has great social influence, (3) the case has great influence over the economic development of the locality, or (4) the case involves vicious crimes (such as serial murders).[26] During the meetings, the three or four heads come up with a plan. The political and legal committee secretary sets the tone and principles, and the three organizations coordinate their actions to implement the plan. The political and legal committee does not intervene in ordinary cases. A court president also commented that it is important for the three heads to reach a consensus on important cases in order to avoid a situation in which the police department makes an arrest, but the procuratorate does not sue and the court does not sentence. In such cases, the court should be involved before the case is filed at the court.[27]

The county government is the "purse" that finances of the basic court. Courts depend on local governments for basic necessities, including judges' salaries and bonuses, office supplies, vehicles, and court buildings. Before 2008, local court expenditures completely depended on local budgets. Each year, the basic court submits its budget to the county government, and the county government allocates a certain proportion of the budget to the court. This proportion varies by location. In economically better-off areas, court funding

---

[25] As commented by a police school chancellor (Hainan Province, March 8, 2010), county court presidents used to chair political and legal committees. But as of 2003, a central party document requires that local police department directors chair the political and legal committees. However, the chancellor also noted that this requirement is not always enforced. In some places, court presidents still chair the political and legal committees, whereas some counties have full-time political and legal committee secretaries.

[26] Interview with a county political and legal committee secretary, Hainan Province, March 15, 2010.

[27] Ibid.

is guaranteed, whereas in underdeveloped areas the funding is often delayed or reduced and, therefore, insufficient to run the court properly. To address this issue, starting in 2008, the central government began allocating ad hoc funding to local courts in underdeveloped areas. However, the money is often misallocated at various levels of government, and by the time it comes to the local courts, there is little left over.[28] The county government also intervenes in individual cases if the case involves a local enterprise. As discussed in the previous section, if a court decision harms a local enterprise, the county government often intervenes to protect the local enterprise for the sake of maintaining economic development and tax revenues.

The county People's Congress is the de jure principal of the county court. This is reflected in three aspects: (1) all the major positions (such as president, vice presidents, adjudication committee members, chief judges, and associate judges of divisions) are appointed by the county congress or the congress standing committee; (2) the county court is responsible for and accountable to the county congress (each year, the court president reports to the county congress, and the report is subject to a vote by the representatives); and (3) the county congress supervises the county court.

But in practice, as discussed in the previous section, party committees at various levels appoint all the major positions. The county congress needs only to pass the nominations. And the local congresses rarely veto the court reports and supervise the courts themselves. This situation has been changing over the last two decades. As Cho (2003) argues, legislative supervision over courts has been strengthened since the 1990s. The supervisory measures include appraisal (*pingyi*) of judicial officers and work, individual case supervision (*gean jiandu*), and the system of investigating the responsibility for misjudged cases (*cuoan zeren zhuijiuzhi*). As documented in Cho (2003, 1073–1074), People's Congresses in Henan investigated 27,964 cases of economic disputes handled by courts and thoroughly appraised 3,055 selected cases in 1999. They also forced courts to redress problems and punish related personnel after the supervision. For individual case supervision, People's Congresses first carefully select targets among public complaints and cases identified through other forms of supervision. Then People's Congresses investigate the cases. Finally, they require courts to correct problems within a certain period and punish related persons, for instance by dismissal (Cho 2003, 1074). As Cho (2003, 1074) argues, "Courts generally accept the demands of People's Congresses when these demands are based on evidence obtained through intensive investigation. So the supervision is evaluated as the most effective measure of dealing with courts." However, during my interviews, a legal work committee[29] director in a county People's Congress commented that it is very difficult for congresses to

---

[28] Interview with the chief of staff at a county's Basic People's Court, Jiangxi Province, April 2, 2010. Chapter 7 provides more detailed information about China's court funding.

[29] The legal work committee (*fagong wei*) in congresses is responsible for supervising courts.

supervise courts due to a lack of human resources, financial resources, and legal knowledge.[30] In addition, most local congresses stopped supervising individual cases after the Supervision Law of Standing Committees of People's Congresses at Various Levels (the Supervision Law hereafter) came into effect on January 1, 2007. The Supervision Law does not grant congresses the authority to supervise individual cases.

The intermediate court is the professional leader of the basic court: they are in a professional (*yewu*) relationship in which the intermediate court cannot issue binding orders to the basic court (Lieberthal 2004, chapter 6). The intermediate court has three ways to control the basic court: (1) the intermediate court, with the municipal party committee, nominates a candidate for the president of the basic court; (2) the intermediate court conducts judicial evaluations of basic courts; (3) the intermediate court corrects misjudged cases after appeal. The evaluation and correction of misjudged cases are two critical methods of monitoring basic courts. So although the intermediate court cannot issue binding orders to the basic court, the lower court often respects the suggestions of the higher-level court.[31]

The county People's Procuratorate (public procurator) is the collaborator of the basic court, which monitors the court in two ways: (1) the chief procurators of the People's Procuratorates at the corresponding levels may attend adjudication committee meetings without voting rights; (2) if the Supreme People's Procuratorate finds errors in a legally effective judgment or order of a People's Court at any level, or if the People's Procuratorate at a higher level finds such an error in a legally effective judgment or order of any People's Court at a lower level, it has the authority to lodge a protest (*kangsu*) in accordance with the procedure of judicial supervision. However, this protest authority is rarely exercised. During the period 2003–08, the second procuratorate of Beijing protested only eighty-nine of more than fifty thousand criminal cases (0.178 percent).[32]

In general, the basic court is embedded in a power network in which the party committees and governments have strong influence over courts and other de jure organizations, such as People's Congresses and procuratorates, and are gaining de facto powers very slowly.

## COURTS, ECONOMIC DEVELOPMENT, AND SOCIAL STABILITY

As discussed in Chapter 2, local officials in China have two major goals: promoting economic growth and maintaining social stability. Since party

---

[30] Interview with a county congress official, Jiangxi Province, April 7, 2010.

[31] Interview with a basic court political work department director, Guangdong Province, March 24, 2010.

[32] Li Liang and Wang Feng, "Liunian wuzui anjian kangsu weishixian lingtupo" [There Is No Breakthrough on Protesting], *Legal Daily (Fazhi ribao)*, April 9, 2009, http://www.legaldaily .com.cn/zmbm/content/2009-04/09/content_1067328.htm?node=7568, accessed January 3, 2010.

committees and governments at various levels control local courts, courts are expected to help local officials fulfill these two goals. This section draws on several cases to illustrate how courts help local governments develop the local economy and maintain social stability.

## Economic Development

Courts are becoming a major avenue of dispute resolution and contract enforcement in China. One strand of the literature on Chinese politics argues that China is able to achieve a high growth rate without a strong legal system because the cadre evaluation system (Clarke, Murrell, and Whiting 2008) and the decentralized fiscal system (Oi 1992) incentivize local officials to protect local business. By contrast, I argue that the courts play an important role in protecting local firms, which contributes to China's rapid economic growth. However, this legal protection is exclusive to businesses that contribute to local tax revenue or have political connections. Legal means of favoring local firms include making unfair adjudications or postponing/expediting case proceedings.

A county political and legal committee secretary told me a story about how he instructed the county court to favor an incoming business:

Several years ago, a state-owned oil and gas exploration company came to the county to explore. During that period, the workers of the exploration company had some conflicts with the local villagers, and five villagers were beaten to death by the workers. The political and legal committee immediately convened a three-heads meeting to discuss this case. The conclusion was that if the court made a harsh verdict against the workers according to the law, it would hurt the exploration company. And if the company could explore oil and gas in the county, it was conducive to the long-term economic development of the county. And also, if the court made a harsh judgment (e.g., death penalty), the villagers' families would not be compensated. So the three-heads meeting set a tone that the court judgment should be lenient. After the case was transferred to the court, the defendants (the workers) were only sentenced to a three-year prison term, and the sentence was suspended. The principle of dealing with this sort of case is that if a court judgment is detrimental to the economic development of the county (for example, the defendant is a local firm), the sentence should be lenient; if a case has provoked significant social reactions, the sentence should be harsh. However, this principle should be carried out in accordance with the law, and this principle is consistent with the party spirit.[33]

Obviously, receiving a suspended three-year prison term after beating five people to death is not "in accordance with the law." To attract a potential "tax payer," the county officials colluded to force the court to make an unfair adjudication.

---

[33] Interview with a county political and legal committee chairman, Hainan Province, March 15, 2010.

Another way to protect local business is to postpone case proceedings if the case is detrimental to local firms and to expedite them if they are beneficial to local firms. A lawyer commented on a case involving Hisense-Kelon, a domestic electrical company located in Guangdong Province. The company produces home appliances such as refrigerators, air conditioners, and TVs. Several years ago, many small stockholders sued the company for hiding information on the stock market. The lawsuit was accepted by a court in Foshan City. To protect the interests of Hisense-Kelon, the local court postponed the case for a long time until the small stockholders agreed to compromise with the company outside the court. The lawyer remarked that this is very common, because companies all have tricks to deal with lawsuits. The lawyer also said that there is an internal court document that spells out the principles of dealing with this sort of sensitive case: "Accept but do not hear the case, hear but do not decide the case, decide but do not enforce the case (*lian bu kaiting, kaiting bu panjue, panjue bu zhixing*)."[34]

Local protectionism (*difang baohu zhuyi*) is particularly strong when the exit of a business would threaten the revenue base of the local government. During the financial crisis in 2008 and 2009, many small manufacturing firms went bankrupt in Guangdong Province. At the same time, because of the newly enacted Labor Contract Law, employees started to use their legal weapons to demand better labor protection and welfare benefits. Local courts, however, were instructed to favor local firms rather than the employees, which violated the spirit of the new Labor Contract Law.

A judge told me about a case in which three people lost their lives because of a minor labor dispute. After a Taiwanese or Hong Kong firm delayed the payment of salaries, a worker sued the firm in the local court for 10,000 *yuan* (about $1,400) in compensation. After the court leadership's intervention, the court ruled against the workers. The firm was informed of this decision before the verdict was even announced. The firm managers showed off this case everywhere. After losing the case, the workers shot and killed two firm managers and were sentenced to the death penalty. The judge remarked:

Because of merely 10,000 *yuan*, three people lost their lives; it is really not worth it. This is completely because of judicial unfairness. The court judgment is directed by the court president to protect the interests of local business rather than the interests of workers. For the firm managers, they didn't care about the money; they wanted to highlight this case to prevent other workers from suing the firm.

The judge also commented that courts have some informal rules to limit workers' ability to pursue their own interests through legal means. For example, for labor disputes, some courts set a 10 percent correction bar – that is, an intermediate court corrects only up to 10 percent of the cases appealed from basic courts. For most cases, if one side (usually the employee) is

---

[34] Interview with a practicing lawyer, Guangdong Province, March 29, 2010.

unsatisfied with the first verdict, she can appeal, but few are changed. Most second verdicts uphold the original judgments to protect the employers' interests.[35]

Local favoritism has become an informal rule that was prevalent during the economic crisis. A lawyer told me that he, through some informal channels, obtained a copy of the internal minutes of an intermediate court meeting. The minutes implicitly state that the court should favor the employers when adjudicating labor disputes. The lawyer remarked that there are two considerations for the court. First, if the court decides in favor of the employees, more employees will follow suit and sue their employers, and these lawsuits will burden the court. Second, courts favor employers to protect local firms, which they can list as one of their achievements when they report to congress.[36]

The rationale of protecting local firms is beyond the consideration of economic development; it is also related to maintaining social stability. A judge in an intermediate court revealed her opinion on the new Labor Contract Law:

After the new Labor Contract Law came into effect, many lawyers urged workers to sue their employers. For example, now there were many cases that involved situations where workers asked for compensation and overtime pay when a formal labor contract was not signed.[37] Lawyers often encouraged workers to file lawsuits. And because the new Labor Contract Law gives a two-year term limit for this sort of dispute, many workers sued on their previous cases. And during the economic crisis, many firms were on the brink of bankruptcy; employees took advantage of this to ask for compensation of overtime pay. Lawyers made lots of money by taking these cases. And under the persuasion of lawyers, workers usually did not accept mediation; many of them then appealed. For this type of case, the court's principle is to expedite adjudication and mediate before the trial. Previously (before the economic crisis), courts tended to protect the interests of laborers; but during the economic crisis, we must take firms' interests into account. For example, if a firm pays its employees well above the minimum wage, even if the workers do not get overtime pay, the workers already make enough money. The court usually does not accept this type of case. In addition, we need to consider the financial resources of a firm. We cannot make a firm bankrupt because of several workers. And if the firm went bankrupt, many more workers would be unemployed, and this would cause social unrest.[38]

In addition to local favoritism, courts also provide regular legal services to local firms to reassure them that the court will be helpful should a dispute arise. An economic division chief judge in a basic court said that his court often visits local enterprises located in the industrial park to provide legal service and

---

[35] Interview with a judge, Guangdong Province, March 28, 2010. The 10 percent correction bar was also verified by an interview with a lawyer, Guangdong Province, March 29, 2010.

[36] Interview with a lawyer, Guangdong Province, March 29, 2010.

[37] The new Labor Contract Law stipulates that employees should receive double overtime pay if a formal labor contract is not signed.

[38] Interview with a judge, Guangdong Province, March 31, 2010.

consultancy. He told me that if the court serves well, the firms will add a term when they sign contracts with firms outside the county: "Should a dispute occur in the future, we agree to settle it in the county Basic People's Court." Firms are reluctant to settle a dispute in the court that is on the other's side, because of local protectionism.[39] These cases suggest that there is (selective and exclusive) legal protection of properties in China.

## Social Stability

A natural question to ask after considering the cases discussed above is: how do authorities control social discontent with such a degree of judicial unfairness? This section discusses ways in which local governments, along with legal institutions, control the social discontent created by the unfair judiciary.

First, the CCP established new institutions to channel social discontent. For example, during the economic crisis in 2008 and 2009, because of the large number of labor disputes, Guangdong Province established the Office of Comprehensive Management, Letters and Visits, and Maintaining Social Stability (*Zongzhi xinfang weiwen bangongshi* or *Zongzhi ban*) at the township level (including street committees in urban areas) to handle minor disputes. Other provinces, such as Zhejiang, also established similar organizations at the local level. *Zongzhi ban* is composed of people from the local police departments, labor bureaus, offices of letters and visits (*xinfang ban*), and legal bureaus. If a dispute occurs, *Zongzhi ban* is the primary channel. Usually, people do not go to court directly, because litigation is costly and time consuming. Settling a dispute in *Zongzhi ban* is free, and because it is a government organization, it is easier to enforce a settlement when coordinating within the government.[40]

As shown in Chapter 2, local officials' careers are tied to the degree of social stability in their jurisdictions. The central government sets several "fire alarms" to monitor local societal problems, such as letters and visits (*xinfang*). By writing letters to or visiting the local offices of letters and visits, citizens can express their grievances caused by unjust government actions or unfair judicial decisions. However, because of the collusion of government organizations, the local offices of letters and visits have neither the incentive nor the ability to help the grieved citizens secure their rights against the government. Many petitioners have to skip levels to petition (*yueji shangfang*), and some of them go directly to Beijing to complain to the central government, because they believe that central leaders are more benevolent than their local counterparts (Li 2004).

A political and legal committee official told me that judicial favoritism and corruption have created a significant amount of letters and visits, which have attracted the attention of the center. As a consequence, governments at all levels

---

[39] Interview with a division chief judge, Jiangxi Province, April 8, 2010.
[40] Interview with a political and legal committee official, Guangdong Province, March 28, 2010.

are concerned with letters and visits and try everything to block petitioners to maintain social stability. The central government has issued a document stipulating that if the number of letters and visits surpasses a certain threshold in a locality, the local officials cannot be promoted. But this type of constraint cannot really reduce judicial unfairness for two reasons. First, judicial unfairness is very difficult to uncover; most unfair cases are covered up at the local level. Second, local governments have ways to prevent petitioners from going to Beijing. For example, one of the important tasks of the local police is to take the petitioners (*jiefang*) into custody. There is a police office beside the State Bureau for Letters and Visits (*guojia xinfang ju*). All local governments need to please the police officers there, because they have the information on the petitioners. Local governments manage to track the information from the police officers and capture the petitioners.[41]

I overheard one of these "catching" actions when I had lunch with a county police chief. It was during the period of "two conferences" (*lianghui*): the annual conferences of the National People's Congress and the Chinese People's Political Consultative Conferences. During this period, people's representatives from all over the country go to Beijing along with thousands of journalists. This is the best time of year for petitioners to get heard. Two petitioners from the county I was visiting had gone to Beijing to petition. The police chief got a call during lunch with this news, and he immediately ordered five policemen to travel to Beijing to catch the petitioners. Several days later, I interviewed the deputy police chief who was sent to Beijing for the task. He said: "To hide from the police, the two petitioners took a train to Baoding City, Hebei Province, and then they took a long-distance bus to Beijing. We took an airplane. We went to the State Bureau for Letters and Visits and Tiananmen Square to search for them. Finally, we found them in a hotel near Tiananmen Square. The petitioners were surprised when they were caught, saying, 'How could you find us in such a large city?'" I asked the deputy chief how they tracked the petitioners, and he said the public security department had its own tactics.[42]

Private entities, such as law firms, are also mobilized to maintain social stability. A lawyer told me that to avoid collective unrest caused by judicial unfairness, the government establishes several "fire alarm" mechanisms. For example, if a lawyer takes a labor dispute case that involves more than ten plaintiffs, the lawyer should report this case to the local legal bureau. The judicial decision on this type of case might be different from cases that involve only a small number of people.[43]

Another way to conceal judicial unfairness is by emphasizing procedural justice. A legal scholar told me that if a judge must make a biased judgment, she

---

[41] Ibid.    [42] Interview with a deputy police chief, Hainan Province, March 15, 2010.
[43] Interview with a lawyer, Guangdong Province, March 29, 2010.

usually follows the legal procedure very strictly so that if the case is appealed, the judge can claim that her legal knowledge or skills are not adequate or that she did not fully understand the nature of the case so that she cannot be punished for a lack of legal professionalism.[44]

This is further verified by a conversation I had with another judge. During the economic crisis, the judge's court accepted many labor disputes. Following the guidelines from the local government, the court adjudicated all the cases in a way that favored the employers. When asked whether he feared provoking collective protests if his court always favors the employers when adjudicating labor disputes, he replied: "In this case, we must follow the legal procedure very strictly. We need to find enough evidence!"[45]

These examples suggest that social stability is a concern for local officials and judges, but that it is maintained through the repressive apparatus rather than by seeking judicial fairness. Judicial fairness is not considered a necessary condition for pacifying litigation-related social unrest.

## DISCUSSION, CONCLUSIONS, AND IMPLICATIONS

China's legal reforms have made significant progress since the 1970s. Many laws have been enacted, more disputes have been brought to courts, judges are more professional, and more people are able to hire a lawyer. However, these developments are uneven across regions and issue areas. Citizens in some regions have easier access to legal services and organizations, while others have to travel long distances to find a lawyer. While the market economy has nurtured a relatively fair, efficient, and effective legal system, the CCP still strongly influences the judiciary to limit citizens' legal rights to challenge the authoritarian state.

Chinese rule of law is still in its premature stage. "Everyone being equal under the law" is not realized due to the unevenness of the quality of legal organizations. This chapter shows that the two most important mechanisms the party-state uses to limit the rule of law are (1) the organizational structure (which prioritizes party intervention in sensitive cases) and (2) the court funding regime (which favors local governments over the courts on financial issues). Even though China is gradually moving away from a rule-of-man regime, the current rule-of-law regime is incomplete.

---

[44] Interview with a legal scholar, Guangdong Province, March 31, 2010.
[45] Interview with a judge, Guangdong Province, March 31, 2010.

# 4

# State-business relations in China

> You're not from the Castle, you're not from the village, you're nobody.
>
> Franz Kafka

## INTRODUCTION: MOTIVATION, FINDINGS, AND A ROAD MAP

The discussion in the rest of the book will focus on actors who demand the rule of law. This chapter addresses the following questions: How do different firms settle disputes? How do they perceive state-business relations in China? And who is subject to discrimination? The demand-side theory implies that foreign firms are more likely to litigate a dispute, less likely to be connected with the government, and less satisfied with the legal system. The key finding of this chapter is that there is a gap between foreign firms' demand for legal protection and the supply of such protection by the Chinese state.

The essential goal of China's legal reforms is to establish a fair and efficient legal system that serves the market economy. A well-functioning market economy requires that economic players compete and cooperate on a level playing field. Therefore, law enforcement organizations need to ensure that everyone abides by the law and that any violations must be punished. A driving force for legal reforms, therefore, comes from an unequal market in which the vested interests monopolize access to rents and the weaker side struggles to level the playing field.

Scholars of the Chinese economy generally believe that China's reforms in the 1980s show a pattern of "reform without losers," in which SOEs were protected, domestic private enterprises were encouraged, township and village enterprises flourished, and FIEs were cautiously accepted (Lau, Qian, and Roland 2000; Qian 2003; Naughton 2007). Nevertheless, many have argued that the diversification of ownership structures in the 1990s has generated disparities among economic actors, which some term as "reform with losers" (Naughton 2007, 100). In this period, small and medium-sized SOEs were privatized, millions of state sector employees were laid off, township and village enterprises decayed, and domestic private enterprises were subject to adverse discrimination.

Students of the Chinese economy debate how foreign companies are treated differently from Chinese domestic companies. Gallagher (2005) argues that the infusion of foreign capital into China's economy changed the nature of the economic debate. A typical transitional economy debate over public versus private industry shifted to a debate that pits Chinese national industry over foreign competition in particular and globalization more generally. Some scholars contend that the Chinese government has favored foreign firms over domestic firms with regard to policies, regulations, and laws. For example, before 1994, the statutory income tax rate on SOEs was 55 percent, whereas the rate on FIEs ranged from 15 to 33 percent, with many tax breaks and exemptions (Fu 2000; Huang 1998, 2008).

In contrast, some claim that the Chinese government evidently favors SOEs at the expense of nonstate firms, including domestic private firms and foreign firms. For instance, Huang (2003) posits that the Chinese state allocates precious financial resources and business opportunities according to a political pecking order of firms, with inefficient SOEs at the top and the more efficient private firms at the bottom. In the same vein, Hsueh (2011, 3) observes, "China only appears to be a more liberal state, for it has complemented liberalization at the aggregate (macro) level with reregulation at the sectoral (micro) level." She argues that in strategic sectors such as telecommunications services, financial services, oil, and petrochemicals, the government centralizes control of the industries and strictly manages the level and direction of FDI. In less strategic sectors, the Chinese government relinquishes control over the industries and encourages private investment and FDI (Hsueh 2011).

Given the theoretical importance of the topic, it is surprising that very few empirical studies have been conducted to assess the literature. This chapter examines how various firms perceive state-business relations based on firm-level evidence.

I have three major findings. First, foreign firms are more likely to settle disputes through the formal legal institutions than other firms. Second, foreign firms believe that their property rights are not protected as well as those of Chinese domestic enterprises and companies owned by ethnic Chinese. Third, foreign firms are not as confident as other firms in China's legal system. The findings suggest that there is a gap between foreign firms' demand for the rule of law and what the Chinese legal system has offered.

The chapter is structured as follows: The next section discusses some recent reforms that contribute to the rising economic inequality among firms in China. The third section introduces the data set and the research design. The fourth section examines firms' dispute resolution strategies with a focus on litigation. The fifth section investigates firms' perceptions/behavior on four dimensions of state-business relations (security of property rights, business relations with the government, public relations with the government, and confidence in the legal system). The last section concludes with a summary of major findings and a discussion of their broader significance.

## ECONOMIC INEQUALITY AMONG FIRMS IN CHINA

Economic inequality comprises disparities in the distribution of property rights protection, political connections, and business opportunities among firms. Many observers of China's reforms have noticed a recent rise in inequality among firms with different ownerships in China. For example, *The Economist* has documented that the twenty-two Chinese companies listed in Forbes's Fortune 500 are unanimously state owned, that the Chinese state is the biggest shareholder in the country's 150 biggest companies, and that state companies make up 80 percent of the value of the stock market in China.[1]

Furthermore, in 2009–10, a government stimulus package of over 40 billion *yuan* (about $6 billion) invested in infrastructure building, in which SOEs were major beneficiaries. In addition, recent reforms and mergers in civil aviation, the steel industry, and coal mines raise the public's concern that there might be a trend of "the state advances, the private retreats" (*guojin mintui*), in which the state-backed conglomerates are expanding and consolidating their territories in critical industries while the private sector is shrinking.[2]

This, however, is only one dimension of China's rising economic inequality: inequality between the state sector and the private sector. The second (arguably greater) dimension is the inequality between domestic and foreign firms.

China is one of the world's most important destinations for FDI. It has by far the highest FDI inflows of any developing country (Naughton 2007, 401). To attract and retain foreign investors, the Chinese government instituted many favorable policies, including tax deductions, discounted land prices, and liberalized entry. With the green light of the government and the advantages of cheap labor and a large market, FIEs have flourished and become a major contributor to China's GDP growth.

But as Huang (2003, 87) argues, China's enormous FDI inflows are more a result of the low competitiveness of indigenous firms than a result of the high competitiveness of foreign firms. The Chinese government does not, however, favor FIEs over SOEs. Hsueh (2011, 3) argues that the Chinese government has

---

[1] "The Visible Hand," *Economist*, January 21, 2012, http://www.economist.com/node/21542931, accessed May 23, 2012.

[2] Please see Xie Peng, "Guojin mintui: jidang 2009" [The State Advances While the Private Retreats: Turbulence in 2009], *Southern Weekend* (*Nanfang zhoumo*), December 25, 2009, http://www.infzm.com/content/39154, accessed December 11, 2011.

adopted a bifurcated strategy in liberalizing FDI: in strategic sectors the government strictly limits FDI, while in less strategic sectors the Chinese government encourages private investment and FDI.

In addition, recent years have also witnessed a backlash on tax policies dealing with foreign investors. For example, the new Corporate Income Tax Law that took effect on January 1, 2008, has equalized the tax rates for FIEs and domestic firms. This series of policies that limit foreign investors' entry into certain industries and eliminate tax benefits raises concerns among foreign investors that the Chinese government is discriminating against FIEs.

Jacques de Boisséson, the President of the European Union Chamber of Commerce in China, once said in an interview: "What we are telling [the Chinese government] is that our companies are willing to invest, and for that, they need to be sure that they will be treated equally. Today they are concerned that this wouldn't be the case."[3]

Recent polices have worried investors both in China and abroad that the Chinese government favors large SOEs over foreign enterprises. Are these anecdotes supported by the empirical evidence? What are the consequences of this policy orientation? The next several sections answer these questions based on an analysis of a firm-level survey.

METHODOLOGY

To address these questions, I analyze data from a firm-level survey: *Governance, Investment Climate, and Harmonious Society: Competitiveness Enhancements for 120 Cities in China* (the World Bank survey, hereafter). The survey was conducted jointly by the World Bank and the Enterprise Survey Organization of the National Bureau of Statistics (NBS) of China in 2005; researchers interviewed 12,400 firms located in 120 cities across all Chinese provinces except Tibet. In each province, the provincial capital was automatically surveyed, and additional cities were selected based on the economic size of the province. One hundred firms were sampled in each city, except for the four provincial-level cities (Beijing, Tianjin, Shanghai, and Chongqing), where two hundred firms were surveyed.

The questionnaire had two parts. The first was filled out by firms' senior managers and asks for qualitative information about the firms in 2004; the second covered financial and quantitative information, much of which went back three years, about the firms' production and operation and was directly obtained from the firms' accounting books through the assistance of the firms' chief accountants.[4]

---

[3] Chengcheng Jiang, "Why Foreign Businesses in China Are Getting Mad," *Time*, September 9, 2010, http://www.time.com/time/world/article/0,8599,2017024,00.html#ixzz1k1krRGxQ, accessed May 23, 2012.

[4] More information about the survey can be found in Appendix A and World Bank (2007).

TABLE 4.1 *Cross Tabulation of Firms' Registration Status and Capital Share*

| Self-Reported Ownership/Average Capital Share (%) | State Capital | Collective Capital | Private Capital | Foreign Capital | Legal Person Capital | N |
|---|---|---|---|---|---|---|
| SOEs | 82.95 | 0.00 | 0.00 | 0.00 | 17.04 | 1,122 |
| Collective | 3.22 | 76.80 | 8.06 | 1.07 | 10.82 | 869 |
| Private | 0.31 | 1.30 | 78.40 | 0.84 | 19.14 | 1,675 |
| China circle | 4.69 | 3.31 | 6.91 | 66.45 | 18.60 | 990 |
| Foreign | 4.96 | 2.43 | 4.39 | 72.11 | 16.07 | 1,398 |
| Mixed | 9.25 | 4.75 | 51.26 | 1.92 | 32.73 | 6,346 |

*Source:* World Bank survey

One advantage of the data set is that it includes questions that address various aspects of state-business relations. It also includes a large number of firms with a wide range of ownerships. A limitation of the survey is that it is cross-sectional in 2004, so it does not provide any insight on reregulation after 2004, nor would it be able to test for change over time. But this is the most recent large-scale firm survey conducted in China, and as shown later, it is new and comprehensive enough to capture some of the recent rounds of reregulation favoring domestic industry vis-à-vis foreign firms before 2004.

### Categorizing Ownership in China

Firm ownership in contemporary China is a complicated issue. After three decades of state sector reforms, private sector development, and opening up policies, very few firms in China have pure ownerships. I rely on two indicators to identify a firm's ownership. The first is the firm's registration status. A firm in China can be registered as an SOE (*guoyou qiye*), a collective enterprise (*jiti qiye*), a private enterprise (*siying qiye*), an FIE (*waizi qiye*), or a mixed-ownership firm (for example, a joint-stock cooperative firm [*gufen hezuo qiye*]).

The World Bank survey also asked the FIEs to state whether their investments are from Hong Kong, Macao, and Taiwan (China circle) or foreign countries. But a large number of firms, especially foreign firms, are joint ventures. So the second indicator is the firm's shareholding structure, which shows who actually controls the firm. The survey asked firm managers about the shares of different shareholders of the firm: state shares, collective shares, legal person shares, private shares, and foreign shares. Table 4.1 shows the cross-tabulation of these two indicators.

The ownership variables are constructed by combining these two indicators. A firm is coded as **SOE** if it is registered as an SOE and its state share is over 50 percent. A firm is coded as **collective** if it is registered as a collective enterprise and its collective share is over 50 percent. A firm is coded as **private**

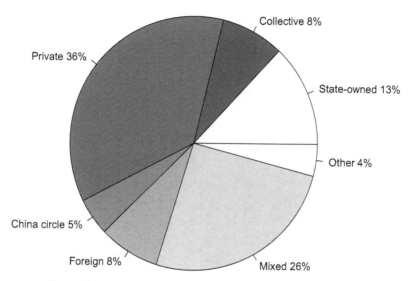

FIGURE 4.1 Share of Firms with Different Ownerships
*Source:* World Bank survey

if it is registered as a private firm and its private share is over 50 percent. A firm is coded as a **China circle** firm if it is registered as a Hong Kong-, Macao-, or Taiwan-invested firm and its foreign share is over 50 percent. A firm is coded as **foreign** if it is registered as a foreign firm and its foreign share is over 50 percent. A firm is coded as **mixed** if it is registered as a mixed firm and no shareholder controls more than 50 percent of its share. Some firms are coded as **others**, since they are registered as others. Figure 4.1 shows the distribution of ownership in the sample.

## DISPUTE RESOLUTION STRATEGY

There are three dispute resolution mechanisms in China. First is the newly enforced formal legal framework (litigation) that emphasizes previously latent legal institutions such as laws, regulations, procedures, court and procuratorate systems, and legal assistance services. Second is the administration intervention-ist arrangement (arbitration), which has been handling legal disputes since the formation of the People's Republic. Government organizations such as commerce bureaus have become the focal point of dispute resolution. With the advent of foreign investors, China has also joined several international conventions to solve disputes through international arbitration centers. These centers are located outside the host country and are therefore believed to be impartial in dealing with commercial disputes. The third dispute resolution mechanism is the informal social network that has functioned as an ADR and sanction enforcement (mediation). There is a long tradition in China that

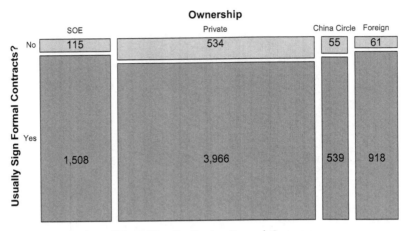

FIGURE 4.2 Proportion of Firms Usually Signing Formal Contracts
*Source:* World Bank survey

socially approved norms and values guide behavior, which is linked with a preference for informality in settling disputes and imposing sanctions. Furthermore, since individual leaders have much more influence over interpreting the loosely defined rules, parties to a dispute use their social contacts to acquire a resolution in their favor. This informal social network is characterized by personal connections and norms of reciprocity, bribery, and mediation through mutual acquaintances.

How do firms choose among these three mechanisms? Is the choice related to a firm's ownership? I show that FIEs are more likely to sign a written contract with their clients and are less likely to have disputes. When disputes arise, FIEs are more likely to rely on litigation than other firms and less likely to use mediation.

## Contracts and Disputes

The survey asked firm managers the following question: "Does your company usually sign formal contracts with your wholesale dealers and clients?" Figure 4.2 shows the result.

As shown, FIEs are the most likely to sign a written contract, followed by SOEs, China circle firms, and domestic private enterprises. Statistical tests show that the differences are significant, which is consistent with our expectation that foreign firms have a contract culture. After all, as Jensen and Meckling's (1976, 310) classic argument holds, a firm is a "nexus of contracts." In contrast, the contract culture is still weak among Chinese firms, especially private firms. This has become an obstacle to building the rule of law, because without written contracts, courts have difficulty finding evidence and making decisions.

The survey results suggest that signing a formal contract helps firms avoid disputes. Figure 4.3 shows that FIEs are the least likely to have a dispute of any

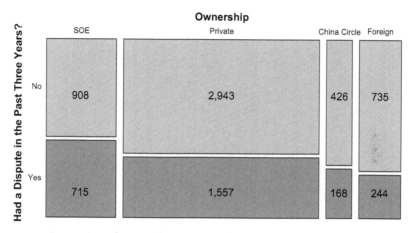

FIGURE 4.3 Proportion of Firms That Have Had a Dispute in the Past Three Years
*Source:* World Bank survey

firms, while SOEs are the most likely. This suggests two possibilities. The first is that FIEs are protected by written contracts. However, this cannot explain the high dispute rate for SOEs, since they are also protected by contracts. The second possibility is that FIEs without strong political connections are more wary of potential disputes, especially with their Chinese competitors. This explanation is more plausible and can account for the high frequency of disputes among SOEs. Since they have strong political connections, SOEs are less attentive to possible conflicts with other firms.

### Dispute Resolution

The survey asked the firm managers how they solved disputes in the last three years. Figure 4.4 shows the litigation rate (percentage of disputes settled through litigation) across ownerships.

As shown, FIEs and SOEs have the highest litigation rate, whereas China circle firms are less likely to go to court. This implies that there is a high demand from foreign firms for China's legal institutions. The high propensity to go to court is also a result of having a formal contract. And interestingly, China circle firms, although technically foreign, are very different from other foreign firms in dispute resolution strategy. This casts doubt on many existing studies that treat all foreign investment the same.[5]

Conversely, domestic private enterprises and China circle firms are more likely to rely on informal social networks to settle disputes. Figure 4.5 shows

---

[5] Hsueh (2011) distinguishes FDI by sector but not by origin. Huang (2003) discusses "ethnically Chinese economies" that include Hong Kong, Macao, and Taiwan, but his argument and data are

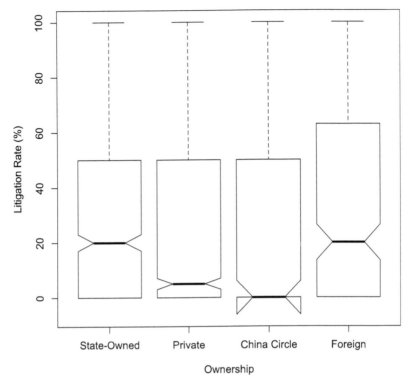

FIGURE 4.4 Litigation Rates across Different Ownerships
*Source:* World Bank survey

the mediation rate (percentage of disputes settled through mediation) across firms. Domestic private companies and China circle firms have the highest mediation rate, while FIEs have the lowest. This implies that domestic and ethnic Chinese firms not only excel at building political connections but also have rich social networking resources to help them solve disputes while avoiding the costly legal process. This suggests that domestic and ethnic Chinese firms have a weak demand for judicial empowerment.

## STATE-BUSINESS RELATIONS

I now examine four dimensions of state-business relations: property rights protection, business relations with the government, public relations with the government, and confidence in the legal system. The demand-side theory

based on the view that foreign investors are under the same FDI regime despite their origins. Naughton (2007) is an exception.

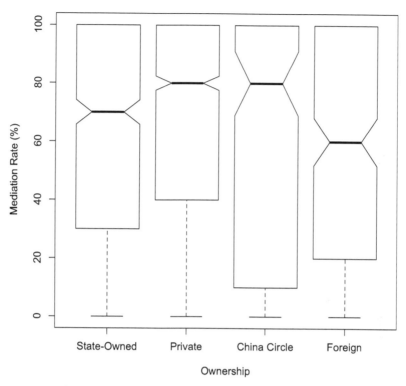

FIGURE 4.5 Mediation Rates across Different Ownerships
*Source:* World Bank survey

predicts that FIEs are not as well connected as domestic and China circle firms and that foreign firms are more frustrated with the legal system.

## Property Rights Protection

The new institutional economics establish that protection of property rights is the key to economic growth (North and Thomas 1973; North 1990). Studies based on developed countries often treat property rights protecting institutions as equivalent to legal institutions (La Porta et al. 1997). The puzzle for China, then, is the coexistence of weak legal institutions and rapid growth. Clarke, Murrell, and Whiting (2008) argue that the answer to this puzzle lies in the institutions that are substituting for formal legal institutions – for example, the decentralized fiscal system and the cadre evaluation system that incentivize local officials to protect property rights. I examine not only to what extent firms believe that their property rights are protected but also whether firms believe that their property rights are protected as well as others.

The survey asked firm managers: "In commercial or other disputes, in how many cases (%) can your company's legal contracts or properties be protected (verdict passed and enforced)?" To investigate whether firms believe that their properties are protected as well as others, I first calculate the city average level of property rights protection (the mean of firms' answers in each city) and then subtract a firm's answer from the city average. The result is a number for each firm that reflects the gap between its perception of property rights security and the city average. For example, firm A perceives that its property rights protection is 60 percent while the city average is 50 percent, so the gap is +10 percent, which means that firm A believes that its property rights are protected 10 percent better than the city average. This new variable is named "**property protection**," where positive values mean better-than-average protection and negative values worse-than-average protection. It is expected that foreign firms and domestic private firms are not as confident in their property rights as SOEs.

## Business Relations with the Government

A second measurement of state-business relations is to examine whether a firm has business relations with the government. Government procurement (*zhengfu caigou*) is an important source of revenue for politically connected firms. Government procurements are often in bulk size, and governments are usually not cost sensitive. Firms with good connections often obtain profitable and long-term contracts from the government, and this has become a hotbed for corruption.

To measure this, the survey asked firm managers: "What percentage of your products was sold to the government in 2004?" I construct a variable called "**sale to the government**" to measure firms' business relations with the government. It is expected that SOEs have more business activities with the government than other firms.

## Public Relations with the Government

It is believed that *guanxi* (connections) is critical in business success in China (Wank 1999). There are various ways to establish *guanxi*. SOEs automatically have close connections with the government because the government appoints most of their managers (Burns 1989). Domestic private enterprises and firms owned by ethnic Chinese are believed to have patron-client ties with local officials (Wank 1999). Dickson (2003) also argues that domestic private entrepreneurs build political connections through joining the CCP or serving in local People's Congresses. Foreign firms are at a disadvantage in terms of building connections with the government. Following the practice of several big multinational corporations, many foreign firms establish ad hoc public relations offices to deal with the government. Multinationals often hire Chinese personnel or even retired government employees to utilize their linguistic and political advantages (Kennedy 2009).

The survey asked firm managers: "Does your company designate special staff to handle government relationships (for example, a government relations office)?" I construct an indicator variable "**government public relations**" to measure whether the firm has such an office. Since this practice originated with foreign firms, it is expected that FIEs are more likely to have a government relations office.

### Confidence in Local Courts

In addition to the bureaucracy, the legal system also serves as an important way to enforce contracts and protect property rights. While many studies have examined local protectionism (e.g., Wedeman 2003), few have paid attention to how courts treat local firms differently.

The survey asked firm managers: "In the case of commercial disputes with the suppliers, clients, or subsidiaries in your locality, how much confidence do you have that the disputes will be settled with justice by the local legal system?" I constructed a continuous variable called "**confidence in courts**" to measure firms' confidence in local courts' fairness in enforcing contracts. It is expected that foreign firms have a lower level of confidence in courts compared with other firms.

### Empirics

How do firms map on these four dimensions of state-business relations? Econometric models are used to estimate differences among firms. The following analysis uses the four state-business relations dimensions as dependent variables and ownerships as independent variables.

The ownership variables are included in the regression analysis one by one, because the interest is in examining the difference between one type of ownership and all other types of ownership.

Alternative explanatory variables are included to tease out the independent contributions of the interested variables. These controls include firm's **age** (log transformed), **tax** paid in 2003 (log transformed), and the number of **employees** in 2003 (log transformed). These variables capture the basic characteristics of a firm: maturity and size. Studies have found that older and larger firms have stronger relations with the government (Cai, Fang, and Xu 2011).

Number of **licenses** (permanent and renewable annually) required for the firm is included to control for the cumbersomeness of regulations. This tests the "speed money" hypothesis, which states that political connections (often via corruption) are the much-needed grease for the squeaking wheels of a rigid administration (Bardhan 1997).

A set of government-business relations variables is also included. **Government-appointed manager** is an indicator variable measuring whether the general manager is appointed by the government. **Interaction with government** is an ordinal variable measuring how many days the general manager or vice general manager spent on interacting with the government every month in 2004.[6]

Industry "fixed effects" are included to control for possible variations in state regulation in various industries (Hsueh 2011). They include dummy variables for each industry, ranging from agriculture and food processing to textiles. City "fixed effects" are also included to account for historical and cultural features of different cities.[7]

Depending on the nature of the dependent variables (continuous or dichotomous), I used ordinary least squares (OLS) or logistic (Logit) regressions. Standard errors are clustered at the city level to remedy the possibility that firms in the same city are interdependent (Moulton 1990). Figure 4.6 presents the main results.[8]

The results show first that SOEs are more likely to have business relations with the government and less likely to establish public relations offices. This is consistent with my expectations. Governments are more likely to sign contracts with SOEs for government procurement, and there is no need for SOEs to have an ad hoc office to deal with the government since their managers are quasi-government officials. It also shows that SOEs do not differ significantly from other firms in their perception of property rights protection and confidence in courts.

As for domestic private enterprises, the results show no significant distinctions in any of the four dimensions, which suggests that private enterprises have an average level of state-business relations. This finding is surprising in the context of existing studies that show the political constraints of private firms (Huang 2003, 2008). One possible explanation is that, given all the constraints and biased policies, only the strong ones survive. "Red capitalists" who are CCP members, People's Congress representatives, or retired government officials have taken advantage of their political connections to aid their companies in an unfair commercial environment (Tsai 2007a).

Firms owned by ethnic Chinese (China circle) are not so different from other firms, except that they sell fewer products to the government. This suggests that

---

[6] The original wording of the question is "How many days does the general manager or vice general manager spend on government assignments and communications per month? (Government agencies include Tax Administration, Customs, Labor Bureau, Registration Bureau, etc.; assignments refer to handling the relationship with the government workers, consolidating and submitting various reports or statements, etc.)" Answers: 1 = 1 day, 2 = 2–3 days, 3 = 4–5 days, 4 = 6–8 days, 5 = 9–12 days, 6 = 13–16 days, 7 = 17–20 days, 8 = over 21 days.

[7] Summary statistics of included variables are shown in Appendix B Table A4.1.

[8] The full model results are presented in Appendix B Table A4.2.

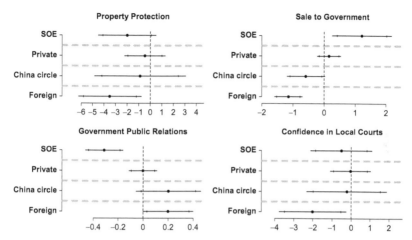

FIGURE 4.6 Ownership and State-Business Relations
*Notes*: Each line represents a *separate* regression. The dependent variable is marked on the top of each panel. SOE, Private, China circle, and Foreign are all dummy variables indicating a firm's ownership. Lines represent the 95% confidence intervals, and the small bars 90% confidence intervals, both based on robust standard errors. The results that generate this graph are presented in Appendix B Table A4.2.
*Source*: World Bank survey

Hong Kong firms and Taiwanese firms more closely resemble domestic firms than foreign firms in this respect. Their property rights are protected as well as those of SOEs and domestic private enterprises. Foreign companies owned by ethnic Chinese are under a very different regime from foreign companies owned by foreigners.

The most significant finding is the real difference between foreign and domestic firms. The results show that foreign firms are different in all four dimensions: they believe that they are poorly protected, they sell significantly fewer products to the government, they are more likely to have public relations offices, and they are less confident in the local courts. This confirms Gallagher's (2005) argument that the dominant debate in China's economic reforms is foreign versus Chinese rather than public versus private. The finding also shows support from the firms' perspective for Hsueh's (2011) argument that China's reregulation of FDI has created a sense of unfairness among foreign investors. This finding contradicts Huang's (2008) observation that the Chinese government favors foreign firms at the expense of indigenous firms. Foreign firms nonetheless believe that they are subject to adverse discrimination.

Several of the control variables need highlighting.[9] First, older firms are more likely to do business with the government, are less likely to have a public

---

[9] Results for the control variables are shown in Appendix B Table A4.2.

relations office, and are less confident in the courts. But older firms' property rights are not better protected. This implies that there is a learning process for conducting business in China. Firms, regardless of ownership, need a relatively long time to build connections with the government and learn the flaws of the legal system. Interestingly, this experience does not guarantee that their property rights will be better protected.

In addition, bigger firms (measured by tax and employees) are better protected, more likely to have a public relations office, and more likely to trust the courts. This suggests that governments differentiate among firms not only by ownership but also by size: governments tend to favor firms that pay a large amount of tax and hire a large number of people. This is intuitive, given that the cadre evaluation system emphasizes tax revenue and social stability as criteria for career advancement. It also shows that firms that pay more taxes sell less to the government, but firms with more employees sell more to the government. This implies that business relations with the government serve as a substitute for tax. Firms doing business with the government are more likely to evade taxes. But the same preferential treatment is not applied to firms with a large number of employees.

The results also show that firms with more licenses are more likely to have a public relations office. This is consistent with the "speed money" argument that cumbersome bureaucracies create higher incentives for corruption (Bardhan 1997).

The government-business relations variables show that firms with government-appointed managers are more likely to conduct business with the government, are less likely to have a public relations office, and are less confident in the local courts. These firms are primarily SOEs, so the findings are very similar to those of SOEs. The results of these variables also show that firms with more interactions with the government are more likely to have a public relations office and less confidence in the courts, while firms with business relations with the government are more likely to have a public relations office. These results are intuitive and manifest how political and economic privileges are intertwined.

I also find some inconclusive patterns regarding the industry fixed effects. A general finding is that there is no significant difference between labor-intensive industries and capital/technology-intensive industries on property rights protection. Using agriculture and food processing as the baseline category, managers of firms in labor-intensive industries (such as textiles, leather, and furniture) and capital/technology-intensive industries (such as chemical and fiber manufacturing, ferrous metals, general equipment, transportation equipment, electric equipment, communication equipment, and computers and other electronic industries) all believe that their property rights are poorly protected. There is also no distinction between strategic and nonstrategic industries. According to the categorization by Hsueh (2011, 42), textiles is a nonstrategic industry, whereas telecommunications equipment is a highly strategic industry, but I do not find any significant difference in terms of property rights protection between these two industries.

There is also no significant distinction between labor-intensive and capital/technology-intensive industries on business relations with the government. It is more about the "usefulness" of the products for the government. For example, clothing, shoes, hats, furniture, printing and media, educational and sporting goods, metal products, electric equipment, communication equipment, and computers and other electronic industries are engaged in business relations with the government more often than other industries.[10]

In summary, an analysis of the firm-level survey data shows that FIEs perceive themselves as disadvantaged compared to their Chinese counterparts. And as an effort to strengthen their *guanxi* with the Chinese government, foreign firms are more likely to establish ad hoc government relations offices.

## DISCUSSION, CONCLUSIONS, AND IMPLICATIONS

After more than three decades of market reforms, ownership reconstruction, opening up, and critical phases of reregulation, the Chinese state has created some interest groups that benefit from the reform policies. But the unevenness of the reforms has led some groups to believe they are subject to severely adverse discrimination. This disparity in the distribution of property rights protection, political connections, and business opportunities among economic actors in China will create both barriers and motives for China's prospective legal reforms. Since a genuine market economy requires a level playing field, the economic inequality of firms will create vested interests that become obstacles for further reforms.

The logic is similar to Hellman's (1998) "partial reform equilibrium" in which the interest groups that benefit from earlier reform policies will block further reforms to maintain their monopolistic position in the market. In the same vein, Pei (2006) argues that the combination of one-party rule and semifinished economic reform creates fertile conditions for local ruling elites to engage in decentralized predation, which undermines governance and creates systemic risks.

---

[10] Results of the industry "fixed effects" are not shown but are available upon request. Industries included in the survey are petroleum, nuclear material processing, agriculture and food processing, ferrous metals (that is, iron, chromium, manganese, and alloys containing them) smelting, nonferrous metals, chemical and fiber manufacturing, chemical material and products manufacturing, clothing, shoes, hats, communication equipment, computer and other electronic industries, crafts and related manufacturing, beverage manufacturing, educational and sporting goods, electric equipment, food manufacturing, furniture, general equipment, instruments, office equipment, leather, hides, feather products, medical equipment, metal products, nonmetal products, mineral manufacturing, paper products, plastic manufacturing, printing and media, recycling, rubber manufacturing, specialized equipment, textiles, transportation equipment, and wood/ bamboo/etc. processing.

However, the uneven distribution of resources among firms also creates hopes for future legal reforms. The analysis shows strong signs of a gap between the demands of foreign firms for the rule of law and the supply of the Chinese state. As the gap widens, foreign investors' impetus for a strong judiciary will become more urgent. And as Schattschneider (1960) shows, the outcome of a conflict will be determined by the success or failure of efforts by the weaker side to enlarge its scope to alter the power balance.

# 5

# Who bribes?

Someone must have traduced Joseph K., for without having done anything wrong
he was arrested one fine morning.

Franz Kafka

## INTRODUCTION: MOTIVATION, FINDINGS, AND A ROAD MAP

This chapter examines the ways in which firms in China build political
connections. I address the following questions in particular: How do firms
build political connections? Do domestic Chinese firms have a comparative
advantage in establishing political connections compared to foreign firms? Do
anticorruption laws and regulations matter in regulating foreign firms' behavior in China? The demand-side theory implies that foreign firms with strict
antibribery and auditing rules bribe much less often than Chinese domestic
firms and China circle firms, holding everything constant.

I use a new measure of graft pioneered by Cai, Fang, and Xu (2011):
entertainment and travel costs (ETC). ETC is listed as a category under
"management fees" (*guanli feiyong*) in firms' accounting books. The World
Bank and the National Bureau of Statistics in China sent survey teams to
12,400 firms operating in China to record the costs on travel (*chailu fei*) and
entertainment (*zhaodai fei*) directly from their accounting books. ETC covers
routine business expenditures on lodging, meals, and travel. However, a significant portion of ETC is spent on building connections with government
officials. This part of ETC takes the form of eating and drinking with officials,
gifts, hotel accommodations and airfare used by officials or their families,
karaoke, sports club memberships, and other recreational activities. Firms in

China often use ETC to bribe officials and get reimbursed by presenting allowable receipts.[1] In China, there is also a large black market for fake receipts. According to an official report, in 2010, an agency designated by the central government detected over 660 million fake receipts. The central government organizations used fake receipts to get reimbursed for over 140 million *yuan* (approximately $20 million) in cash. In addition, more than 70,000 firms were found to use fake receipts.[2] Obviously, this is just the tip of the iceberg.

Based on a quantitative analysis and qualitative interviews, I demonstrate that foreign firms spend less on ETC to bribe officials, which suggests that FIEs have a limited capability to build political connections with Chinese officials, while Chinese SOEs, domestic private enterprises, and China circle firms have a comparative advantage in doing so. The finding is consistent with the implication of the demand-side theory.

The second section theorizes about the relationship between a firm's incentive structure and its bribing behavior. The third section discusses a new measure of bribery based on a firm-level survey. The fourth section investigates the variation of bribery across firms with different ownerships. The fifth section summarizes major findings and discuss their broader implications.

## INTERNAL INCENTIVE STRUCTURE AND BRIBERY

Bribes are prices firms are willing to pay to obtain a government good, such as protection. Prices are determined by a set of institutions governing firms' capacity and incentives, along with the demand for and supply of the good. Firms calculate the costs and benefits of paying bribes, and the incidence and amount are explained by the variation in the institutional environment in which the firm is embedded.

I examine the briber's side and argue that firms' internal institutions, among which auditing rules are the most crucial part, affect their incentive to engage in bribery. A firm's auditing rules determine the transparency of its accounts to the public, shareholders, partners, regulators, and/or mother companies. A stricter auditing system will significantly decrease a firm's tendency toward discretionary spending (for example, bribery) by increasing the costs of graft.

---

[1] The author's experience with Chinese firms is that the reimbursement requirements are very flexible. Almost everything can be reimbursed. What's worse is that the issuers of receipts are also very flexible. For example, many hotels operate boutiques for expensive gifts, and those gifts can be invoiced as room charges.

[2] Please see "2010 Quanguo jiaohuo 6.6 yi jiafapiao" [China Detected and Confiscated 660 Million Pieces of Fake Receipts in 2010], *Xinhua News*, May 16, 2011, http://news.xinhuanet.com/video/2011-05/16/c_121423162.htm, accessed January 12, 2012.

A firm's internal auditing rules are highly associated with ownership of the firm. As I argue in Chapter 2, FIEs from outside the China circle are subject to strict antibribery and auditing rules instituted by their countries of origin.

The most salient example is the Foreign Corrupt Practices Act (FCPA). The FCPA was enacted in 1977 by the United States to halt the use of bribery as a means of obtaining or retaining foreign business. The statute generally prohibits US companies and citizens, foreign companies listed on the US stock exchange, or any person acting in the United States from corruptly paying, offering to pay, or authorizing the payment of money, a gift, or anything of value, directly or indirectly, to a foreign official in order to obtain or sustain business (the "anti-bribery provisions").[3] The Act also requires companies that issue debt or equity in the United States to maintain books and records that accurately reflect the disposition of corporate assets, and to devise and maintain internal controls sufficient to provide reasonable assurances, among other things, that transactions are executed in accordance with management's authorization (the "Books and Records and Internal Control provisions").[4]

The US Department of Justice (DOJ) and the Securities and Exchange Commission (SEC) jointly enforce the FCPA. The DOJ is responsible for criminal enforcement of the statute and for civil enforcement of the antibribery provisions against nonpublic companies and foreign companies and nationals. The SEC is responsible for civil enforcement of the antibribery provisions with respect to issuers as well as overall responsibility for the books and records and internal control provisions (Koehler 2007).

FCPA compliance poses a special challenge for American firms operating in China. The Chinese business culture values the provision of gifts, meals, trips, and entertainment, and the exchange of favors drives successful business development (Warin, Diamant, and Pfenning 2010). Yet the broad scope of the Act – its "anything of value" and "foreign official" elements in particular – exposes American firms to high risk.

"Anything of value" includes not only cash or a cash equivalent but also discounts; gifts; use of materials, facilities, or equipment; entertainment; drinks; meals; transportation; lodging; insurance coverage; and the promise of future employment, among other things (Koehler 2007, 402). However, the Chinese approach to conducting business greatly values personal relationships and requires a certain level of gift exchange. *Oriental Outlook* magazine published a diary kept by two Hunan entrepreneurs who attempted to open a fireworks business. The diary chronicles the many payments for gifts, dinners, and entertainment that the two men had to make over eight months to secure permits and licenses for their nascent business. In the end, the entrepreneurs spent over 300,000 *yuan* (about $44,000) on gifts and

---

[3] Foreign Corrupt Practices Act of 1977, 78dd-1.    [4] Ibid., 78m(b).

hospitality – nearly every day they treated officials to dinner, paid them cash, or presented gifts such as cigarettes, alcohol, or dried tofu.[5]

There are many cases in which American firms exchanged gifts with Chinese government officials and are under investigation for potential FCPA violations.

From 1995 to 2004, Schnitzer Steel Industries' South Korean subsidiary made payments to private companies in South Korea and private companies and government officials in China to induce them to purchase scrap metal. In May 2004, after Schnitzer's compliance department uncovered the payments, company executives authorized Schnitzer employees to increase the entertainment expenses they paid for government employees and privately owned customers, in lieu of cash payments. According to the SEC order, the gifts that Schnitzer provided included $10,000 gift certificates and a $2,400 watch. The Korean subsidiary pled guilty to violations of the antibribery and books and records provisions and paid a $7.5 million penalty, and Schnitzer entered into a deferred prosecution agreement with the DOJ. In the SEC proceeding, Schnitzer consented to a cease-and-desist order and agreed to pay disgorgement and prejudgment interest totaling $7.7 million.[6]

Many FCPA actions involved US companies paying trips to their Chinese partners. For example, Paradigm's subsidiary used an agent to make payments to a subsidiary of the China National Offshore Oil Company in connection with the sale of software. It also retained oil and gas employees to test its software and paid them in cash for their services, hoping their companies would then purchase the software. Paradigm also paid for sightseeing trips for Chinese state oil and gas company officials. These customer "training" trips included paying for hotels, meals, airfare, sightseeing, and entertainment, as well as providing cash per diems and cash for the officials to shop.[7]

In another case, Lucent Technology paid for 315 trips to the United States and other benefits for Chinese government officials who were employees of Chinese state-owned or state-controlled telecommunications enterprises. Some trips were characterized as "factory inspections" or "training" in the contracts with government customers, although they usually involved little of either, focusing instead on sightseeing in major US cities or

---

[5] Huang Zhijie, "The Gift Diary of a Small, Private Company," *Oriental Outlook*, November 28, 2007, http://www.danwei.org/business/what_it_takes_to_register_a_bu.php, accessed June 15, 2012.

[6] Jaymes Song, "Schnitzer Steel Industries Inc.'s Subsidiary Pleads Guilty to Foreign Bribes, Agrees to $7.5 Million Criminal Fine; Parent Company Enters Into Deferred Prosecution Agreement Following Exceptional Cooperation with Justice Dept.," US Newswire, October 16, 2006; see also Warin, Diamant, and Pfenning (2010, 49–50).

[7] US Department of Justice, "Paradigm B.V. Agrees to Pay $1 Million Penalty to Resolve Foreign Bribery Issues in Multiple Countries," news release, September 24, 2007, http://www.justice.gov/opa/pr/2007/September/07_crm_751.html, accessed June 15, 2012; also see Warin, Diamant, and Pfenning (2010, 50).

at the Grand Canyon, Disneyland, or Universal Studios. Lucent improperly booked these expenses as business trips.[8]

In addition, the "foreign official" element of the FCPA makes compliance in China a unique challenge compared to other countries, given the prevalence of state-owned or state-controlled enterprises in China. The Act's antibribery provisions broadly define the term "foreign official" to include "any officer or employee of a foreign government or any department, agency, or instrumentality thereof, or of a public international organization, or any person acting in an official capacity for or on behalf of any such government or department, agency or instrumentality, or for or on behalf of any such public international organization."[9]

As many cases demonstrate, US enforcement agencies view Chinese SOEs as being "instrumentalities" of the Chinese government and employees of the SOEs as being "foreign officials" under the FCPA. In June 2008, Faro Technologies, a Florida-based public company, agreed to pay combined fines and penalties of $2.95 million in connection with improper payments made to employees of Chinese SOEs in order to help obtain and retain business, in violation of the FCPA.[10]

Similarly, in May 2005, Diagnostic Products Corporation (DPC), a producer and seller of diagnostic medical equipment, along with its Chinese subsidiary, DPC Tianjin, agreed to settle an FCPA enforcement action in connection with alleged payments of approximately $1.6 million in the form of illegal commissions to physicians and laboratory personnel employed by government-owned hospitals in China.[11]

OECD members were also required to implement laws criminalizing the bribery of foreign officials (Pedersen 2008). The 1997 OECD Convention on Combating Bribery of Foreign Public Officials in International Business Transactions is a binding convention on all member states.

The EU, World Bank, International Monetary Fund, World Trade Organization, US Agency for International Development, UN Development Programme, and the Asian Development Bank all enacted similar regulations to fight corruption and promote transparency (Sandholtz and Gray 2003).

---

[8] US Department of Justice, "Lucent Technologies Inc. Agrees to Pay $1 Million Fine to Resolve FCPA Allegations," news release, December 21, 2007, http://www.justice.gov/opa/pr/2007/December/07_crm_1028.html, accessed June 15, 2012; also see Warin, Diamant, and Pfenning (2010, 51).

[9] Foreign Corrupt Practices Act of 1977, 78dd-1(f)(1)(A).

[10] US Department of Justice, "Faro Technologies Inc. Agrees to Pay $1.1 Million Penalty and Enter Non-Prosecution Agreement for FCPA Violations," news release, June 5, 2008, http://www.justice.gov/opa/pr/2008/June/08-crm-505.html, accessed June 15, 2012; also see Koehler (2007, 407).

[11] US Department of Justice, "DPC (Tianjin) Ltd. Charged with Violating the Foreign Corrupt Practices Act," news release, May 20, 2005, http://www.justice.gov/opa/pr/2005/May/05_crm_282.htm, accessed June 15, 2012; also see Koehler (2007, 409).

In contrast, Chinese indigenous firms are not subject to strictly enforced anticorruption and auditing rules. Studies have shown that local and central SOEs tend to hire small local auditors for opportunistic reasons and that governments use political pressure to coerce small local auditors to collude with their SOEs (Wang, Wong, and Xia 2008). Domestic private firms are in a more liberal regime. Similarly, ethnic Chinese investors – taking advantage of their linguistic advantage, understanding of Chinese culture, and close family ties – are more likely to rely on informal connections with Chinese officials to conduct business and settle disputes.

Do anticorruption acts matter in curbing firms' corrupt behavior? Although the contents and implications of anticorruption laws are well documented,[12] few studies have tested the effect of these laws on foreign firms' behavior. Based on a large firm-level survey and a new measure of bribery, I test the following hypothesis:

*Hypothesis 5.1: FIEs from outside the China circle are less likely to bribe than other firms in China*, ceteris paribus.


## MEASURING BRIBERY

In a review article of corruption studies, Treisman (2007, 213) concludes that "the challenge of the next wave of research will be to refine and gather more experience-based measures of corruption and to examine the patterns they reveal."

The three most widely used corruption measures are based on the subjective evaluations of experts or survey respondents. These include the Corruption Perception Index (CPI) constructed by Transparency International (TI), a rating of control of corruption published by a team led by Daniel Kaufmann at the World Bank (*Governance* scores), and a rating by Political Risk Services, based on evaluations by its network of experts and published in its *International Country Risk Guide*. These measures are subject to perception bias and introduce significant measurement errors (Knack 2006; Treisman 2007).

Recent years have seen a surge in experience-based measures: TI's "Global Corruption Barometer," the United Nations Interregional Crime and Justice Research Institute, and the World Bank's World Business Environment Survey have asked respondents about their experience of paying a bribe or being expected to pay a bribe. These measures are, however, also subject to biases. As Treisman (2007, 239) argues, "Respondents in some countries are more

---

[12] Urofsky, Philip, and Danforth Newcomb, "Recent Trends and Patterns in the Enforcement of the Foreign Corrupt Practices Act," Shearman & Sterling LLP, October 1, 2009, http://www. shearman.com/files/Publication/bb1a7bff-ad52-4cf9-88b9-9d99e001dd5f/Presentation/Publication Attachment/6ec0766a-25aa-41ec-8731-041a672267a6/FCPA-Digest-Trends-and-Patterns-Jan 2012.pdf, accessed June 15, 2012.

reluctant to admit paying bribes and so would reply 'don't know' or 'no answer' rather than 'yes' to survey questions about this."

Following the practice of Cai, Fang, and Xu (2011), I use firms' ETC to measure bribery; this measure is not subject to perception bias or nonresponse bias, because it was collected directly from accounting books, and every firm has an accounting book.

However, the measure is subject to another measurement error; that is, ETC includes not only bribery but also routine business trip expenses and meals. Cai, Fang, and Xu (2011) distinguished between four components of ETC. The first is *normal business expenditures*, denoted by $x_r$, to build relational capital with suppliers and clients. The second is *managerial excess*, denoted by $x_c$, which goes directly to the manager's or employees' own pockets or to their families and friends. SOEs and domestic private firms with low levels of oversight and transparency might use ETC as an informal compensation scheme for employees. This would allow SOEs to compensate employees at higher levels than is usually permissible under regulations. The third is *grease money*, denoted by $x_g$, which refers to bribes paid to service-related government agencies, such as licensing and utilities agencies, in exchange for better government services. The fourth is *protection money*, denoted by $x_p$, which refers to bribes to government tax agency officials in exchange for lower government expropriation. Thus, ETC is the sum of these four components: $x_r$, $x_c$, $x_g$, and $x_p$. I am interested in $x_g+x_p$: that is, the costs of bribery. The weights of different components in ETC generate different observable implications:

> **Implication 1:** If ETC is spent as normal business expenditures, then it should increase as the firm's geological scope of business activities expands; otherwise, ETC should not be correlated with the geological scope of business activities.
>
> **Implication 2:** If ETC is spent as managerial excess, then it should increase as the manager's salary or employees' salaries decrease; otherwise, ETC should not be correlated with the manager's or employees' salaries.
>
> **Implication 3:** If ETC is spent as "grease money" or "protection money," then it should increase as the internal auditing rules loosen; otherwise, ETC should not be correlated with the stringency of internal auditing rules.

The rationale for Implication 1 is that if a firm has a large geographical scope of business activities, such as suppliers or clients outside the locality where the firm is based, then its routine business expenditures (lodging, transportation, and meals) should be higher than those of a firm that conducts business only locally. The rationale for Implication 2 is the efficient wage logic: employees with higher pay are less likely to embezzle company funds or be compensated. The rationale for Implication 3 is a direct derivation of Hypothesis 5.1.

WHO BRIBES?

The data are derived from the World Bank survey analyzed in Chapter 4. To recap, the survey was conducted in 2005 and interviewed 12,400 firms in 120 cities across all Chinese provinces except Tibet. In each province, the provincial capital was automatically surveyed, and additional cities were selected based on the economic size of a province. One hundred firms were sampled in each city, except for the four provincial-level cities (Beijing, Tianjin, Shanghai, and Chongqing), where two hundred firms were surveyed.[13]

The questionnaire had two parts: the first part was completed by the firms' senior managers and asked for qualitative information about the firm in 2004. The second part covered financial and quantitative information, much of which went back three years, about the firms' production and operation and was directly obtained from the firms' accounting books with the help of their chief accountants.

## The Dependent Variable

The dependent variable of the analysis is the firms' 2004 ETC normalized by the firms' total revenues in 2004. ETC, in the rest of the chapter, refers to this percentage. It varies significantly across firms and cities. At the firm level, ETC has a mean of 1.09 and a standard deviation of 2.25 (range 0–45.51). One percent of firms has ETC higher than 9.72. To avoid having a few high-leverage cases that could potentially distort the regression line, these cases are excluded from the analysis. At the city level, ETC has a mean of 1.14 and a standard deviation of 0.45 (range 0.4 [Suzhou, Jiangsu Province] to 2.4 [Haikou, Hainan Province]). Cities and their ETC are mapped in Figure 5.1; darker colors indicate higher levels of ETC (more corruption).[14]

## The Independent Variables

The first set of independent variables measures a firm's ownership. I use the same set of ownership variables introduced in Chapter 4. They take into account both a firm's registration status and its shareholding structure.

The ownership variables are included in the regression analysis one by one, because we want to examine the difference between one type of ownership, such as foreign, and all other types of ownership. Only SOE, private, China circle, and foreign are included in the analysis, because these firms have clearly specified auditing rules. I expect to see a negative sign on foreign and a positive sign on SOE and private. The effect of China circle on ETC is difficult to predict.

---

[13] Please see Appendix A for more information about the survey.
[14] The full results are presented in Appendix B Table A5.1.

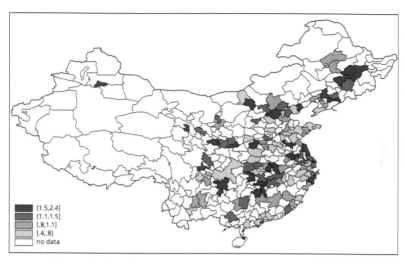

FIGURE 5.1 Cities and Their ETC Levels
*Notes*: Darker color indicates a higher level of ETC (city average ratio of firms' ETC spending as a percentage of total revenues). The full results are presented in Appendix B Table A5.1.
*Source*: World Bank survey

## Controls

Alternative explanatory variables are included to tease out the independent contributions of the interested variables. These controls include the firm's **age** (log transformed), **taxes** paid in 2003 (log transformed), and number of **employees** in 2003 (log transformed). These capture the basic characteristics of firms: maturity and size.

To differentiate between the various components of ETC, the "percentage of **sales outside the province** in 2004" is controlled to test Implication 1. Business relations outside the province reflect the geographical scope of a firm's business activities. If ETC is spent as a normal business expenditure, it should increase as sales outside the province increase. In addition, **CEO pay in 2004** (log transformed)[15] and average monthly **employee wages** (log transformed) in 2004 are included to test Implication 2. If ETC is spent as managerial excess, then it should decrease as CEO pay or employee wages increase.

The number of **licenses** and registrations (permanent and renewable annually) required for the firm is included to test the "speed money" hypothesis

---

[15] CEO pay is not directly observed in the survey. The survey asked the relative ratio of CEO pay to the average middle manager pay and the ratio of the latter to the average worker pay. CEO pay is computed as the product of the two ratios and the average wage of the firm. Firms' average wages are measured directly in the survey.

(Bardhan 1997), which holds that corruption is the much-needed grease for the squeaky wheels of a rigid administration.

A set of government-business relations variables is also included. **Government-appointed manager** is an indicator variable measuring whether the government appoints the general manager. **Interaction with government** is an ordinal variable measuring the number of days that the general manager or vice general manager spent on interacting with the government every month in 2004.[16] This variable indicates the extent of "red tape." **Sale to government** is a continuous variable indicating the percentage of a firm's products sold to the government in 2004. **Confidence in courts** is a continuous variable measuring a firm's level of confidence in the local legal system.[17] **GDP per capita** (log transformed) of cities is included to test the relationship between economic development and corruption (Treisman 2007).

Industry fixed effects are included to control for possible variation in state regulations in various industries (Hsueh 2011). City fixed effects are also included to account for the historical and cultural features of different cities.[18]

## Results

Before conducting regression analysis, I first show the descriptive pattern of ETC across different ownership types. Figure 5.2 shows box plots of ETC across various ownership types.[19] As shown, firms with China circle ownership and foreign ownership have a noticeably lower level of ETC compared to all other types of firms. Meanwhile, SOEs and private firms have a marginally higher level of ETC than other firms. This lends preliminary support to Hypothesis 5.1 – that foreign firms characterized by strict internal auditing rules are less likely to bribe. This also implies that a significant proportion of ETC is not spent as normal business expenditures, since foreign firms (which have a larger geological scope of business activities than domestic firms) spend less on ETC.

The results also increase confidence in the survey data. Scholars and pundits are skeptical of data from authoritarian regimes, especially survey data (Wintrobe 2000, 20), because respondents may overreport or underreport due to political fear, social desirability, or political correctness. In this case, firm

---

[16] The original wording of the question was "How many days does the general manager or vice general manager spend on government assignments and communications per month? (Government agencies include Tax Administration, Customs, Labor Bureau, Registration Bureau, etc.; assignments refer to handling the relationship with the government workers, consolidating and submitting various reports or statements, etc.)" Answers: 1 = 1 day, 2 = 2–3 days, 3 = 4–5 days, 4 = 6–8 days, 5 = 9–12 days, 6 = 13–16 days, 7 = 17–20 days, 8 = over 21 days.

[17] The wording of the question was "In the case of commercial disputes with the suppliers, clients, or subsidiaries in your locality, how much confidence (%) do you have that the disputes will be settled with justice by the local legal system?"

[18] Summary statistics of the included variables are shown in Appendix B Table A5.2.

[19] Outside values are excluded in the plots.

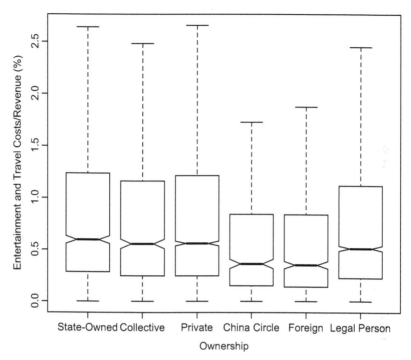

FIGURE 5.2 ETC across Different Ownerships
*Source:* World Bank survey

managers might underreport their ETC spending to make their firms look more professional. I acknowledge this possibility, but the analysis shows that this is not a major concern. If firm mangers tend to underreport, it is illogical to see higher reported ETC among Chinese private firms with lax oversight and transparency. If they lied and nobody could check, why would they not hide more? In addition, scholars who have used this data set and verified its credibility also make me more confident (Cai, Fang, and Xu 2011). Figure 5.3 shows the regression results.[20]

For the independent variables, the marginal effect of SOE is positive, but it fails to pass hypothesis testing at any conventional level. The marginal effect of private firms is positive and significant at the 0.05 level. On average, a private firm spends 0.056 more on ETC than all other types of firms. This effect is substantial, given that the mean ETC among firms is 1.09, which means that an average private firm spends 27 million *yuan* (about $4 million) more on

---

[20] The full model specification and results are presented in Appendix B (under "OLS Regression to Predict ETC") and Table A5.3.

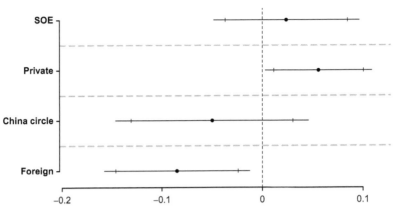

FIGURE 5.3 OLS Estimates of the Determinants of ETC
*Note*: Each line represents a *separate* regression. The dependent variable is the percentage of a firm's total revenue represented by entertainment and travel costs in 2004. SOE, Private, China circle, and Foreign are all dummy variables indicating a firm's ownership. Lines represent the 95% confidence intervals, and the small bars 90% confidence intervals; both are based on robust standard errors. The results that generate this graph are presented in Appendix B Table A5.3.
*Source:* World Bank survey

entertainment and travel each year than an average nonprivate firm. The marginal effect of a China circle firm is negative but insignificant. The marginal effect of a foreign firm is negative and significant at the 0.05 level. On average, a foreign firm spends 0.085 less on ETC than other types of firms. An average FIE spends 43 million *yuan* (about $6 million) less each year on entertainment and travel than an average nonforeign firm. This supports Hypothesis 5.1 – that foreign firms bribe less because of stricter internal auditing rules. This also supports Implication 3 – that a significant portion of ETC is spent as "grease money" and "protection money" in building political connections.

Among the controls, firm age is significantly positive; this implies that ETC is not a one-off fixed cost to establish relationships with officials and/or clients. Taxes paid in 2003 and the number of employees in 2003 both have negative and significant effects: bigger firms bribe less. This implies that bigger firms have stronger bargaining power with the government, so they do not need to pay a higher price (for example, bribes) for political protection. This also implies that taxes and bribes substitute for each other, which confirms an observation from qualitative interviews that tax evasion is prevalent among firms that have political connections.

The two variables that are included to test the two implications show mixed results. Sale to another province, which measures the geological scope of a firm's business, has a significantly positive effect on ETC. This supports Implication 1, which states that if ETC is spent as normal business expenditures, it should increase as the firm's geological scope of business expands. This means that part of ETC is spent as routine business expenditures on lodging, meals, and travel for firm managers. However, there is no evidence to support Implication 2. Neither CEO pay nor employee wages is correlated with ETC, so there is no strong support for the hypothesis that firm managers or employees are embezzling or compensated by company funds.

Among the government-business relations variables, a government-appointed manager, interaction with the government, and sale to the government all have significantly positive effects on ETC. However, the government-appointed manager variable fails to show any significant effect after controlling for SOE. This has three implications. First, it makes no difference for SOEs whether they have a government-appointed manager, but it matters for non-SOEs such as private enterprises. Many private enterprises in China are privatized SOEs, and some of their managers still have very strong government connections. Managers with connections have better access to the government than managers without connections. Second, this lends extra support to Implication 3 – that a big chunk of ETC is spent on interacting with government officials. This supports the "red tape" argument that cumbersome bureaucracy invites corruption (Bardhan 1997). Third, obtaining a government contract requires extra bribery costs. Firms that sell their products to the government must spend money to buy this privilege. The number of licenses does not show any significant effects. There is no support for the "speed money" hypothesis. Finally, confidence in the courts does not affect a firm's tendency to bribe, which suggests that formal legal institutions have not functioned as a curb on graft. This supports Manion's (2004) observation that party organizations have triumphed over state institutions (for example, courts and procuratorates) in handling corruption cases.

## DISCUSSION, CONCLUSIONS, AND IMPLICATIONS

Weak institutions cause corruption. Based on an analysis of a large-scale firm survey and qualitative interviews, I show that firms with lax internal auditing rules are more likely to bribe. The results show that Chinese private enterprises spend more money on bribery than any other type of firm, whereas foreign firms spend less.

The findings have important implications for China's legal reforms. Scholars have argued that private-property-protecting mechanisms such as bribery or gangs serve as a substitute for formal mechanisms. Frye and Zhuravskaya (2000), based on a survey of shopkeepers in three cities in Russia, find that shopkeepers view private-protection organizations primarily as a substitute for state-provided police protection and state-provided courts. Sonin (2003) developed a formal model suggesting that company managers who benefit from privatization prefer to keep the rule of law weak because they have a comparative advantage in using private means, including bribing government officials, to protect their property. Hoff and Stiglitz (2004) argue that managers with access to rents may prefer to delay the establishment of the rule of law because there is no guarantee that everyone will coordinate on a strategy that improves their individual gain.

Both domestic private enterprises and FIEs are subject to discrimination, but this chapter shows that Chinese private firms are able to build informal connections through bribery. The availability of informal protection weakens Chinese firms' incentives to seek the rule of law. However, the Chinese state's favoring of SOEs, and its close ties with private firms, puts foreign firms in a particularly disadvantaged position. Constrained by anticorruption regulations, foreign firms' strategy is to push for judicial fairness that helps level the playing field to protect their contract and property rights. This is the focus of the next chapter.

# 6

# When do authoritarian rulers build less corrupt courts?

I have important contacts in the Castle, and shall have even more in the future; these will. . .guarantee that I shall be in a position to return in full any small favor you may do me.

Franz Kafka

## INTRODUCTION: MOTIVATION, FINDINGS, AND A ROAD MAP

The demand-side theory predicts that localities with significant foreign investment are more likely to have less corrupt courts, whereas areas with investment from Chinese domestic or China circle companies are likely to have corrupt courts. The theory also hypothesizes that judicial corruption should vary across issue areas: foreign firms' demand should affect only courts' handling of economic cases but not administrative cases. This chapter tests these hypotheses by examining variations in judicial corruption at the county and municipal levels. The analysis shows that FDI reduces judicial corruption in the economic, but not the political, realm.

Judicial corruption is a global disease. Transparency International, a global organization that promotes clean government, polled 59,661 people in sixty-two countries in its 2006 Global Corruption Barometer survey and found that in one-third of these countries, more than 10 percent of respondents who had interacted with the judicial system claimed that they or a member of their household had paid a bribe to obtain a "fair" outcome in a judicial case (Transparency International 2007).

Public perceptions of judicial corruption are more prevalent than experience. In fifty-five of the sixty-two countries polled, a higher percentage of people perceived extreme judicial corruption than had paid a bribe. In thirty-three of the sixty-two countries polled, a majority of respondents described the judiciary/legal system of their country as corrupt (Transparency International 2007).

The negative effects of judicial corruption cannot be overemphasized. It denies citizens (especially the poor) access to justice, jeopardizes economic growth by delaying cases and favoring politically connected firms, violates human rights by physically abusing litigants, and erodes the ability of the international community to tackle transnational crime and terrorism. In China, judicial corruption has become an increasingly salient social and political issue. According to Li's (2010, 201) calculation, the number of court personnel investigated and punished for corruption increased in the latter half of the 1990s and peaked in 1998 at 2,512 cases. The first half of the first ten years in the twenty-first century witnessed a decline in the number of corruption cases. However, Li (2010, 202) also noted the discrepancy between national figures and local figures and warned that the national figures might be underestimated.

In addition to the number of corruption cases involving court personnel, the impact of individual judicial corruption cases has been significant. The investigation of Huang Songyou, a former vice president of the Supreme People's Court, revealed the extent of corruption at the highest level of the judicial system. Some recent cases that stimulated large-scale demonstrations show the public's mistrust of the judicial system and the detrimental effect of judicial corruption on social stability.[1] Judicial corruption has been a major obstacle for China to transition to a rule-of-law regime.

What explains judicial corruption and its regional variation in China? Previous studies have focused on China's authoritarian political system and insufficient court funding. For example, Gong (2004) and Li (2011) argue that a lack of judicial independence and accountability, and collective decision-making mechanisms, led to China's judicial corruption. He (2008) and Wang (2010) point to China's inadequate court funding as a source of judicial corruption. He (2008) identifies three reasons why insufficient court funding can lead to judicial corruption. First, it induces judges to engage in "profit-making" activities, such as collecting arbitrary litigation fees and selecting cases with high litigation fees. Second, underfunded courts are more susceptible to government interference, since courts are funded by governments at the same territorial level. Third, underfunded courts are more likely to take advantage of legal reforms to maximize rent-seeking opportunities. Wang's (2010) study is focused more on Chinese judges' low wages and their corrupt activities.

The demand-side theory provides new insights into the occurrence of and variation in judicial corruption in China. I argue that the diversification of

---

[1] A salient case is the protest in Weng'an County in Guizhou Province in 2008. The death of a female middle school student and the subsequent legal investigation provoked a riot involving tens of thousands of local residents. Rioters smashed government buildings and torched several police cars to protest against an alleged police cover-up of the girl's death.

ownership structure in the reform era causes the various levels of judicial corruption across regions in China. I test the hypothesis that regions with a strong FDI presence in the economy are less likely to have corrupt courts.

However, the impact of FDI is limited to a certain realm. Judicial justice in one realm does not automatically spill over to another realm. I show that the "cleaning up" effect of FDI on Chinese courts exists only in the economic realm. With its enormous agenda-setting power, the CCP still manipulates courts' handling of political cases. Through the *nomenklatura* and fiscal systems, the Chinese government at various levels still micromanages legal cases involving the state. I rely on a subnational research design and test hypotheses quantitatively using original data sets of 102 counties and 120 cities.

The next section discusses general patterns of China's judicial corruption. The subsequent section discusses how FDI reduces judicial corruption in the commercial realm and how the CCP micromanages the judicial system to limit citizens' use of the judiciary to challenge the state. The fourth section tests the theory using an original cross-sectional data set of 102 randomly selected Chinese counties. The fifth section addresses the potential endogeneity issue using genetic matching. The sixth section tests the robustness of the findings by replicating the county-level results using a city-level data set and an instrumental variable approach. The seventh section tests an empirical implication of the theoretical model. The final section concludes with a summary of the findings and a discussion of the broader significance of the research.

## JUDICIAL CORRUPTION IN CHINA

Corruption is broadly defined as the abuse of public power for private gain (Bardhan 1997). There are various typologies of judicial corruption. Transparency International differentiates between two types of corruption that most often affect judiciaries: political interference in judicial processes by either the executive or legislative branch of government, and bribery (Transparency International 2007). In a similar vein, Volcansek, De Franciscis, and Lafon (1996) distinguish political corruption (judges compromise legal standards under external political pressure) from personal corruption (judges bend rules to secure private gains for themselves). This definition is also adopted by Gong (2004). Li (2010, 198) classifies judicial corruption into three types. Type A involves cases in which corrupt judges have physically abused litigants, illegally seizing and detaining them by force. Type B represents corrupt conduct without exchange between the judge and litigants, such as embezzlement, misappropriation of assets, swindling litigants, and serious negligence. Type C represents mainly bribery and favoritism.

The distribution of cases across the three types is uneven. According to Li (2010, 207), the majority of cases are Type C, where an exchange between judges and litigants is involved. Within Type C, the occurrence of corruption is unbalanced across the different stages of litigation.

It is more likely to take place in the adjudication and enforcement stages, and less likely in the registration stage.

The type of corruption is related to the institutional configurations of the Chinese judicial system. As Gong (2004) argues, the source of political corruption is the lack of judicial independence, whereas personal corruption is mainly due to a lack of accountability. Li (2011) argues that judicial corruption in China is a product of its particular decision-making mechanisms, which are guided by the CCP's instrumental rule-by-law ideal.


## FDI AND JUDICIAL CORRUPTION

Globalization's effect on China is debated. In 2001, China's decisive reformer, then prime minister Zhu Rongji, told provincial officials in one now-declassified speech, "Western hostile forces are continuing to promote their strategy of Westernizing and breaking up our country." He accused such people of conducting "infiltration and sabotage."[2]

What is the effect of globalization on a hosting country's politics? While "dependentistas" of the 1970s argue that foreign investment distorts host countries' political processes (Moran 1978), many current studies point out the benevolent effects of economic integration on a hosting country's governance. Examples include Cao and Prakash's (2010) and Zeng and Eastin's (2007) studies on globalization and environmental protection; Apodaca's (2002) study on FDI and human development; Borensztein, De Gregorio, and Lee's (1998) study on FDI and economic growth; de Soysa and Oneal's (1999) study on FDI and productivity; Malesky's (2008) study on FDI and regional autonomy; Mosley and Uno's (2007) research on FDI and workers' rights; Neumayer and de Soysa's (2006) study on FDI and human rights; and Rudra's (2005) research on export and democratization.

However, many others find that economic openness also creates "race to the bottom" pressures on governments to engage in grand corruption (Pinto and Zhu 2008), reduce social spending (Kaufman and Segura-Ubiergo 2001), violate labor rights in less developed countries (Rudra 2002), and threaten worker security (Scheve and Slaughter 2004). Sheng (2007) also finds that economic integration increases the center's incentive to control local government and decrease regional autonomy in China.

My theory implies that FDI is conducive to China's "long march" toward the rule of law (Peerenboom 2002). However, I argue that the impact of FDI is complicated, so we need to examine its effects in different issue areas.

My case studies show that foreign investors' influence has a measurable impact on the country's legal institutions. To respond to complaints from some

---

[2] "No Change: Hopes of Sparking Political Change Have Come to Nothing So Far," *Economist*, December 10, 2011.

foreign companies that certain judges are connected to some SOEs and several large domestic private enterprises, an Intermediate People's Court in Guangzhou City reformed its case-allocation rules in 2002. Before the reforms, the president of the court assigned cases to a panel of three judges; the case-assignment process presented opportunities for corruption. Judges with close ties to an enterprise could request to sit on the panel. This is still normal practice in many local courts in China. In many places, judges' salaries are tied to how many cases they adjudicate each year. This creates incentives for judges to seek cases that involve high stakes (which bring higher litigation fees) and select which cases they adjudicate.[3] The connections between the judges and one side of the litigation are a hotbed of corruption and judicial unfairness. In 2002, the Intermediate People's Court in Guangzhou introduced a computer-based random assignment system to allocate cases to judges, which significantly minimizes opportunities for corruption.[4]

However, the impact of FDI on China's judicial system is limited to the commercial realm. Local governments have no incentive to strengthen courts in every respect. A fair court system would not only protect investors whose assets are crucial for local officials' political advancement; it would also provide openings for discontented citizens and social groups to challenge the state, which undermines officials' careers. Therefore, the best strategy for the government is to curb corruption in the commercial realm while imposing constraints on citizens' rights to sue the authoritarian state through legal channels. *Ex ante*, this is achieved through the CCP's agenda-setting power to selectively intervene in judicial decisions, as shown in Chapter 3. Or, as an *ex post* remedy, the CCP can manipulate the setup of the anticorruption agencies to gain a first-mover advantage to protect corrupt party officials (Manion 2004).

In summary, although FDI is expected to curb corruption in the judicial system, its impact is limited to the commercial realm. The political realm is still under the strict control of the CCP.

## EMPIRICS

I rely on a subnational research design and an analysis of quantitative data. The quantitative data are drawn from a mass survey conducted in 2003 with 7,714 ordinary citizens. The advantage of the mass survey is that it differentiates between judicial corruption in different types of cases: civil, economic, and administrative. Thus the analysis can disaggregate the effect of FDI on judicial corruption in different realms. The disadvantage of the mass survey is that it reflects the opinions of ordinary citizens, which

---

[3] Interview with a former judge in Guangzhou City, Guangdong Province, March 30, 2010.

[4] Interview with a judge in an Intermediate People's Court in Guangzhou City, Guangdong Province, March 31, 2010.

could differ from those of investors. I will also test the robustness of the analysis using the results of a firm-level survey.

## Testable Hypotheses

Based on the demand-side theory, two hypotheses are generated:

> *Hypothesis 6.1: Foreign capital reduces corruption in the commercial realm in local courts. As the weight of foreign capital increases in a local economy, the degree of judicial corruption in the commercial realm decreases*, ceteris paribus.
>
> *Hypothesis 6.2: Foreign capital has a smaller effect on corruption in the political realm in local courts. The weight of foreign capital in the local economy is not strongly related to the degree of judicial corruption in the political realm*, ceteris paribus.

## The Data

The quantitative data used in this section are drawn from a 2003 survey of the Institutionalization of Legal Reforms in China (ILRC), conducted by the Research Center of Contemporary China at Peking University. The survey interviewed a national probability sample of 7,714 respondents on a wide range of items related to their attitudes and behavior in dispute resolution. It employed a spatial sampling technique to compile the sample[5] to overcome coverage problems in sample frames based on formal household registration (*hukou*), due to the fact that 11.1 percent of the total population in China is unregistered migrants. All respondents were Chinese adult citizens.[6]

We surveyed 102 counties in China, across all thirty-one provinces and provincial-level units of the country, and from the coastline areas to the remote western regions. They vary a great deal in terms of their level of economic prosperity and openness. I compiled a unique cross-sectional data set using the survey data and data collected from various sources ranging from year-books to government websites. All variables in the data set are measured using 2003 data.

I use respondents' subjective evaluation of Basic People's Courts to measure the degree of judicial corruption, which is the dependent variable.[7] I use Basic

---

[5] For more details about the spatial sampling technique used in the ILRC survey, please see Yan, Landry, and Ren (2009). For a general introduction of spatial sampling, please see Landry and Shen (2005).

[6] Please see Appendix A for more information about the survey.

[7] Most existing measures of corruption are subjective. Two indexes of perceived corruption have become the most commonly used in empirical work: the CPI constructed by Transparency International and a rating of control of corruption published by a team led by Daniel Kaufmann at the World Bank. A third cross-national corruption rating is produced by the firm Political Risk

TABLE 6.1 *Three Vignettes That Describe Three Types of Disputes*

### Civil dispute

Since you have not had such experiences, let's use a hypothetical case to understand your views. The labor contractor of a construction site has been embezzling the workers' wages, and the workers were denied their demands for payment numerous times. If you were one of the workers, what would you do? Would you take action to settle the dispute, or would you not do anything?

### Economic dispute

Since you have not had such experiences, let's use a hypothetical case to understand your views. To help a township business through some financial difficulties, a township government borrows 100,000 *yuan* from villager Wang Lin. The agreement lays down that this amount should be repaid in two years. But two years go by, and the amount has still not been repaid. If you were Wang Lin, what would you do? Would you take action to settle the dispute, or would you not do anything?

### Administrative dispute

Since you have not had such experiences, let's use a hypothetical case to understand your views. Zhang Jie is an individual industrial household with a license to set up his stall. But the relevant authority found his stall detrimental to the aesthetic of the city, and thus confiscated his goods and fined him. If you were Zhang Jie, what would you do? Would you take action to settle the dispute, or would you not do anything?

*Source:* ILRC 2003

People's Courts as the focus of this study, because they are the first hurdle in the Chinese legal system for the majority of litigants. Most legal cases in China are dealt with daily by over three thousand Basic People's Courts all over the country.

The survey questionnaire includes three vignettes, as shown in Table 6.1, which highlight three types of disputes to solicit respondents' evaluation of local courts. The survey asked the respondents whether they would choose to go to court if faced with the hypothetical scenarios, and why. One quantity pertinent to my interest is the proportion of respondents in each county that responded "court is corrupt."[8]

The dependent variable is measured using two disaggregate measures and one aggregate measure. The two disaggregate measures are the proportion of respondents in each county that said "court is corrupt" in economic (**"Econ-corruption"**) and administrative (**"Admin-corruption"**) cases, respectively.

---

Services, based on evaluations by its network of experts and published in its *International Country Risk Guide*. All three of these measures are based on the subjective evaluations of experts or survey respondents of how widespread or costly corruption is in particular countries. For a review of ratings of corruption, please see Treisman (2007).

[8] The analysis is weighted by taking into account sampling design effects.

TABLE 6.2 *Correlation Matrix of Three Dependent Variables*

| Variable | Corruption | Econ-corruption | Admin-corruption |
|---|---|---|---|
| Corruption | 1.000 | | |
| Econ-corruption | 0.855 | 1.000 | |
| | (0.000) | | |
| Admin-corruption | 0.670 | 0.378 | 1.000 |
| | (0.000) | (0.000) | |

*Source:* ILRC 2003

The key difference between these two types of cases is that administrative cases directly involve the state, whereas economic cases do not.[9] The aggregate measure "**Corruption**" is constructed by adding up the proportion of respondents that chose "court is corrupt" in all three types of disputes and then normalizing to 1.[10]

Table 6.2 shows the correlation matrix (with levels of significance in parentheses) of the three measures. As shown, the aggregate measure (Corruption) is highly correlated with the two disaggregate measures (with correlation coefficients greater than 0.6). However, Admin-corruption is weakly correlated with Econ-corruption (with correlation coefficients smaller than 0.4). This provides preliminary evidence that in the same court, administrative cases are treated differently from economic cases, and that ordinary citizens are aware of this difference.

The advantage of using survey data to measure judicial corruption is that posing the questions as hypothetical cases makes them less controversial and enhances their validity. However, there are at least two potential challenges to the validity of the measure. First, respondents' evaluations might simply be the result of media influence (Zhu, Lu, and Shi 2013). For example, if many corrupt cases were uncovered by the public media, respondents would be more likely to report that their local courts were corrupt. Likewise, positive media propaganda could increase confidence in local courts. A second challenge to validity is social desirability. Since questions about corruption are sensitive, respondents who grew up in that locality are more likely to save face by not saying "court is corrupt" (thus giving the interviewer a bad impression of the county) than respondents who did not grow up in that locality.

To validate the measure of judicial corruption using survey data, I examine individual-level characteristics that could potentially influence respondents'

[9] On many occasions, economic cases are also political when politically connected firms are involved. But I distinguish these two types based on the assumption that the Chinese state is willing to tie its hands in the commercial realm to make a credible commitment to foreign investors while still avoiding being directly challenged in the political realm.

[10] I did not include corruption in civil cases, as it is not in the scope of this analysis.

evaluations of the courts. The auxiliary analysis is presented in Appendix B.[11] The results show that none of the media-related variables is significant, either individually or jointly, which does not provide positive evidence that respondents' evaluations of judicial corruption were influenced by the public media. The results also show that respondents who grew up in the locality were more likely to say "court is corrupt" than those who came from outside. This suggests that respondents were not trying to save face for the local court when asked about judicial corruption. In summary, there is no empirical evidence that respondents' subjective evaluations were biased by media influence or social desirability.

*Independent variables.* **Foreign capital** is measured by "foreign capital actually used," which includes FDI and foreign loans. Foreign loans usually comprise a small proportion of foreign capital; the majority is in the form of FDI. Since what matters for local officials is the importance of foreign capital in the local economy, I use the percentage of "foreign capital actually used" to measure the weight of foreign capital in relation to overall GDP. The variable is collected using sources provided by the University of Michigan's China Data Center. While it would be ideal to also differentiate between types and origins of FDI, these data are not available at the county or city level in China.

A court's performance depends to a large extent on what resources it has (Wang 2013). In China, a court's income completely relies on the local government's budget. When facing budget constraints, local courts have to seek more cases to make money. In some courts, judges' wages also hinge on how many cases they can find. As a result, judges need to keep informal ties with all intermediaries of litigation, including lawyers, corporate managers, and officials in the local legal bureau.[12] Corruption often occurs in the process of transactions between cases and money.

The variable "**Finances**" is constructed to measure how much financial support a court obtains from the local government. The 2003 *Statistical Report on Finance in All Chinese Counties*, edited by the Ministry of Finance, provides data on the total amount that each county government spends on the police, procurator, court, and legal bureau. "Finances" is calculated as the proportion that these expenditures represent in the overall government budget to measure the priority that local governments give to legal affairs generally. It is not a perfect measure, but there is no disaggregated data available.

As a developing country, China still has a remarkable rural-urban divide. I expect to discover different degrees of judicial corruption in rural and urban

[11] Please see "Individual Determinants of Perceived Corruption" in Appendix B.

[12] Interview with a court official, Guangdong Province, March 23, 2010. Interview with a government official, Guangdong Province, March 30, 2010. Interview with a legal scholar, Guangdong Province, March 31, 2010. Interview with a court official, Jiangxi Province, April 2, 2010. Interview with a court official, Jiangxi Province, April 8, 2010.

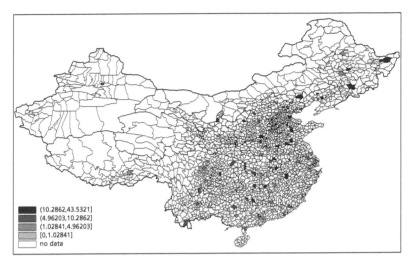

FIGURE 6.1 Level of Judicial Corruption across Chinese Counties (2003)
*Note*: Darker color indicates a higher level of judicial corruption, which is measured by ordinary citizens' responses to survey questions. The numbers indicate the percentages of respondents in each county who answered "Court is corrupt" in the survey.

areas. The variable "**Rural**" measures the proportion of agricultural products in the county's overall GDP to assess how rural it is.

Modernization theorists predict that a rule-of-law regime should emerge as a country becomes economically better off (Peerenboom 2007). A recent study by Michelson and Read shows that subjective evaluation of court performance improves with economic development (Michelson and Read 2011). Is it simply a matter of development? To test this hypothesis, I included log-transformed GDP per capita (**GDP pc [logged]**) in the model. All variables in the data set were measured at the county level in 2003.[13] Figure 6.1 maps the measure of judicial corruption; darker colors indicate highly corrupt counties.

### Analysis and Results

Using the data set I compiled at the county level, this section tests the theory empirically. The observations are from 102 randomly sampled Chinese counties. Figure 6.2 shows the regression results.[14] At this point, let us focus on the left panel that shows the OLS estimates. As shown in the upper left panel where the dependent variable is the aggregate measure of judicial corruption, foreign

---

[13] Appendix B Table A6.2 shows summary statistics of these variables.
[14] The full model specification and discussion are in Appendix B, "OLS Regression to Predict Perceived Judicial Corruption at the County Level."

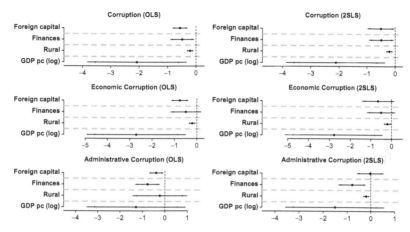

FIGURE 6.2 Determinants of Judicial Corruption among Chinese Counties
*Notes*: The dependent variable is perceived judicial corruption in the upper panel, perceived judicial corruption in economic cases in the middle panel, and perceived judicial corruption in administrative cases in the lower panel. The left panel shows OLS estimates, and the right panel shows two stage least squares (2SLS) estimates. Lines represent 95% confidence intervals, and the small bars 90% confidence intervals, both of which are based on robust standard errors. The results that generate this graph are presented in Appendix B Table A6.3.
*Source*: Data set compiled by the author

capital has a negative effect, and the effect is distinguishable from zero. Substantively, a 1 percent increase of foreign capital in the overall GDP will result in a 0.565 percent decrease in people who think the local court is corrupt. Government financial support has a significantly negative effect. A 1 percent increase in the proportion of government legal expenditures in the overall fiscal budget will result in a 0.488 percent decrease in people who think the local court is corrupt. The magnitude of the agricultural industry has a negative sign as well and passes the 0.01 level of significance. Substantively, a 1 percent increase in the weight of agriculture in the overall economy will bring a 0.210 percent decrease in people who think the local court is corrupt. Finally, the level of economic development has a significantly negative impact, which is consistent with modernization theory's predictions.

A more interesting picture is shown in the middle left and lower left panels when the dependent variable is disaggregated. The marginal effect of foreign capital is largest in magnitude (-0.759) when Econ-corruption is the dependent variable (middle left panel). The effect is smaller and less significant (-0.388) when Admin-corruption is the dependent variable (lower left panel). This provides preliminary support that foreign capital plays an important role in reducing judicial corruption in the commercial realm but less so in the political realm.

## TESTING FOR CAUSALITY: GENETIC MATCHING

Despite the strength of the evidence, there is a possible endogeneity problem: foreign capital might be endogenous to judicial corruption. It might be argued that foreign asset holders would take into account the quality of local legal systems when choosing where to invest. However, as Clarke, Murrell, and Whiting (2008, 399) argue, "Indeed, 'The Development of Law during the Era of Economic Reform' contains more evidence for the proposition that economic change spurred legal change than for the opposite relation."

I employ matching techniques to test this possibility. This approach facilitates the estimation of causal effects using observational data by choosing observations that approximate the counterfactual quantities of interest. In this case, I wish to compare the level of judicial corruption in counties with a strong FDI presence to the level of corruption in counties with a weak FDI presence. Because FDI cannot be randomly assigned to counties, I create a "control" group of counties that are as comparative as possible to the "treated" counties. I accomplish this by using observed data about each county to create a sample of counties that differ as little as possible, aside from having a strong FDI influence or not. I then evaluate the effects of FDI on judicial corruption using the matched data set. Importantly: using this approach, I sacrifice some precision, because I am able only to estimate the effect of a binary treatment (above- or below-average FDI) on judicial corruption.

I employ Diamond and Sekhon's genetic matching procedure, which is shown to achieve a better balance between the "control" and "treatment" groups (Diamond and Sekhon 2013). My results indicate dramatic improvements in balance, which suggest that the genetic matching algorithm provides data that approximates the counterfactual question: what would the level of judicial corruption in FDI-heavy counties have been had they not been influenced by FDI?

Using the matched data, I investigate this counterfactual by conducting genetic matching. The treatment variable is a binary indicator of FDI ($1$ = above-average FDI and $0$ = below-average FDI). The results are in Figure 6.3. The effect of FDI on general judicial corruption is still significantly negative. The coefficient of FDI on Econ-corruption is negative and statistically significant, while the coefficient of FDI on Admin-corruption is negative but insignificant, once again confirming my hypotheses.

## ROBUSTNESS CHECKS

I rely on two methods to test the robustness of my findings. First, I replicate the findings at the county level using a city-level data set aggregated from a firm survey. This survey provides more insights from the investors' side. Second, I employ an instrumental variables approach to verify the matching results to complement some weaknesses of matching.

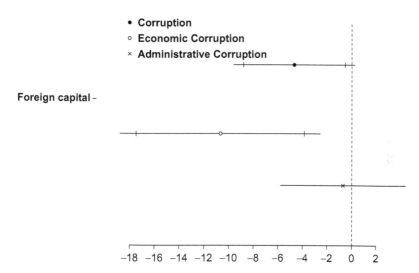

FIGURE 6.3 FDI and Judicial Corruption, Matched Data
*Notes*: Each line represents a *separate* regression. The dependent variable is perceived judicial corruption in the upper panel, perceived judicial corruption in economic cases in the middle panel, and perceived judicial corruption in administrative cases in the lower panel. Results are estimated using genetic matching. Lines represent the 95% confidence intervals, and the small bars 90% confidence intervals, both of which are based on robust standard errors. The results that generate this graph are presented in Appendix B Table A6.4.
*Source*: Data set compiled by the author

### Evidence from City-Level Data

One potential problem with the county-level survey data is that the survey respondents are ordinary citizens, whose perception might be different from that of investors. And because the theory is based on the incentives of foreign investors, I want to know whether the findings still hold if I use investors' perception as a measure of judicial corruption.

I analyze the data from the survey *Competitiveness Enhancements for 120 Cities in China*, which was designed and implemented by the World Bank and China's National Bureau of Statistics in 2005 (World Bank 2007). The survey interviewed senior managers in 12,400 firms in 120 major Chinese cities. Therefore it provides a relatively comprehensive view of judicial corruption from the business side.[15]

The survey asked firm managers: "In the case of commercial disputes with the suppliers, clients or subsidiaries in your locality, how much confidence do you have that the disputes will be settled with justice by the local legal system?"

[15] Please see Appendix A for more information about the survey.

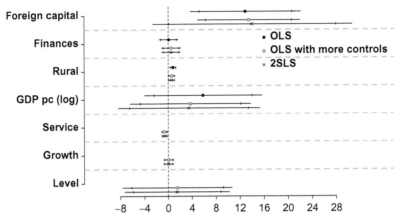

FIGURE 6.4 Determinants of "Confidence in Courts" in 120 Cities
*Notes*: The dependent variable is the city average confidence in courts measured by firm managers' response to a survey question. Black dots represent estimates using OLS with few controls, white dots show OLS results with more controls, and crosses represent 2SLS estimates. Lines represent 95% confidence intervals, and the small bars 90% confidence intervals, both of which are based on robust standard errors. The results that generate this graph are presented in Appendix B Table A6.5.
*Source*: Data set compiled by the author

A continuous variable, **Confidence in courts,** is constructed based on firms' answers aggregated at the city level. It is a percentage measure ranging from 27 to 98 percent. Unfortunately, the survey does not ask firms' evaluation of their confidence in the courts' handling of administrative cases, so I cannot test Hypothesis 6.2 using the city-level data.

To verify the empirical findings from the county-level analysis, I use a similar set of explanatory variables to explain the variation of "Confidence in courts" among Chinese cities, including **"Foreign capital," "Finances," "Rural,"** and **"GDP pc (log)."** Except for being measured at the prefectural level, they are constructed in the exact same way as the county-level variables.

Due to better data availability at the municipal level, I also control for an alternative set of variables. To account for the overall economic structure of the locale, a variable **"Service,"** which measures the weight of the service industry in the overall GDP, is listed on the right-hand side. GDP growth rate (**"Growth"**) is also included. As there are four provincial-level cities and 116 prefectural-level cities in the sample, a dichotomous variable **"Level"** is included to distinguish the cities' administrative levels (1 = provincial level and 0 = prefectural level). All variables were measured in 2005 at the city level.

The black dots in Figure 6.4 show OLS regression results of the city data. Foreign capital has a positive effect, and the effect is distinguishable from zero.

Government financial support has a positive effect, but the effect is indistinguishable from zero. This is different from the findings in the county-level regressions. One potential reason is that the spending combines expenditures on the public security department, procuratorate, court, and the legal bureau, which does not directly reflect government spending on courts. "Rural" has a positive effect, and the effect is significant. This is consistent with my county-level finding. GDP per capita has a positive sign but does not pass hypothesis testing at any conventional level of significance.

The white dots show the results with extra controls. The weight of the service industry is negative and significant. This might be because the service industry in China is mainly composed of private enterprises that rely on patron-client ties to conduct business. Economic growth, surprisingly, has a negative sign. But the effect is very small and not significant. Finally, provincial-level cities have higher confidence in courts than prefectural-level cities, as expected, but this difference is not significant. Overall, the empirical evidence from prefectural-level business survey data reconfirms my finding about the reducing effect of FDI on judicial corruption.

### Instrumental Variables Approach

Matching is no panacea. It cannot correct for endogeneity. Its strength is in reducing the model dependence of the counterfactual inferences about the effect of a treatment on an outcome when data are not generated via a randomized experiment. Instrumental variables regressions can correct for endogeneity. I combine both matching and instrumental variables approaches to confirm that FDI reduces judicial corruption in China.

I use two instrumental variables. **Distance** is the distance to the nearest special economic zone or coastal open city. As argued before, China's FDI is very concentrated in these special administrations where sweetheart deals are offered to foreign companies. And as Malesky (2008) shows, distance to the coast is exogenous to FDI and should influence judicial corruption only through FDI. Thus it meets the two conditions for a good instrument.

**Migrant population** measures a county's migrant population as a percentage of the entire population. Since China's development in FDI is labor intensive, the more free labor an area is endowed with, the more likely it is to attract investors.[16]

---

[16] As Cameron and Trivedi (2005, 96) show, an instrument variable $z$ has the property that changes in $z$ are associated with changes in the endogenous variable (FDI in this case) but do not lead to change in the outcome variable (corruption) aside from the indirect route via the endogenous variable (FDI). As for distance, there is no empirical evidence showing that the geographical location of a court is related to the level of corruption, except that regions with more FDI are less corrupt, as I argue. For the migrant population variable, as Gallagher and Wang (2011) show, migrants working in the private sector have a more favorable view of the

The right panel in Figure 6.2 shows the results of two stage least squares (2SLS) regressions. As shown in the upper right panel, after instrumented by two exogenous variables, the effect of foreign capital is still significantly negative. And the magnitude of the effect has not changed very much.[17]

In addition, as presented in the middle right panel, the marginal effect of foreign capital when Econ-corruption is the dependent variable remains significant. However, the effect fails to pass any conventional significance tests when Admin-corruption is the dependent variable, as shown in the lower right panel. This confirms the matching results, which adds more evidence that Chinese local governments seek only to clean up courts in the commercial realm but not in the political realm.

Similarly, I conduct 2SLS regressions for the city-level data using the same instrumental variables. Crosses in Figure 6.4 show the results of these tests. As is shown, after instrumented by two exogenous variables, the effect of foreign capital is still positive, and the effect is significant.[18]

## AN EMPIRICAL IMPLICATION OF THE THEORETICAL MODEL

If my theory holds, the presence of foreign capital in the local economy should not increase *government* corruption as well, because foreign investors do not rely on clientelist ties with local governments to conduct business in China.

Students of Chinese political economy have long argued that business and the state have strong patron-client ties (*guanxi*) through which private firms are protected (Wank 1999). Oi (1992) has argued that the impressive growth of collective rural industrial output between 1978 and 1988 is in large measure a result of local government entrepreneurship. Fiscal reform has assigned local governments property rights over increased income and has created strong incentives for local officials to pursue local economic development. In the process, local governments have taken on many characteristics of a business corporation, in which officials act as the equivalent of a board of directors. This merger of state and economy characterizes a new institutional development that Oi (1992) labels "local state corporatism." The "developmental state" literature has also noted the importance of administrative protection of business in East Asian economies (Evans 1995; Johnson 1982; Woo-Cumings 1999; Kohli 2004). Meanwhile, these scholars have also observed massive

---

judicial system than urban permanent residents working in the public sector. So the migrant population is associated only with perceived corruption through FDI. These two variables constitute strong instruments, because two instruments have significant effects on foreign capital in regression analysis and explain 28 percent of the variation in foreign capital. The first-stage regression results are in Appendix B Table A6.6.

[17] The Hausman test shows that $\chi^2 = 0.054$, $p = 0.816$. This suggests that the null hypothesis (that the OLS and 2SLS estimates are the same) cannot be rejected.

[18] The Hausman test shows that $\chi^2 = 0.078$, $p = 0.780$. This suggests that the 2SLS estimate of $\beta_1$ is not significantly different from the OLS estimate.

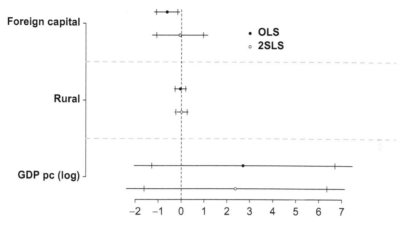

FIGURE 6.5 Foreign Capital and Government Corruption
*Notes*: The dependent variable is perceived government corruption measured by ordinary citizens' response to survey questions. Black dots represent OLS estimates, and white dots show 2SLS results. Lines represent the 95% confidence intervals, and the small bars 90% confidence intervals, both of which are based on robust standard errors. The results that generate this graph are presented in Appendix B Table A6.7.
*Source*: Data set compiled by the author

corruption in "transactions of commercial wealth for political power" that Kang (2002) terms "crony capitalism."

Under pressure to stimulate economic growth, have Chinese local state agents relied on *guanxi* (connections) to protect foreign asset holders? If so, we would expect to observe more government corruption in regions where foreign capital is important in the local economy.

I test this empirical implication of the theoretical model using the county survey data. The variable "Gov-corruption" is constructed in the same way as judicial corruption. Respondents were asked whether they would choose to go to the government if they were confronted with three types of disputes. The variable Gov-corruption is constructed by adding the proportion of respondents who chose "Government is corrupt" in three types of disputes and then normalizing to 1. I then include a similar set of independent variables including **foreign capital, rural,** and **GDP per capita** (log transformed).

Figure 6.5 shows estimates of the model with Gov-corruption as the dependent variable using both OLS and 2SLS. If the implication were plausible, we would expect that the effect of foreign capital on government corruption is not significantly positive, all else being equal. As shown, the effect of foreign capital on government corruption is significant but negative in the OLS results (black dots), which suggests that foreign capital decreases government corruption. It becomes insignificant in the 2SLS results but remains negative (white dots).

Overall, competition for foreign capital has not made Chinese local governments more corrupt. The test adds more evidence to the demand-side theory.

## DISCUSSION, CONCLUSIONS, AND IMPLICATIONS

This chapter examines the effect of foreign investors' influence on the degree of judicial corruption across subnational regions and issue areas in China. I argue that FDI reduces judicial corruption in the commercial realm. I also show that foreign capital has influence only in the commercial realm, whereas judicial unfairness is still prevalent in the political realm to prevent ordinary citizens from challenging the authoritarian state.

Discoveries in this chapter contribute to the literature on globalization and governance. While the majority of the literature focuses on how a host country's policy, institutional, and cultural environments influence the inflows of foreign investment, few examine how economic integration changes the host country's governance and policies. And even fewer studies have examined globalization's impact on judicial politics. This research reveals that foreign investor interactions with the host country's institutions and actors induce Chinese local officials to promote judicial honesty in the commercial realm. Meanwhile, the demands of foreign investors are confined to the economic area so that they will not threaten the CCP's grip on political power.

Despite the strong evidence, I acknowledge one weakness. Data on the county and prefectural levels do not allow this research to differentiate FDI from within and outside the China circle, which in theory should have different impacts on the judicial system. The quantitative results may measure the outcome of the weighted average of all foreign capital combined. I address this problem using provincial-level data in the next chapter.

This chapter poses a new question: if court funding reduces judicial corruption, what determines the government's incentive to fund courts? As the theory implies, court spending is one mechanism that governments use to strengthen courts. We would expect that in regions where there is a large share of foreign enterprises from outside the China circle, governments should have a positive incentive to finance courts; in regions where there is a large share of SOEs, domestic private enterprises, and ethnic Chinese investors, governments should have a negative incentive to finance courts. The next chapter tests this proposition empirically.

# 7

# When do authoritarian rulers invest in courts?

Any day not spent in court is a day lost for them.

Franz Kafka

## INTRODUCTION: MOTIVATION, FINDINGS, AND A ROAD MAP

Why do some Chinese local governments invest more money in courts while others invest less? The demand-side theory posits that with foreign investors' demand, Chinese local governments can increase court funding to enable courts to run more efficiently and effectively. Yet Chinese domestic enterprises and China circle enterprises would want to keep the courts weak and vulnerable to corporate capture. This chapter, using a panel data set of court funding, shows that provinces with more FDI are more likely to fund their courts, while provinces with more domestic and ethnic Chinese investors are less likely to fund courts.

Financial resources largely determine the incentive and behavior of judges in China. Courts with guaranteed and sufficient funding have more resources to achieve efficiency, implement reforms, and hire professional judges, and have less incentive to engage in corrupt activities. Courts with uncertain and insufficient funding are less likely to be independent of economic interests and more likely to engage in corrupt activities. However, courts in China do not control their own purse strings. The power of budgeting lies in the hands of territorial governments.

Budget is the key to understanding politics. Since financial resources are limited, budget becomes a mechanism for making choices among alternative expenditures. The budgetary process always involves competing players with distinctive preferences and conflicting goals. The budget, therefore, resembles a contract that reflects how the government prioritizes alternatives and makes commitments to various clashing powers. Government spending on courts indicates the priority that regional governments give to the judiciary. However, little is known about budgeting in authoritarian regimes, and even less is known about court budgeting. The lack of research is partly due to the opacity of the budgetary process in authoritarian regimes. Using newly released "internal" data on provincial budgets published by the PRC's Ministry of Finance, I am able to systematically examine government spending on courts both across space and over time.[1] This chapter explains the subnational variation in government spending on courts among China's thirty-one provinces from 1995 to 2006.

I argue that Chinese local officials prioritize court spending only when courts can serve the purposes of the officials. And the utility of courts depends on the demands of local elites. In provinces that have a large share of SOEs and domestic private enterprises, governments are less likely to finance courts, because these types of companies do not frequently rely on courts to enforce contracts. SOEs and domestic private enterprises instead resort to the administrative branch or informal mechanisms for dispute resolution and contract enforcement. In provinces where there is a large share of foreign firms, governments have a strong incentive to finance courts, because the legal system is a useful tool for foreign firms to enforce contracts and settle disputes. I also argue that foreign investors from within the China circle – Hong Kong, Macao, and Taiwan – resemble domestic investors on the ground that they rely on kinship connections and clientelist ties to conduct business in mainland China. Therefore, they do not exert a positive pressure on court funding, although they are FIEs in the technical sense.

To test these hypotheses, I compiled an original time-series cross-section data set on provincial court funding across China's thirty-one provinces from 1995 to 2006.

The next section provides a detailed description of institutions governing court finance; the third section discusses the empirical strategies and shows the analytical results; the fourth section addresses a potential endogeneity problem using an instrumental variable approach and tests an alternative explanation; and the last section concludes with a summary of major findings and a discussion of their broader significance.

## SUBNATIONAL COURT FUNDING IN CHINA

This section introduces how China's court finance system works and why court funding is important to understanding China's legal reforms.[2]

---

[1] Please see Ministry of Finance of People's Republic of China (Various years). The reports are now available in Beijing's National Library. Appendix A provides more information about the reports.

[2] The findings in this section are consistent with He (2008), Wang (2010), and Wang (2013). These studies, based on case studies or large-N analysis, show that court funding is highly correlated with judicial fairness and efficiency.

Chinese territorial governments finance local courts. Courts depend on local governments for basic necessities, including judges' salaries and bonuses, office supplies, vehicles, and court buildings. In 1998, a dual-track system (*shouzhi liangtiaoxian*) was applied to court revenues and expenditures in which all court income, including litigation fees and fines, is turned over to the territorial government; each year the court submits a budget to the government, and the government distributes funds according to its financial situation and the needs of the court. The core principle of the dual-track system is that a court's spending should be independent of its income; that is, how much money a local government allocates to the court in the budget should be unrelated to how much money the court turns over to the government.[3]

Since court finance is highly decentralized, court funding is to a large extent determined by the financial resources of the local government – and especially by the local officials' perception of the court's importance. The budget data shows several patterns of court funding in subnational China (Figure 7.1). First, the share of court funding in provincial budgets demonstrates significant stability over time: the lines are smooth except with spikes in certain years. Second, in most provinces, the shares are increasing over time, except in Hainan and Qinghai. Third, a spike in court funding occurred around 2002 in most provinces. One possible cause is China's joining the World Trade Organization in 2001, which imposed international standards of trade and investment on China and significantly attracted more foreign investors. Finally, court funding reveals significant variations both across space and over time.

Court funding has great implications for judicial efficiency and judicial fairness.[4] I asked a court official in Guangdong who had traveled to many courts in China "Why are some courts clean, efficient, and professional, while others are corrupt, incompetent, and inept?" His answer was simple but illuminating: "It's all about money!"[5] Whether a court can secure funding from the government to a large extent determines its "quality." This insight is confirmed by my field research in two municipalities in China.[6]

---

[3] For details about the dual-track system, please see "Guanyu renzhen guanche luoshi 'shouzhi liangtiaoxian' guiding de tongzhi" [On Implementing the "Dual-Track" Regulations], issued by the Supreme People's Court on June 9, 1998.

[4] The consensus is that insufficient funding is often correlated with inefficient and unfair court decisions, judicial corruption, and a lack of professionalization. Please see He (2008), Li (2010), Wang (2010), and Wang (2013).

[5] Interview with a court official, Guangdong Province, March 23, 2010.

[6] The two cases were not randomly selected and therefore cannot be used to generate generalizable conclusions for China. The interviews conducted in these two cities are utilized primarily to uncover the black box of court funding and its relationship with court performance. Please see Appendix A for a methodological discussion.

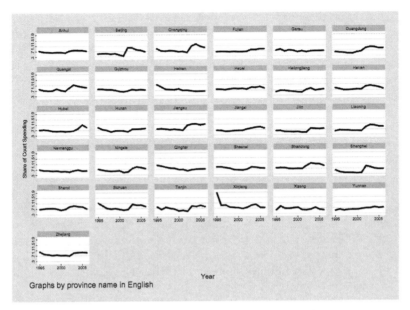

FIGURE 7.1 Court Funding across China's Provinces (1995–2006)
*Source:* Ministry of Finance of People's Republic of China (Various years)

Water Grass is one of the richest cities in China. I visited a Basic People's Court there in March 2010. The court is located in a town[7] and has 159 judges and staff members; of these, 131 have bachelor degrees and thirteen went to graduate school. In 2009, the court received 31,728 cases and completed 30,518 cases (completion rate 96.19 percent). The average number of cases that one of the court's judges completed is 402, nine times the national average of forty-six cases per judge. The court has a newly built nine-floor building. A court official told me that the town government paid 70 million *yuan* (approximately $10 million) for its construction. The court did not pay a cent for the building.[8] I interviewed the president of the court, who told me that the court relies completely on the city government for financial resources, and that luckily for her court, the city government is economically better off, so she "can focus on work rather than finding money for the court!" Her court simply submits a budget at the beginning of each year to the city government, which "always gives us what we ask for!" The president also said that the dual-track regulation was strictly enforced, so the government decides on the budget based

---

[7] Water Grass is a prefecture-level city but does not have districts or counties. So the basic courts (county level) are located in towns.
[8] Interview with a court official, March 23, 2010.

only on how much the courts need, rather than on how many fees the court collects and hands over to the government.[9]

I did not have to travel too far to find a court vastly different from this one. In April 2010, I arrived in Youth Town, located in a neighboring province. I visited the Basic People's Court in Youth Town, which has only thirteen judges, four of whom are officials who do not usually adjudicate cases. In 2009, the court completed about six hundred cases, and each judge completed about sixty cases. I talked to the chief of staff in her office. She said that the court revenue came from two sources: the local government and the central government. Usually, the transfer from the central government was guaranteed, but local funds rarely arrived in time. She added, "The dual-track regulation is never enforced here: the city government always returns 100 percent of what we turn in, and that's it, they give us no more! But now the litigation fees are too low to run the court."

As a consequence of its poor financial condition, the court had no money to investigate cases. The chief of staff said:

We have to postpone cases. We don't have many cars. Judges have to walk or ride a bike to investigate a case. Sometimes, if it is too far, we just don't go. We don't like people coming to our court to start a case. The fee is 5 or 10 *yuan* for a case, but the cost is 500 *yuan*. We sometimes don't let them register, of if they register, we just postpone it![10]

The court's fiscal system governs judges' incentive structure. Due to their pay structure, local judges are more likely to be focused on the *quality* of cases if their courts have sufficient funding, whereas they are more likely to be focused on the *number* of cases if their courts have insufficient funding. In wealthy courts, judges' salaries depend on rank and performance, which is assessed by an evaluation system based on indicators such as number of errors and completion rate.[11] However, where courts cannot secure government funding, judicial pay is tied to how many cases the judge can attract to the court. The cases have to involve high stakes, because the litigation fees are proportional to the stakes involved. The chief of staff in a court in Hunan Province revealed:

Judges have to make money on their own! For example, in the court that I was working for, we had a policy called "return." The way it works is that judges usually go to talk to people working in banks and ask them to transfer their debt disputes to the court. Those debt cases often involve large amounts of money, so the litigation fees would be high. Although there is this dual-track system, my court had a deal with the district government that part of the litigation fees would be returned to the court. And the court paid judges based on the number of cases they adjudicated. Their wages were fixed, but bonuses were very flexible. Some

[9] Interview with a court president, March 23, 2010.
[10] Interview with a court official, Jiangxi Province, April 2, 2010.
[11] Interview with a court official, Guangdong Province, March 23, 2010.

judges had very close connections with lawyers, and lawyers always gave cases to the judges with whom they are friends.[12]

In summary, government funding has a significant impact on courts and judges in a way that can potentially determine the efficiency and fairness of judicial judgments.

## EMPIRICAL EVIDENCE FROM PROVINCIAL-LEVEL DATA

As implied by the demand-side theory, I test the following four hypotheses:

> *Hypothesis 7.1: As the contribution of FDI from outside the China circle to the provincial GDP increases, provincial governments in China are more likely to provide financial support to courts*, ceteris paribus.
>
> *Hypothesis 7.2: The proportion of FDI from within the China circle in the provincial GDP has a negative impact on provincial governments' financial support to courts*, ceteris paribus.
>
> *Hypothesis 7.3: As the share of SOEs in the local economy increases, local governments' financial support to courts decreases*, ceteris paribus.
>
> *Hypothesis 7.4: As the share of domestic private enterprises in the local economy increases, local governments' financial support to courts decreases*, ceteris paribus.

### Data and Measurement

I will test the effect of FDI on court funding using an original time-series cross-section data set on FDI and court funding of thirty-one Chinese provinces during 1995–2006. I limit my data collection efforts to these twelve years mainly because the core dependent variable, court funding, is available only from *Statistical Reports on Local Finance* (*Difang caizheng tongji ziliao*), which was published by the Ministry of Finance of the PRC for these twelve years. The unit of analysis is province/year. I focus on provinces, because reliable data regarding sources of FDI and court funding exist only at the provincial level.

The dependent variable "court funding" is measured in two ways. The first is **court funding per capita** (*yuan*/person), which captures the magnitude of court funding adjusted by population size. When included in the regressions, this variable is log transformed to reflect the fact that, say, a 5 percent increase in the FDI/GDP ratio will have a smaller effect on court funding in an FDI-rich province than in an FDI-poor one. The second measurement is **court funding as a proportion of the overall government budget**. This captures the "willingness" of local governments to finance courts. Financial support from territorial governments is a crucial way to keep courts running, as discussed in the

---

[12] Interview with a former court official, Guangdong Province, March 30, 2010.

previous section. If a local government has the inclination to empower the local court, it must allocate a larger percentage of the overall budget to the court.

FDI is measured in two ways. To distinguish FDI from within and outside the China circle, I collected the amounts of FDI inflows from Hong Kong, Macao, and Taiwan (**China circle**) in 1995–2006 across China's thirty-one provinces and provincial-level cities. FDI from outside the China circle is measured using the amount of FDI inflows from all other countries (**foreign**). The sources of FDI data are provincial yearbooks of thirty-one provinces published in 1996–2007. Both variables are *divided by the provincial GDP* to adjust for size of the economy, so the variables that are eventually included in the regressions are all percentages.

I also account for other types of ownership. The share of SOEs in the local economy (**SOE**) is measured as *the percentage of the total urban labor force that is employed in urban SOEs*. SOE is expected to have a negative impact on government spending on courts, because SOEs are backed by the government, and therefore they do not rely on courts to settle disputes and enforce contracts.

The share of private enterprises in the local economy (**private**) is measured by *the percentage of the total urban labor force that is employed in the urban private sector (including private enterprise employees and self-employed workers)*. The effect of the private sector is expected to be negative, because it is well known that private entrepreneurs in China have strong patron-client ties with local governments (Wank 1999), which will only undermine formal legal institutions.

Controls include: **total fiscal expenditure per capita** (log transformed), **GDP per capita** (log transformed), weight of the service sector in the overall GDP (**service**), GDP growth rate (**GDP growth**), share of rural population (**rural pop**), log-transformed population (**population**), log-transformed number of cases accepted by first-instance courts (**cases**), log-transformed number of law offices (**law offices**), and log-transformed number of lawyers (**lawyers**).

## Descriptive Analysis

Before engaging in regression analysis, I will first show some descriptive patterns using a comparison of two cases: Guangdong Province and Jiangsu Province.

Guangdong and Jiangsu are in many aspects very similar: both are coastal provinces, both have attracted a large amount of FDI in the last three decades, and both are very rich. In 2005, per capita GDP in Guangdong Province was 28,332 *yuan*/person and 28,814 *yuan*/person in Jiangsu Province. The levels of economic development were almost identical. The size of the 2005 fiscal budget were also similar in these two provinces. For example, Guangdong had a per capita fiscal expenditure of 3,172 *yuan*/person, whereas in Jiangsu the figure was 2,667 *yuan*/person. Thus we would expect their court funding to also be at similar levels; however, the levels are vastly different. As Figure 7.2 shows, from

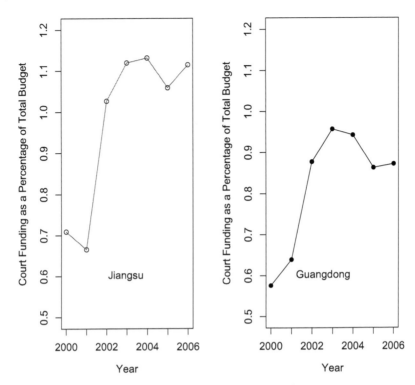

FIGURE 7.2 Levels of Court Funding in Jiangsu and Guangdong (2000–06)
*Source:* Ministry of Finance of People's Republic of China (Various years)

1995 to 2006, Jiangsu's government consistently allocated a bigger share of its fiscal budget to courts than Guangdong's government.

The reason, as I argue, lies in the composition of FDI in these two provinces. Guangdong, due to its geographical proximity and linguistic advantages,[13] has attracted a large amount of FDI from within the China circle, primarily Hong Kong and Taiwan. In contrast, Jiangsu Province has attracted foreign investors from outside the China circle, primarily the United States and Japan. Figure 7.3 shows the foreign/GDP ratios in these two provinces in 2000–06, and Figure 7.4 shows the China circle/GDP ratios.

Although Guangdong and Jiangsu are similar in many respects, their governments give very different priorities to court funding due to the composition of FDI in the two economies.

---

[13] Cantonese, which is the local dialect in Guangdong Province, is the dominant language in Hong Kong, because many Hong Kong residents were originally from Guangdong Province.

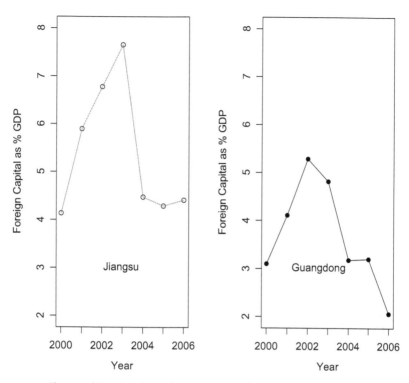

FIGURE 7.3 Shares of Foreign Capital in Jiangsu and Guangdong (2000–06)
*Source:* National Bureau of Statistics of People's Republic of China (Various years)

## Model Specification and Econometric Issues

This section tests the hypotheses using multiple regressions. The data set is compiled from various sources. An inevitable problem is missing data.[14] While most variables are complete, some major independent variables have nonignorable missing values, for example, China circle, foreign, cases, law offices, and lawyers.

A conventional way to deal with missing data is listwise deletion. However, as King et al. (2001, 51) argue, if the missing process is *nonignorable* – that is, if the probability that a cell is missing depends on the unobserved value of the missing response – listwise deletion can bias conclusions. The missing process is highly likely to be nonignorable in this case. For example, provinces with less FDI are less likely to report information on FDI. To create balanced matrices

---

[14] A "missing data map" of major variables used in the model is presented in Appendix B Figure A7.1.

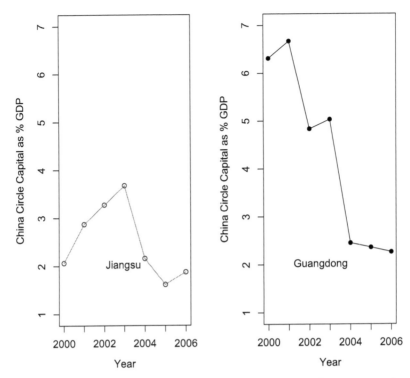

FIGURE 7.4 Shares of China Circle Capital in Jiangsu and Guangdong (2000–06)
*Source:* National Bureau of Statistics of People's Republic of China (Various years)

for time-series cross-section analyses, I employed the multiple imputation technique to impute five multiple matrices with complete data on each variable.[15]

A pooled time-series cross-section analysis will allow us to examine the
variation in court funding both across space and over time. All thirty-one
provinces over the time period 1995–2006 (N = 31, T = 12) are included in
the following analysis.

## Results

Figure 7.5 shows the results of OLS estimates with two different measures of
the dependent variable. The black dots show estimates when per capita court
funding (log transformed) is the dependent variable, while the white dots show

[15] For multiple imputation, I used Amelia II (Version 1.2–14, built: 2009-11-16) designed by James
Honaker, Gary King, and Matthew Blackwell. Please refer to http://gking.harvard.edu/amelia/
for more information. For analyses of multiple imputed data sets, I used the STATA package
"*miest*" developed by Kenneth Scheve.

the estimates when the percentage measure is the dependent variable. Both models include province and year fixed effects. All regressions include the lagged dependent variable. This is a very stringent test, because inclusion of lagged dependent variables usually suppresses the significance of other independent variables (Achen 2000). As shown in Figure 7.5, the point estimates of the marginal effect of China circle are all negative. In both regressions, this effect is distinguishable from zero. The negative effect is especially significant when both province dummies and year dummies are included. This indicates that after controlling for all sources of heterogeneity across space and over time, FDI from within the China circle still exerts a negative impact on court funding. The significant results indicate that a change in FDI from within the China circle will cause an immediate change in court funding. A concrete example is that a 1 percent increase in China circle/GDP ratio in Beijing from 2005 to 2006 would bring a 12,699,737 *yuan* ($\approx$ \$1.7 million) immediate decrease in court funding (0.01 × 0.012 × 105,831,140,000).

In addition, using De Boef and Keele's (2008) formula, the long-term effect of China circle is calculated to be -0.019, and this effect is also distinguishable from zero. The long-run effects and their standard errors are presented using crosses in Figure 7.5. This suggests that besides its short-run effect, FDI from within the China circle also has a long-term influence on government spending on courts. Using the Beijing example as a benchmark, a 1 percent increase in China circle/GDP ratio from 2005 to 2006 would bring a 20,107,917 *yuan* ($\approx$ \$2.8 million) decrease in court funding in the long run (0.01 × 0.019 × 105,831,140,000).

On the other hand, the point estimates of the marginal effect of Foreign are all positive. In both regressions, the effect is distinguishable from zero. Based on the white dot results in Column 2, a 1 percent increase in FDI/GDP ratio in, say, Beijing from 2005 to 2006 would bring an immediate 12,699,737 *yuan* ($\approx$ \$1.6 million) increase in court funding. Furthermore, Foreign also has a long-run effect on court funding, which is presented using crosses. The magnitude of the effect is 0.028 (slightly greater than that of China circle), and hypothesis testing shows that it is significant at the 0.01 level. Using the Beijing example again, a 1 percent increase in FDI/GDP ratio from 2005 to 2006 would bring a 29,632,719 *yuan* ($\approx$ \$3.7 million) increase in court funding in the long run, of which roughly 45 percent of the effect would take place immediately and 55 percent would be over time.

Using the formula given by De Boef and Keele (2008), I can also calculate the lags of the dynamic effect of Foreign on court funding. Figure 7.6 shows the lags of the dynamic effect. Approximately 43 percent of the effect will be realized immediately, and another 37 percent will be realized in the next period. The whole effect will disperse over six years.

In addition, the point estimates of Private and SOE are all negative. Interestingly, Private fails to show any short-term effect, while exerting a significantly negative effect in the long run. Conversely, the effect of SOE fails to show

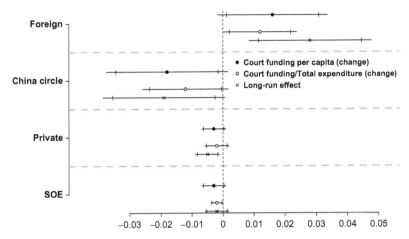

FIGURE 7.5 Effects of FDI on Court Funding across Chinese Provinces (1995–2006)
*Notes*: This graph shows the OLS results of an error correction model using court funding as the dependent variable. Black dots represents estimates using provincial court funding per capita as the dependent variable, and white dots present results using court funding as a percentage of total expenditure as the dependent variable. Both measure changes rather than levels. The crosses show calculated long-term effects based on the black dots results. Lines represent the 95% confidence intervals and the small bars 90% confidence intervals, both of which are based on robust standard errors. The results that generate this graph are presented in Appendix B Table A7.1.
*Source*: Data set compiled by the author

significance in either the short term or the long run. The magnitudes of the effects of Private and SOE are smaller than those of foreign enterprises. This suggests that foreign investors have stronger bargaining power than their domestic counterparts, probably due to their mobility and large contribution to China's GDP.

As for other controls, some deserve special mention.[16] First, the one-year lag for court funding shows consistent significance across all regressions. This is consistent with the well-known argument that the budgetary process is incremental. The negative sign simply confirms the intuition that high-level spending grows slower. Second, the long-run effect of GDP per capita is significantly negative, which contradicts the prediction of modernization theory. At the same time, Law Offices shows a significantly long-run effect, whereas Lawyers has no effect. This might suggest that lawyers as a group can make a difference, while lawyers as individuals – because of collective action problems and

---

[16] The full model results are presented in Appendix B Table A7.1.

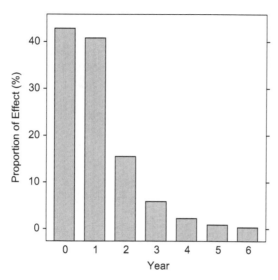

FIGURE 7.6 Lags of the Long-Term Effect of Foreign Capital on Court Funding
*Source:* Author's calculation

political constraints – are powerless. Generally speaking, the results shown in Figure 7.5 support the four hypotheses.

## IDENTIFICATION STRATEGY AND ROBUSTNESS CHECKS

This section addresses a potential endogeneity issue and tests the robustness of the findings against an alternative explanation and various model specifications.

### Endogeneity

It might be argued that foreign investors from different points of origin site their investments differently, depending on the quality of the legal organizations. Therefore, better-funded courts disproportionately attract certain types of investors rather than the other way around. Theoretically, this is possible, but this is not the case in China. As the demand-side theory suggests, foreign investors were attracted by China's labor costs, market size, and access to Asian markets, rather than its good courts. It is only after they have invested – and especially when they have disputes – that they start to pay attention to the country's legal institutions.

The ethnic Chinese investors in particular were attracted by geographical proximity, kinship connections, and a linguistic advantage. Thus, most China circle capital is clustered in provinces such as Guangdong and Fujian, which are close to Hong Kong and Taiwan and where most local residents speak Cantonese or Minnan dialect.

To ease the endogeneity concern, I employ an instrumental variable (IV) approach. I need an IV that is both contemporaneously uncorrelated with the error term from the original model and correlated with the endogenous regressor for which it is to serve as an instrument.

I use the five-year lag of the number of foreign tourists in a province as an instrument for FDI. Foreign investors, before they build a factory in a foreign country and put money into it, might take an "investment tour" to familiarize themselves with the local environment. Some tours are unplanned but end up becoming a location of investment, because the investor likes the place after the vacation. The instrument is also valid because tourism is not directly related to judicial empowerment: a strong court is the least important concern for a tourist when choosing where to vacation.

Figure 7.7 shows the results of the IV-2SLS procedure.[17] Foreign capital (instrumented) still has a positive effect on both measures of judicial empowerment, and the effect is significant.[18] The effects of the controls are largely consistent with my original model, except that some effects lose significance because of a smaller sample size.

## An Alternative Explanation

One competing explanation is that it is not the origin of FDI that matters but the *type* of FDI. It might be argued that firms investing in tertiary industry (for example, service) to access local consumer markets behave differently from those setting up to manufacture (or extract) for export. China circle firms are disproportionately in one set of activities, whereas firms outside the China circle are doing the opposite. This is plausible in the sense that multinational

---

[17] Implementing an IV-2SLS regression using panel data with missing values is tricky, because many procedures dealing with multiple imputed data sets are not compatible with IV-2SLS. For example, the *miest* package in STATA designed by Kenneth Scheve is not compatible with *xtivreg*. I therefore exclude the variables with missing values. Fortunately, this brings only minor changes to my original model, because most major independent variables are included. Furthermore, with a strong instrument, I am less concerned about omitted variable bias as a result of this exclusion. The model was also transformed from ECM to a restricted autoregressive distributed lag model to facilitate the execution without changing the substance of the estimation (De Boef and Keele 2008).

[18] To confirm this finding, I also conduct the Granger causality test, a standard analytic technique for tests of causal direction at the macro level (Freeman 1983; Freeman, Williams, and Lin 1989; Keele 2005). The essence of the Granger test is a standard partial *F* test that is used to determine whether past values of one series affect subsequent values of another series. I perform two Granger tests. The first is a test of whether FDI causes court funding (my theory), and the second is a test of whether court funding causes FDI (competing theory). I found strong evidence that FDI causes court funding rather than the other way around, regardless of whether I use the one-year or two-year lag of court funding.

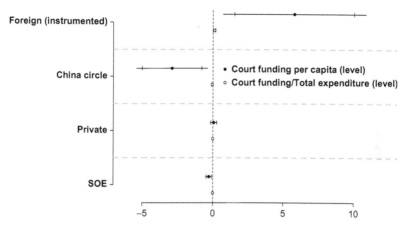

FIGURE 7.7 2SLS Estimate of the Effect of Foreign Capital on Court Funding
*Notes*: This graph shows the 2SLS results of a restricted autoregressive distributed lag model using court funding as the dependent variable. Black dots represents estimates using provincial court funding per capita as the dependent variable, and white dots present results using court funding as a percentage of total expenditure as the dependent variable. Both measure levels rather than changes. Lines represent the 95% confidence intervals, and the small bars represent 90% confidence intervals, both of which are based on robust standard errors. The results that generate this graph are presented in Appendix B Table A7.2.
*Source*: Data set compiled by the author

corporations in the tertiary industry care more about the quality of governance, and since they are mobile, they can exert a strong influence on government policies. In contrast, multinationals in other immobile industries have "obsolescing bargain" problems and therefore cannot influence government policies (Vernon 1971).

To test this alternative hypothesis, I collect data on foreign capital invested in the tertiary sector. The variable, **FDI in tertiary**, is again divided by provincial GDP to adjust for the size of the economy. To test the impact of this variable on court funding, I replace other measures of FDI in the original model with this variable to avoid multicollinearity. If the alternative theory were true, we would expect to see a positive effect of FDI in the tertiary sector on court funding. Figure 7.8 shows the results. FDI in the tertiary sector has a very small positive effect, and this effect is nowhere near significant. This suggests that it is not the type, but the origin, of FDI that matters.

## DISCUSSION, CONCLUSIONS, AND IMPLICATIONS

The empirical evidence from regional economy and provincial court funding in 1995–2006 is consistent with the demand-side theory. While foreign capital

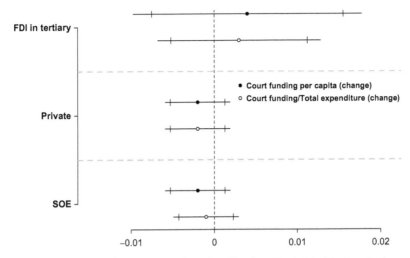

FIGURE 7.8 Testing an Alternative Explanation: Foreign Capital in Tertiary Industry and Court Funding
*Notes:* This graph shows the OLS results of an error correction model (ECM) using court funding as the dependent variable. Black dots represent estimates using provincial court funding per capita as the dependent variable, and white dots represent results using court funding as a percentage of total expenditure as the dependent variable. Both measure changes rather than levels. Lines represent the 95% confidence intervals, and the small bars represent 90% confidence intervals, both of which are based on robust standard errors. The results that generate this graph are presented in Appendix B Table A7.3.
*Source:* Data set compiled by the author

from outside the China circle pushes Chinese local governments to strengthen courts by providing more financial support, Chinese indigenous firms and ethnic Chinese firms prevent local governments from spending money on courts.

The findings, first of all, reconcile the debate between the "race to the top" and "race to the bottom" arguments. The analysis shows that whether there is a "race to the top" or "race to the bottom" effect depends on the *origin* of foreign investors. There is "race to the top" pressure among the competing provinces for foreign capital from outside the China circle, and a "race to the bottom" effect among the competing provinces for investors from within the China circle, domestic private enterprises, and SOEs.

The implications of this finding also partly contradict the new institutional economics, which argues that property holders will demand a limited government under which the ruler and asset holders share power (North and Weingast 1989). In China, domestic investors and investors from within the China circle have been found to be blocking legal reforms. A strong legal system is conducive not only to the protection of domestic capital, but also to the protection of foreign capital. Facing competition from the foreign side, domestic and ethnic Chinese investors have no interest in pushing for legal reforms. Instead, they have a strong incentive to obstruct legal reforms to consolidate their comparative advantages in conducting business in China. Domestic firms and firms run by ethnic Chinese who have political connections with the Chinese government have hindered China's progress toward the rule of law.[19]

---

[19] This finding is consistent with the "partial reform equilibrium" argument by Hellman (1998).

# 8

# Conclusion

Everyone strives to reach the Law.

Franz Kafka

## TOWARD A GENERAL THEORY OF THE RULE OF LAW

Many scholars, pundits, journalists, and policy makers believe that the rule of law is a panacea for all the world's troubles: crime, underdevelopment, corruption, human rights violations, environmental degradation, and war. Carothers (1998, 95) wrote:

How can US policy on China cut through the conundrum of balancing human rights against economic interests? Promoting the rule of law, some observers argue, advances both principles and profits. What will it take for Russia to move beyond Wild West capitalism to more orderly market economics? Developing the rule of law, many insist, is the key. How can Mexico negotiate its treacherous economic, political, and social transitions? Inside and outside Mexico, many answer: "establish once and for all the rule of law." Indeed, whether it is Bosnia, Rwanda, Haiti, or elsewhere, the cure is the rule of law, of course.

However, if the rule of law is so beneficial, then why is it so rare? More precisely, under what conditions would politicians be willing to constrain their discretionary power in order to respect the rule of law?

Various answers have been offered. Policy makers believe in the supply of international aid. The "law and development" project that started in the 1960s and waned in the 1970s received substantial support from the Ford Foundation, the Agency for International Development, and its own foundation, the International Legal Center (Merryman 1977, 457). In recent years, rule-of-law reform has become a major category of international aid. Russia's legal and judicial reforms, for example, have been supported by a variety of US assistance projects, extensive German aid, a $58 million World Bank loan, and numerous smaller World Bank and European Bank for Reconstruction and Development initiatives, as well as many efforts sponsored by Great Britain, the Netherlands, Denmark, and the European Union. Asia and Latin America are also major recipients of rule-of-law aid, while Africa and the Middle East have received less attention (Carothers 1998, 103).

However, the net effects of this rule-of-law aid have been modest. As Carothers (1998, 104) contends, "After more than ten years and hundreds of millions of dollars in aid, many judicial reforms in Latin America still function poorly. Russia...is not even clearly moving in the right direction." Many policy makers have realized that aid must interact with domestic institutions and interest groups to bring real changes to the judiciary.

Scholars, on the other hand, have focused on the supply from domestic politicians. Realizing that the judiciary has neither the power of the purse nor the ability to take up arms, many argue that the empowerment of the judiciary must come from the delegation of powerful politicians. Some suggest that legislators have an interest in creating an independent judiciary that can enforce the deals struck by enacting legislatures, thereby increasing the value of campaign contributions that legislators can extract from contributors on whose behalf they made those deals (Landes and Posner 1975). Some point to politicians' desire to duck blame for unpopular policies (Graber 1993; Salzberger 1993; Whittington 2009). McCubbins and Schwartz (1984) suggest that an independent judiciary can help the legislature prevent executive agencies from veering from legislative intent. Some contend that an incumbent legislative majority might willingly transfer some of its power to the judiciary as political insurance against being dominated by a future majority (Ramseyer and Rasmusen 1997; Finkel 2008).

These delegative models of judicial empowerment have two evident problems. First, since politicians can delegate power to the judiciary under certain conditions, they can also withdraw their support under other conditions. Judicial empowerment as a temporary solution to power balance is not sustainable in the long run. The second problem, as Helmke and Rosenbluth (2009) argue, stems from ignorance of the fact that courts, like legislators, are strategic actors.

As a remedy, a new strand of the rule-of-law literature focuses on the strategic actions of judges. For example, Helmke (2002) argues that under certain conditions – for example, at the end of weak dictatorships and weak democratic governments – the lack of judicial independence motivates judges to "strategically defect" against the government to ensure their status in the new government.

However, the strategic defection of judges can bring only temporary independence to the judiciary. Without an institutionalized power balance between the judicial branch and other political organizations, the transient rule of law will be easily abandoned by self-interested politicians.

As Widner (2001, 35) points out, having important and vocal constituencies is critical for sustained rule of law. My demand-side theory of the rule of law emphasizes interest groups as constituencies of the rule of law. I show that authoritarian rule of law is a result of the bargaining process between authoritarian rulers and organized interest groups. In this bargaining process, the rule of law is more likely to be enforced when authoritarian rulers need the cooperation of organized interest groups that control valuable and mobile assets but are not politically connected.

However, authoritarian rulers are not keen on promoting full-scale rule of law. The rule of law not only serves as a credible commitment to assets holders, whose cooperation is urgently needed by authoritarian states, but also provides ways for discontented citizens to challenge the state. Therefore, a partial form of the rule of law is often enforced in authoritarian regimes: judicial impartiality is respected in the commercial realm but violated in the political realm, where the state is directly in danger of being challenged. As a consequence, although authoritarian rulers tie their hands in the economic realm, promoting partial rule of law does not significantly threaten their grip on power.

I examine this theory in contemporary China. I show that the Chinese state and its local agents are revenue maximizers. Incentivized by the cadre evaluation system instituted by the CCP, Chinese local officials must cooperate with investors both at home and abroad to advance their political careers and personal well-being. However, investors' policy preferences vary. An analysis of a large firm-level survey shows that Chinese SOEs, domestic private enterprises, and enterprises owned by ethnic Chinese have stronger political connections and are more likely than FIEs to settle disputes through informal social networks. In addition, despite their reliance on the formal judicial system, FIEs have a lower level of confidence in Chinese courts. The gap between what foreign investors demand and what the Chinese judiciary offers is a driving force of China's legal reforms.

Foreign investors are less politically well connected than their Chinese counterparts for two reasons. First, FIEs are constrained by strict internal auditing rules and anticorruption regulations instituted by their countries of origin, and are thus less likely to bribe Chinese officials to build clientelist ties. Second, extending political connections to foreign investors would depreciate the privileges held by Chinese indigenous investors and decrease the rents shared by indigenous investors and the state.

I then show that a strong presence of FDI in a region's economy will significantly decrease perceived judicial corruption. Using statistical techniques, I show that this connection is causal and that the results stand at both the county and prefectural levels. However, I also find that FDI has an impact on judicial corruption only in the economic realm; the effect is weak (or even null) in the political realm.

Next I explore a causal mechanism through which Chinese governments empower the judiciary: court funding. I demonstrate that provinces with a large share of FDI in their economy are more likely to fund courts, whereas provinces with a large proportion of SOEs, domestic private enterprises, and China circle firms are less likely to fund courts. I also show that it is the ownership rather than the type of firms that matters: foreign investors in the tertiary industry have no impact on court funding.

These optimistic findings do not suggest that a rule-of-law regime has been built in China. China's legal institutions are far from perfect, and most progress has been in the economic arena. Through the *nomenklatura* system and its fiscal muscle, the CCP still firmly controls the judiciary so that it can limit citizens' rights to challenge the state. Therefore promoting the partial rule of law does not undermine authoritarian rule in China.

## AUTHORITARIAN RULE OF LAW BEYOND CHINA

The demand theory of authoritarian rule of law was developed in China, but it also has great explanatory power for other authoritarian regimes or even new democracies. Latin America is probably the continent that has received the most attention and international aid in building the rule of law. From the "law and development" project in the 1960s to the Washington Consensus in the 1990s, legal reform has been a central issue on policy makers' agenda to build democracy and a market economy in Latin America. Sutil (1999) lists some common trends in these reforms, including amendments to the constitution to guarantee a percentage of the budget for the judiciary; revising the rules that govern how judges are appointed and their terms of and conditions in office; adopting more oral and less inquisitorial procedures; and introducing measures to improve the education of judges.

Despite this progress, equity before the law is the key issue in the reforms. As Pinheiro (1999, 11) shows, a large percentage of Latin American citizens does not believe that their government implements, or attempts to implement, the law with equality and impartiality for all citizens. In Latin American countries, the poor often see the law as an instrument of oppression in the service of the wealthy and the powerful.

Therefore, similar to China, the law has become the "weapon of the weak" in Latin America. Sutil (1999) demonstrates that there is a clear trend, caused by the opening of markets, toward increasing the importance of the judiciary as a forum for dispute resolution. In this process, some marginalized groups in the region start to use the judicial system, through public interest litigation, to advance their interests. As Sutil (1999) concludes, judicial reform in Latin America is probably motivated by social demands for a wider and stronger role, and the underprivileged may benefit from that process.

Another active region for rule-of-law reform is Eastern Europe and the former Soviet Union. The legal reforms in this region are consistent with the demand-side theory in its negative sense; that is, privileged groups in these countries have become obstacles to meaningful legal reforms. Most Eastern

European regimes have made progress in de-Sovietizing their legal systems, and many have achieved partial judicial independence – such as the Czech Republic and Hungary – whereas Croatia, Serbia, and Slovakia are still falling short. The post-Soviet states are still struggling to distance themselves from their Soviet habits. Russia's legal reforms have been the weakest link in the post-Communist world. As Carothers (1998, 102) argues, the Russian government's attempts to reform "have been neutralized, however, by the ruling elite's tendency to act extra-legally and by the new private sector's troubling lawlessness."

One of the problems in post-Communist Russia is the rise of the racket in the unofficial economy. Frye and Zhuravskaya (2000) demonstrate that private business owners face very high levels of predatory regulation and have frequent contacts with private protection rackets. Russian private business owners view private protection organizations primarily as a substitute for state-provided police protection and courts, which echoes the finding in this book: that indigenous Chinese investors primarily rely on informal mechanisms such as mediation to settle disputes and, therefore, negatively affect the formal legal institutions.

In Western Europe, a more institutionalized form of private protection – the Mafia – constitutes a similar obstacle for the rule of law in Southern Italy. In Diego Gambetta's famous study of the Sicilian Mafia, he defines the Mafia as "a specific economic enterprise, an industry which produces, promotes, and sells private protection" (Gambetta 1993, 1). His analysis also provides insights on characteristics of informal protection. For example, mafiosi only offer their protection to a selective group of sellers in the market. Gambetta (1993, 22) analyzes why – since the more sellers the mafiosi protects, the higher their rents – they protect only a limited number of sellers at the expense of all others. This question is relevant to the study of political connections in China: if the Chinese government can extract rents from politically connected firms, why does it not extend its protection to all investors, including foreigners? Gambetta's answer is the problem of scale. He argues that if the mafiosi's guarantees were too public, and available to a potentially infinite number of sellers, they would be unable to enforce the collection of their rents from all their clients, who would thus find "tax evasion" easier. As with all public goods, every seller would have an interest in having mafiosi supply guarantees but without paying for that supply. In addition, mafiosi would find it difficult to police all the transactions they guaranteed, thus risking the loss of their reputation (Gambetta 1993, 22–23). I agree with Gambetta's logic, except that I also argue that making political connections a public good would increase competition among all connected firms and hence decrease the rents the government can extract.

The continent that has received the least attention regarding its rule-of-law reforms is probably Africa. With the exception of South Africa, very few, if any, sub-Saharan African countries have moved forward toward the rule of law in any meaningful way. In the oft-cited study of judicial independence in

Africa, Jennifer Widner calls our attention to the importance of building constituencies for the rule of law. Widner (2001, 34–37) notices that increases in judicial independence usually begin with a temporary "deal" between the executive and judiciary. There needs to be an initial delegation of authority from the executive branch or sometimes from the legislature. But the commitments are unreliable and the arrangements unstable. Therefore, Widner (2001, 35) contends, "Having important and vocal constituencies was critical for sustained independence. The courts needed friends who could keep political leaders from reneging on their grants of independence to the judiciary." Widner emphasizes the public as constituencies of judicial independence; I instead examine how foreign investors as an interest group push for China's legal reforms.

It is logical to conclude our world tour by coming back to my starting point: Asia. The strong state-business ties that obstruct the rule of law are not at all unique to China. The East Asian "developmental states" have manifested long-lasting patterns in which political power and business interests are intertwined (Johnson 1982). Kang (2002) shows how strong business interests represented by Japanese *keiretsu*, Korean *chaebol*, and Philippine family conglomerates collude with their states to manipulate prices and cause them to diverge from competitive levels, and how the existence of rents leads to corruption by various actors attempting to gain access to the rents. Kang (2002, 180) contends that a principal way to generate rents is through state intervention: the state uses its power to manipulate prices and markets to create rents. By intervening, the government creates incentives for businesses to attempt to influence policy decisions; corruption occurs when businessmen use bribery, personal connections, or other means to influence policy decisions. In this crony capitalism, the entanglement of business and politics has created a weak rule-of-law regime in East Asia.

The strong state-business connection becomes more extreme in Taiwan, where politicians, businessmen, and gangsters are linked in a nexus. Chin (2003), in his famous book *Heijin*, shows that Taiwanese enterprises that maintain a close relationship with powerful politicians are more likely to secure government contracts, less likely to be targeted by law enforcement authorities for irregular business practices, and more likely to receive government aid when they are in financial distress. These entrepreneurs also welcome the affiliation with gangsters because in Taiwan, which has fierce and unfair competition, many business disputes are most efficiently settled in private. Meanwhile, gang leaders are eager to be connected with politicians who can protect them from law enforcement authorities. Chin (2003, 17) notices that in Taiwan, elected deputies often show up in police stations to express their "concern" whenever a person is arrested. They see this as one of their many "services" to their constituents, regardless of why the person has been arrested. Many people also view the presence of elected deputies in police stations as the most effective way to obtain a quick release, which is much needed by gangsters. Organized crime, business, politics, and their union have become a significant threat to judicial fairness in Taiwan.

## THE RULE OF LAW, AUTHORITARIANISM, AND BEYOND

I challenge the conventional wisdom that the rule of law is a natural enemy of authoritarian regimes. A partial form of the rule of law can actually make authoritarianism more robust by making a credible commitment to investors (whose assets are needed by authoritarian rulers) and limiting citizens' ability to use the judiciary to challenge the state.

My findings also cast doubt on the literature on the politics of reforms. The dominant view of economic reform is that interest groups that benefited from economic reforms received tangible benefits and pushed the reforms forward, while those that did not benefit had to be compensated or repressed in order for economic liberalization to proceed (Rodrik 1996; Garrett 1998; Haggard 1990; Roland 2000). However, I show that interest groups represented by indigenous Chinese investors who benefit from the existing political and economic arrangement would block further reforms to eliminate competition and maintain their privileged position in rent seeking. So the therapy for the "partial reform equilibrium" (Hellman 1998) is not to repress the losers but to weaken the winners.

My research presents an optimistic past and a cautiously optimistic future for the rule of law in authoritarian regimes. While some autocrats are willing to tie their hands by respecting the rule of law, authoritarian rule of law is incomplete. It is still impossible to have full-scale rule of law in an authoritarian regime as long as the autocrat sets the legal agenda. Incremental improvement in legal institutions in certain realms will not spread gradually throughout the system. To make the rule of law complete, autocrats not only need to tie their hands but also have to dig their own graves to make democratic transitions.

# Appendix A

## Research Methods

This project has drawn broadly from the diverse methodological tool kit of modern social sciences.

### FIELDWORK AND QUALITATIVE INTERVIEWS

I independently did the fieldwork in the summer of 2007, talking with ordinary citizens in Wuxi (Jiangsu Province), Foshan (Guangdong Province), and Shenyang (Liaoning Province). Most of my interviewees were people who had litigation experience. They were identified using Prof. Mary Gallagher's 2004 Rule of Law survey. The 2007 trip gave me a general sense of who used the courts and why, but the interviews were not cited in this book; it motivated me to conduct a more systematic study of judicial institutions in China. My 2010 trip was more systematic and better prepared; I spoke with elites including party/government officials, judges, investors, and scholars. I visited a county in Hainan Province; two municipalities in Guangdong Province; and two counties/districts each in Jiangxi Province, Shanghai, and Beijing. Obviously, the sites were not selected randomly. I relied on my personal connections to select the sites and establish initial contact. I then used snowball methods to recruit more respondents. The goal of the qualitative fieldwork and interviews was not to make any causal inference, which was not possible, because the cases and interviewees were not randomly selected. I did not seek to infer any conclusions from a comparison between, for example, county A and county B, because A and B are different in every respect; it was not a controlled experiment. In contrast, the goal of the fieldwork and qualitative interviews was to make sense of the quantitative analyses and provide insight into how the Chinese legal system works in practice, how investors feel about the rule of law, and what government officials think they should do to keep investors.

### SURVEY ON INSTITUTIONALIZATION OF LEGAL REFORMS IN CHINA

The survey on the Institutionalization of Legal Reforms in China (ILRC) was conducted by the Research Center of Contemporary China at Peking University in 2003. The principal investigators of the survey include Professors Pierre Landry, Yanqi Tong, Wenfang Tang, and a team at the Center including Professors Shen Mingming, Yang Ming, and Yan Jie, and Ms. Chai Jingjing. This survey interviewed a national probability sample of 7,714 respondents (that is, completed interviews) on a wide range of items related to their attitudes and behavior in dispute resolution. All respondents were Chinese adult citizens, of whom 79.3 percent live in rural areas.

The ILRC survey employed a spatial sampling technique to draw a national sample of Chinese adults in 2003/14. The primary sampling units (PSUs) were counties and county-level units (county-level cities or urban districts). Using provinces as strata, 102 PSUs were selected by PPS (probability of selection proportional to measure of size – population), and within each county, two townships were also drawn by PPS. Tertiary sampling units (TSUs) are cells of spatial grids drawn for each township, namely a half square minute of latitude and longitude. This method is based on population density rather than population size. To be specific, the sample space (township) was divided into a geographic information system grid that linked specific cells to the boundary map of the township. TSUs were drawn using the PPS technique. Trained surveyors equipped with GPS receivers were then sent to locate and enumerate the sampled spatial square seconds, or SSS. In order to maintain equal probabilities of selection across households, all dwellings enumerated in the SSS were included in the sample. Respondents were selected from each dwelling using the Kish grid method. The advantage of using spatial sampling is that it overcomes coverage problems in sample frames based on formal household registration (*hukou*), since 11.1 percent of the total population in China is migrants who are not registered.

We surveyed a total of 102 counties, across all thirty-one provinces and provincial-level units. They vary a great deal in terms of their levels of economic prosperity and fiscal conditions. I compiled a unique cross-sectional data set using the survey data and data collected from various sources ranging from yearbooks to government Web sites. All variables in the data set were measured in 2003.

WORLD BANK INVESTMENT CLIMATE SURVEYS
OF CHINESE CITIES

The Investment Climate Survey was jointly conducted by the World Bank and the PRC's National Bureau of Statistics in 2005. They interviewed firms in 120 cities located in all provinces except Tibet. It is important to note that neither the cities nor the firms were randomly selected. However, the 120 cities included in this survey accounted for 70–80 percent of China's GDP. For all but the four provincial-level cities, the survey sampled 100 firms. For each of the four megacities (Beijing, Tianjin, Shanghai, and Chongqing), the survey sampled

200 firms. Thus the sample included 12,400 firms. For each city, the top ten industries in terms of sales revenue were drawn. For each industry, all firms in the sample universe were divided into large, middle, and small firms, each of which accounted for one-third of the total industry revenue. Then, from each of these three types of firms, an equal number of firms was drawn. Firms were required to have a minimum of ten employees to enter the sample.[1]

## PANEL DATA SET ON PROVINCIAL COURT FUNDING

This is an original time-series cross-section data set of thirty-one Chinese provinces from 1995 to 2006. I limited my data collection efforts to these twelve years mainly because the core dependent variable, court funding, is available only from Statistical Reports on Local Finance (*Difang caizheng tongji ziliao*) published by the Ministry of Finance for these twelve years. These reports used to be classified but are now public and available in the National Library in Beijing and some university libraries in China and the United States. The unit of analysis is province/year. I chose to focus on provinces because reliable data regarding sources of FDI and court funding exist only at this level.

---

[1] For more information about the survey, please see World Bank (2007).

# Appendix B

## Technical Details

CHAPTER 4

TABLE A4.1 *Summary Statistics*

| Variable | N | Mean | Std. Dev. | Min | Max |
|---|---|---|---|---|---|
| Property Protection | 9,469 | 0.36 | 35.17 | −95.00 | 73.05 |
| Sale to Government | 12,399 | 2.33 | 10.05 | 0.00 | 100.00 |
| Government Public Relations | 12,400 | 0.27 | 0.44 | 0.00 | 1.00 |
| Confidence in Courts | 11,598 | 78.47 | 26.33 | 0.00 | 100.00 |
| Firm Age (log) | 12,395 | 2.13 | 0.88 | 0.69 | 4.93 |
| Tax (log) | 12,207 | 7.17 | 2.30 | −1.61 | 16.94 |
| Employees (log) | 12,399 | 5.55 | 1.49 | 0.00 | 11.70 |
| License | 12,400 | 6.48 | 6.82 | 1.00 | 258.00 |
| Government-Appointed Manager | 12,368 | 0.12 | 0.32 | 0.00 | 1.00 |
| Interaction with Government | 12,265 | 2.57 | 1.27 | 1.00 | 8.00 |

*Source*: World Bank survey

TABLE A4.2  *Ownership and State-Business Relations*

| Dependent Variable | OLS Property Protection | | | | OLS Sale to Government | | | | Logit Government Public Relations | | | | OLS Confidence in Local Courts | | | |
|---|---|---|---|---|---|---|---|---|---|---|---|---|---|---|---|---|
| | (1) | (2) | (3) | (4) | (5) | (6) | (7) | (8) | (9) | (10) | (11) | (12) | (13) | (14) | (15) | (16) |
| SOE | -1.999 (1.271) | – | – | – | 1.217** (0.489) | – | – | – | -0.312*** (0.077) | – | – | – | -0.509 (0.819) | – | – | – |
| Private | – | 0.464 (0.900) | – | – | – | 0.156 (0.192) | – | – | – | -0.002 (0.057) | – | – | – | -0.035 (0.540) | – | – |
| China Circle | – | – | 0.880 (2.011) | – | – | – | -0.586* (0.310) | – | – | – | 0.202 (0.132) | – | – | – | -0.219 (1.070) | – |
| Foreign | – | – | – | -3.505** (1.396) | – | – | – | -1.146*** (0.229) | – | – | – | 0.199** (0.102) | – | – | – | -2.011** (0.896) |
| Firm Age (log) | -0.444 (0.500) | -0.545 (0.514) | -0.558 (0.516) | -0.609 (0.517) | 0.597*** (0.121) | 0.679*** (0.127) | 0.672*** (0.128) | 0.657*** (0.127) | -0.103*** (0.031) | -0.122*** (0.031) | -0.122*** (0.031) | -0.119*** (0.031) | -0.830*** (0.276) | -0.863*** (0.268) | -0.862*** (0.269) | -0.891*** (0.270) |
| Tax (log) | 0.525** (0.249) | 0.538** (0.251) | 0.537** (0.250) | 0.569** (0.247) | -0.206** (0.079) | -0.207** (0.081) | -0.214*** (0.080) | -0.197** (0.079) | 0.024 (0.014) | 0.024* (0.015) | 0.026* (0.015) | 0.022 (0.015) | 0.314** (0.159) | 0.315** (0.159) | 0.314* (0.159) | 0.336** (0.156) |
| Employees (log) | 2.985*** (0.453) | 2.918*** (0.448) | 2.896*** (0.448) | 2.887*** (0.443) | 0.212 (0.129) | 0.260** (0.131) | 0.260* (0.133) | 0.253* (0.132) | 0.128*** (0.024) | 0.117*** (0.023) | 0.115*** (0.023) | 0.117*** (0.023) | 1.716*** (0.301) | 1.696*** (0.299) | 1.699*** (0.295) | 1.693*** (0.296) |
| Licenses | -0.027 (0.053) | -0.027 (0.053) | -0.028 (0.053) | -0.024 (0.053) | 0.045*** (0.017) | 0.045*** (0.017) | 0.045*** (0.017) | 0.046*** (0.017) | 0.007** (0.003) | 0.007** (0.003) | 0.007** (0.003) | 0.006** (0.003) | 0.019 (0.042) | 0.019 (0.042) | 0.019 (0.042) | 0.022 (0.042) |

Table A4.2 (*cont.*)

| Dependent Variable | OLS | | | | OLS | | | | Logit | | | | OLS | | | |
| --- | --- | --- | --- | --- | --- | --- | --- | --- | --- | --- | --- | --- | --- | --- | --- | --- |
| | Property Protection | | | | Sale to Government | | | | Government Public Relations | | | | Confidence in Local Courts | | | |
| Government-Appointed Manager | -2.408 (1.477) | -2.930** (1.369) | -3.024** (1.342) | -3.190* (1.350) | 1.300** (0.532) | 1.738*** (0.493) | 1.689*** (0.479) | 1.651*** (0.480) | -0.095 (0.081) | -0.196*** (0.078) | -0.191** (0.076) | -0.186** (0.077) | -1.157 (0.829) | -1.330* (0.765) | -1.327* (0.784) | -1.408* (0.791) |
| Interaction with Government | -0.262 (0.300) | -0.268 (0.300) | -0.262 (0.300) | -0.278 (0.298) | 0.027 (0.079) | 0.025 (0.079) | 0.026 (0.078) | 0.023 (0.078) | 0.130*** (0.017) | 0.130*** (0.018) | 0.130*** (0.017) | 0.131*** (0.018) | -0.861*** (0.203) | -0.861*** (0.204) | -0.861*** (0.203) | -0.867*** (0.203) |
| Sale to Government | -0.017 (0.041) | -0.02 (0.040) | -0.019 (0.041) | -0.022 (0.041) | — | — | — | — | 0.003* (0.002) | 0.003 (0.002) | 0.003* (0.002) | 0.003* (0.002) | -0.037 (0.036) | -0.037 (0.035) | -0.037 (0.035) | -0.039 (0.035) |
| Industry Dummies | YES | YES | YES | YES | YES | YES | YES | YES | YES | YES | YES | YES | YES | YES | YES | YES |
| City Dummies | YES | YES | YES | YES | YES | YES | YES | YES | YES | YES | YES | YES | YES | YES | YES | YES |
| N | 9,224 | 9,224 | 9,224 | 9,224 | 12,037 | 12,037 | 12,037 | 12,037 | 11,737 | 11,737 | 11,737 | 11,737 | 11,275 | 11,275 | 11,275 | 11,275 |
| (Pseudo) $R^2$ | 0.029 | 0.029 | 0.029 | 0.029 | 0.065 | 0.064 | 0.064 | 0.065 | 0.062 | 0.061 | 0.061 | 0.061 | 0.176 | 0.176 | 0.176 | 0.177 |

P-values are based on two-tailed tests: *** $p < 0.01$; ** $p < 0.05$; * $p < 0.10$.

*Source:* World Bank survey

CHAPTER 5

TABLE A5.1 *Ranking of Surveyed Cities on ETC*

| Rank | Province | City | ETC | Rank | Province | City | ETC |
|------|----------|------|-----|------|----------|------|-----|
| 1 | Jiangsu | Suzhou | 0.4 | 60 | Liaoning | Jinzhou | 1.1 |
| 2 | Shandong | Linyi | 0.4 | 61 | Heilongjiang | Daqing | 1.1 |
| 3 | Shandong | Weihai | 0.4 | 62 | Heilongjiang | Qiqihaer | 1.1 |
| 4 | Hebei | Tangshan | 0.5 | 63 | Anhui | Hefei | 1.1 |
| 5 | Guangdong | Shenzhen | 0.5 | 64 | Yunnan | Kunming | 1.1 |
| 6 | Hebei | Handan | 0.6 | 65 | Jiangsu | Lianyungang | 1.1 |
| 7 | Fujian | Xiamen | 0.6 | 66 | Hunan | Chenzhou | 1.1 |
| 8 | Sichuan | Leshan | 0.6 | 67 | Beijing | Beijing | 1.2 |
| 9 | Shanxi | Yuncheng | 0.6 | 68 | Shaanxi | Baoji | 1.2 |
| 10 | Henan | Nanyang | 0.6 | 69 | Fujian | Zhangzhou | 1.2 |
| 11 | Shandong | Yantai | 0.6 | 70 | Jiangsu | Nanjing | 1.2 |
| 12 | Zhejiang | Hangzhou | 0.6 | 71 | Hubei | Yichang | 1.2 |
| 13 | Guangdong | Jiangmen | 0.6 | 72 | Sichuan | Mianyang | 1.2 |
| 14 | Sichuan | Deyang | 0.6 | 73 | Jiangsu | Nantong | 1.2 |
| 15 | Zhejiang | Jinhua | 0.6 | 74 | Tianjin | Tianjin | 1.2 |
| 16 | Liaoning | Dalian | 0.7 | 75 | Zhejiang | Ningbo | 1.2 |
| 17 | Shandong | Taian | 0.7 | 76 | Shanghai | Shanghai | 1.3 |
| 18 | Jiangxi | Shangrao | 0.7 | 77 | Hunan | Yueyang | 1.3 |
| 19 | Guangdong | Foshan | 0.7 | 78 | Shanxi | Taiyuan | 1.3 |
| 20 | Guangdong | Huizhou | 0.7 | 79 | Ningxia | Yinchuan | 1.3 |
| 21 | Hubei | Xiangfan | 0.7 | 80 | Jiangsu | Changzhou | 1.3 |
| 22 | Henan | Zhoukou | 0.7 | 81 | Hubei | Jingmen | 1.3 |
| 23 | Guangdong | Guangzhou | 0.7 | 82 | Shanxi | Datong | 1.3 |
| 24 | Henan | Shangqiu | 0.7 | 83 | Jiangxi | Jiujiang | 1.3 |
| 25 | Guangdong | Maoming | 0.7 | 84 | Guangxi | Nanning | 1.4 |
| 26 | Fujian | Fuzhou | 0.7 | 85 | Jiangsu | Yangzhou | 1.4 |
| 27 | Yunnan | Yuxi | 0.7 | 86 | Jiangxi | Yichun | 1.4 |
| 28 | Shandong | Weifang | 0.7 | 87 | Jilin | Jilin | 1.4 |
| 29 | Chongqing | Chongqing | 0.7 | 88 | Guangdong | Zhuhai | 1.5 |
| 30 | Hubei | Jingzhou | 0.8 | 89 | Henan | Xinxiang | 1.5 |
| 31 | Hebei | Shijiazhuang | 0.8 | 90 | Liaoning | Fushun | 1.5 |
| 32 | Shandong | Zibo | 0.8 | 91 | Guangxi | Guilin | 1.5 |
| 33 | Anhui | Wuhu | 0.8 | 92 | Shaanxi | Xianyang | 1.5 |
| 34 | Zhejiang | Shaoxing | 0.8 | 93 | Hebei | Baoding | 1.6 |
| 35 | Shandong | Jining | 0.8 | 94 | Jilin | Changchun | 1.6 |
| 36 | Zhejiang | Jiaxing | 0.8 | 95 | Zhejiang | Taizhou | 1.6 |

Table A5.1 *(cont.)*

| Rank | Province | City | ETC | Rank | Province | City | ETC |
|------|----------|------|-----|------|----------|------|-----|
| 37 | Neimenggu | Baotou | 0.8 | 96 | Jiangsu | Xuzhou | 1.6 |
| 38 | Hebei | Langfang | 0.8 | 97 | Hubei | Wuhan | 1.6 |
| 39 | Henan | Xuchang | 0.9 | 98 | Sichuan | Chengdu | 1.6 |
| 40 | Jiangxi | Ganzhou | 0.9 | 99 | Liaoning | Benxi | 1.6 |
| 41 | Sichuan | Yibin | 0.9 | 100 | Xinjiang | Wulumuqi | 1.6 |
| 42 | Fujian | Quanzhou | 0.9 | 101 | Hubei | Huanggang | 1.6 |
| 43 | Jiangxi | Nanchang | 0.9 | 102 | Gansu | Tianshui | 1.7 |
| 44 | Liaoning | Anshan | 0.9 | 103 | Shaanxi | Xian | 1.7 |
| 45 | Hubei | Xiaogan | 0.9 | 104 | Hebei | Qinhuangdao | 1.7 |
| 46 | Henan | Zhengzhou | 0.9 | 105 | Liaoning | Shenyang | 1.8 |
| 47 | Hebei | Cangzhou | 0.9 | 106 | Hunan | Changde | 1.8 |
| 48 | Shandong | Jinan | 0.9 | 107 | Qinghai | Xining | 1.8 |
| 49 | Fujian | Sanming | 0.9 | 108 | Guizhou | Guiyang | 1.8 |
| 50 | Jiangsu | Wuxi | 1.0 | 109 | Guizhou | Zunyi | 1.8 |
| 51 | Gansu | Lanzhou | 1.0 | 110 | Henan | Luoyang | 1.8 |
| 52 | Zhejiang | Huzhou | 1.0 | 111 | Heilongjiang | Haerbin | 1.9 |
| 53 | Anhui | Anqing | 1.0 | 112 | Jiangsu | Yancheng | 1.9 |
| 54 | Hebei | Zhangjiakou | 1.0 | 113 | Neimenggu | Huhehaote | 1.9 |
| 55 | Ningxia | Wuzhong | 1.0 | 114 | Hunan | Hengyang | 2.0 |
| 56 | Yunnan | Qujing | 1.0 | 115 | Anhui | Chuzhou | 2.0 |
| 57 | Guangxi | Liuzhou | 1.0 | 116 | Hunan | Zhuzhou | 2.0 |
| 58 | Shandong | Qingdao | 1.1 | 117 | Hunan | Changsha | 2.3 |
| 59 | Zhejiang | Wenzhou | 1.1 | 118 | Hainan | Haikou | 2.4 |

*Source:* World Bank survey

TABLE A5.2 *Summary Statistics*

| Variable | N | Mean | Std. Dev. | Min | Max |
|----------|---|------|-----------|-----|-----|
| ETC | 12,400 | 1.09 | 2.25 | 0.00 | 45.51 |
| Firm Age (log) | 12,395 | 2.13 | 0.88 | 0.69 | 4.93 |
| Tax 2003 (log) | 12,207 | 7.17 | 2.30 | −1.61 | 16.94 |
| Employee 2003 (log) | 12,399 | 5.55 | 1.49 | 0.00 | 11.70 |
| Sale to Another Province | 12,399 | 39.41 | 34.80 | 0.00 | 100.00 |
| CEO Pay 2004 (log) | 12,002 | 8.49 | 1.01 | −0.11 | 13.62 |
| Employee Wages (log) | 12,400 | 6.87 | 0.49 | −0.92 | 9.52 |
| License | 12,400 | 6.48 | 6.82 | 1.00 | 258.00 |

Table A5.2 *(cont.)*

| Variable | N | Mean | Std. Dev. | Min | Max |
|---|---|---|---|---|---|
| Sale to Government | 12,399 | 2.33 | 10.05 | 0.00 | 100.00 |
| Government-Appointed Manager | 12,368 | 0.12 | 0.32 | 0.00 | 1.00 |
| Interaction with Government | 12,265 | 2.57 | 1.27 | 1.00 | 8.00 |
| Confidence in Courts | 11,598 | 78.47 | 26.33 | 0.00 | 100.00 |

*Source:* World Bank survey

## OLS REGRESSION TO PREDICT ETC

OLS regression is employed to estimate the following models:

$$ETC = \alpha + \beta_1 \, SOE + X\beta + \sum Industry_i + \sum City_j + \varepsilon \tag{A5.1}$$

$$ETC = \alpha + \beta_1 \, Private + X\beta + \sum Industry_i + \sum City_j + \varepsilon \tag{A5.2}$$

$$ETC = \alpha + \beta_1 \, China\, circle + X\beta + \sum Industry_i + \sum City_j + \varepsilon \tag{A5.3}$$

$$ETC = \alpha + \beta_1 \, Foreign + X\beta + \sum Industry_i + \sum City_j + \varepsilon \tag{A5.4}$$

Columns 1–4 in Table A5.3 report the results of OLS estimates of models A5.1–A5.4. Because firms in the same city are not independent, standard errors of the estimates clustered at the city level are reported in parentheses.

TABLE A5.3  OLS *Estimates of the Determinants of ETC*

| Explanatory Variables/ Dependent Variable | OLS | | | |
|---|---|---|---|---|
| | Entertainment and Travel Costs/Total Revenue | | | |
| | (1) | (2) | (3) | (4) |
| SOE | 0.024 | – | – | – |
| | (0.037) | | | |
| Private | – | 0.056** | – | – |
| | | (0.027) | | |
| China Circle | – | – | –0.050 | – |
| | | | (0.049) | |
| Foreign | – | – | – | –0.085** |
| | | | | (0.037) |
| Firm Age (log) | 0.057*** | 0.060*** | 0.058*** | 0.057*** |
| | (0.013) | (0.013) | (0.013) | (0.013) |

Table A5.3 *(cont.)*

| Explanatory Variables/ Dependent Variable | OLS | | | |
|---|---|---|---|---|
| | Entertainment and Travel Costs/Total Revenue | | | |
| Tax 2003 (log) | −0.035*** | −0.035*** | −0.036*** | −0.035*** |
| | (0.009) | (0.008) | (0.008) | (0.008) |
| Employee 2003 (log) | −0.156*** | −0.153*** | −0.155*** | −0.156*** |
| | (0.016) | (0.016) | (0.016) | (0.016) |
| Sale to Another Province | 0.005*** | 0.005*** | 0.005*** | 0.005*** |
| | (0.000) | (0.000) | (0.000) | (0.000) |
| CEO Pay 2004 (log) | −0.010 | −0.010 | −0.010 | −0.006 |
| | (0.019) | (0.019) | (0.019) | (0.019) |
| Employee Wages (log) | 0.039 | 0.047 | 0.039 | 0.042 |
| | (0.056) | (0.056) | (0.056) | (0.056) |
| License | 0.002 | 0.002 | 0.002 | 0.002 |
| | (0.002) | (0.002) | (0.002) | (0.002) |
| Government-Appointed Manager | 0.055 | 0.077** | 0.063* | 0.061** |
| | (0.037) | (0.038) | (0.037) | (0.037) |
| Interaction with Government | 0.018** | 0.018* | 0.018** | 0.018** |
| | (0.009) | (0.009) | (0.009) | (0.009) |
| Sale to Government | 0.005*** | 0.005*** | 0.005*** | 0.005*** |
| | (0.001) | (0.001) | (0.001) | (0.001) |
| Confidence in Courts | −0.000 | −0.000 | −0.000 | −0.000 |
| | (0.001) | (0.001) | (0.001) | (0.001) |
| Industry Dummies | YES | YES | YES | YES |
| City Dummies | YES | YES | YES | YES |
| N | 10,857 | 10,857 | 10,857 | 10,857 |
| $R^2$ | 0.154 | 0.155 | 0.154 | 0.154 |

*Note:* The dependent variable is ETC as the percentage of a firm's total revenue in 2004. Standard errors clustered at the city level are reported in parentheses. P-values are based on two-tailed tests: *** $p < 0.01$; ** $p < 0.05$; * $p < 0.10$.

*Source:* World Bank survey

## CHAPTER 6

### INDIVIDUAL DETERMINANTS OF PERCEIVED CORRUPTION

The two potential challenges discussed in the text can be phrased as two null hypotheses:

Null Hypothesis A6.1: *Respondents' exposure to public media is correlated (positively or negatively) with their evaluations of judicial corruption in local courts,* ceteris paribus.

Null Hypothesis A6.2: *Respondents who grew up in the locality are less likely to say that the "court is corrupt" than those who came from outside,* ceteris paribus.

For the measure to be valid, both null hypothesis A6.1 and A6.2 should be rejected.

Using individual-level data collected in the same survey, I estimate a model to test these two null hypotheses. I coded the dependent variable "perceived corruption" as a dichotomous variable that equals 1 if the respondent chose "the court is corrupt" in any of the three hypothetical cases and 0 otherwise. The explanatory "media exposure" variable is the sum of a battery of ordinal scales measuring the respondents' usage of various media outlets, including newspapers, magazines, TV, and the radio. Higher values indicate more media exposure. To capture whether a respondent was interested in the political and legal issues covered by public media specifically, two other variables are constructed. One dichotomous "attention" variable was coded 1 if the respondent chose "current issues" or "legal issues" as one of the top three attended topics in the media and 0 otherwise.[1] Another variable, "interest," measures the respondents' interest in politics. It is on an ordinal scale; larger values indicate more interest.[2] The dichotomous "local" variable equals 1 if the respondent grew up in that locality and 0 otherwise. Controls include the respondents' party membership, satisfaction with their local leaders,[3] trust in courts, and connections with officials in the police department, procurator, and court. The demographic variables include age, sex, and education.

An econometric model is specified as follows:

$$Perceived\ Corruption = \beta_1 + \beta_2 Media + \beta_3 Attention + \beta_4 Interest$$

$$+ \beta_5 Local + X'B + \varepsilon \qquad (A6.1)$$

Table A6.1 reports the results of the logistic regression. As shown, none of the media-related variables (media, attention, and interest) is significant

---

[1] The original question was "Among the types of information provided by these various media, which three are you most concerned with?" Options include: current issues, economy, culture and sports, life, education, society, legal issues, technology, health, and others.

[2] The original question was "Some people care deeply about the affairs of the government, while others are not too interested. With regards to affairs of the government, are you very concerned, somewhat concerned, not very concerned, or not concerned at all?"

[3] The question was "In general, are you satisfied with the leadership of this village or this unit?"

TABLE A6.1 *Who Said the "Court is Corrupt": Complex Survey Design Effects Logistic Regression*

| Variable | Coefficient | | Std. Err. |
|---|---|---|---|
| Age | −0.124 | ** | 0.061 |
| Age$^2$ | 0.002 | ** | 0.001 |
| Sex | 0.067 | | 0.280 |
| Education | −0.106 | | 0.154 |
| CCP Member | 0.714 | | 0.470 |
| Media Exposure | −0.057 | | 0.069 |
| Attention | 0.316 | | 0.272 |
| Interest in Politics | 0.089 | | 0.152 |
| Local | 1.214 | ** | 0.478 |
| Connection | 0.928 | *** | 0.303 |
| Satisfaction | −0.567 | *** | 0.154 |
| Trust in Courts | −0.679 | *** | 0.196 |
| Intercept | 1.335 | | 1.825 |
| N | 2,276 | | |
| Population size | 2.64E+08 | | |
| Design df | 2275 | | |
| $F_{(12,2275)}$ | 4.925 | | |

P-values are based on two-tailed tests: *** $p < 0.01$; ** $p < 0.05$; * $p < 0.10$.

TABLE A6.2 *Summary Statistics*

| Variable | N | Mean | Std. Dev. | Min. | Max. |
|---|---|---|---|---|---|
| Corruption | 102 | 6.782 | 7.241 | 0 | 43.532 |
| Econ-corruption | 102 | 7.406 | 9.866 | 0 | 61.683 |
| Admin-corruption | 102 | 5.105 | 7.036 | 0 | 27.654 |
| Foreign Capital | 101 | 3.193 | 5.583 | 0 | 35.409 |
| Finances | 102 | 5.962 | 2.617 | 1.8 | 18.04 |
| Rural | 96 | 23.131 | 15.349 | 0 | 57.041 |
| GDP pc (logged) | 101 | 8.895 | 0.836 | 7.322 | 10.784 |

*Source:* Data set compiled by the author

either individually or jointly ($F_{(3,2273)} = 0.86$, $p = 0.46$). This rejects null hypothesis A6.1. This finding suggests that the respondents' evaluations of judicial corruption were not influenced by the public media. In addition, the "local" variable has a significantly positive effect, which means that respondents who grew up in the locality were more likely to say that the "court is corrupt" than those who came from outside. This rejects null hypothesis A6.2 and suggests that the respondents were not trying to save face for the local court when they were asked about judicial corruption. In sum, there is no empirical evidence that the respondents' subjective evaluations were biased by media influence or social desirability.

## OLS REGRESSION TO PREDICT PERCEIVED JUDICIAL CORRUPTION AT THE COUNTY LEVEL

Based on Hypotheses 6.1 and 6.2, a benchmark model is specified as follows:

$$Y = \beta_1 + \beta_2 \text{Foreign capital} + \beta_3 \text{Finances} + \beta_5 \text{Rural} + \beta_6 \text{GDP pc} + \varepsilon$$

$$(A6.2)$$

where Y includes three measures of judicial corruption, and $\beta_2$ is expected to be negative as it is the marginal effect of foreign capital, which should reduce corruption. As the theory implies, $\beta_2$ is expected to be significant when Econ-corruption is the dependent variable, while it should be insignificant or smaller in magnitude when Admin-corruption is the dependent variable, as foreign capital reduces judicial corruption only in the commercial realm. $\beta_3$ is expected to be negative: it is the marginal effect of government financial support, which should also reduce corruption. $\beta_4$ is expected to be negative, as corruption should be more rampant in urban areas than in rural areas. $\beta_5$ is expected to be negative as well, because corruption should become less frequent as the economy develops.

Table A6.3 shows regression estimates of Model A6.2.[4] Columns 1, 3, and 5 present the OLS regression results with different dependent variables. Columns 2, 4, and 6 show the 2SLS estimates.

---

[4] Prior to estimating the model, I carried out a diagnosis using Cook's methods (Cook 1977) to identify highly influential cases. Two observations were highly influential and were therefore dropped in the following analysis. In addition, Cameron and Trivedi's (1990) decomposition of IM-test rejects the null hypothesis of homoscedasticity ($\chi^2 = 21.9$, p <.1). Thus, robust standard errors are estimated in the regression analysis.

TABLE A6.3 *Determinants of Judicial Corruption among Chinese Counties*

| Variable | DV = Corruption OLS Coefficient (Robust S.E.) | DV = Corruption 2SLS Coefficient (Robust S.E.) | DV = Econ-corruption OLS Coefficient (Robust S.E.) | DV = Econ-corruption 2SLS Coefficient (Robust S.E.) | DV = Admin-corruption OLS Coefficient (Robust S.E.) | DV = Admin-corruption 2SLS Coefficient (Robust S.E.) |
|---|---|---|---|---|---|---|
| Foreign Capital | -0.565 *** (0.131) | -0.504 ** (0.240) | -0.759 *** (0.188) | -0.650 * (0.390) | -0.388 ** (0.156) | -0.028 (0.285) |
| Finances | -0.488 ** (0.220) | -0.492 ** (0.217) | -0.494 (0.343) | -0.501 (0.341) | -0.772 *** (0.273) | -0.794 *** (0.287) |
| Rural | -0.210 *** (0.052) | -0.205 *** (0.054) | -0.210 *** (0.073) | -0.201 ** (0.081) | -0.226 (0.615) | -0.196 *** (0.064) |
| GDP pc (log) | -2.080 ** (0.889) | -2.116 ** (0.893) | -2.712 ** (1.130) | -2.778 ** (1.191) | -1.287 (1.127) | -1.505 (1.051) |
| Intercept | 34.201 *** (8.967) | 34.265 *** (8.876) | 41.037 *** (11.328) | 41.150 *** (11.489) | 27.063 ** (10.976) | 27.437 ** (10.648) |
| N | 94 | 94 | 94 | 94 | 94 | 94 |
| $R^2$ | 0.215 | 0.214 | 0.172 | 0.170 | 0.185 | 0.143 |
| F | 7.000 | 4.760 | 5.530 | 3.390 | 4.530 | 3.200 |
| Durbin-Wu-Hausman $\chi^2$ test | – | $\chi^2=0.054$, $p=0.816$ | – | $\chi^2=0.084$, $p=0.772$ | | $\chi^2=1.624$, $p=0.203$ |

P-values are based on two-tailed tests: *** $p < 0.01$; ** $p < 0.05$; * $p < 0.10$.
*Source:* Data set compiled by the author

TABLE A6.4 *FDI and Judicial Corruption, Matched Data*

| Variable | DV = Corruption Coefficient (S.E.) | | DV = Econ-corruption Coefficient (S.E.) | | DV = Admin-corruption Coefficient (S.E.) |
|---|---|---|---|---|---|
| Foreign Capital | −4.677 | * | −10.656 | ** | −0.695 |
| | (2.512) | | (4.141) | | (2.605) |
| N | 94 | | 94 | | 94 |

P-values are based on two-tailed tests: *** p < 0.01; ** p < 0.05; * p < 0.10.
*Source:* Data set compiled by the author

TABLE A6.5 *Determinants of "Confidence in Courts" in 120 Cities*

| Variable | OLS Coefficient (S.E.) | | OLS Coefficient (S.E.) | | 2SLS Coefficient (S.E.) | |
|---|---|---|---|---|---|---|
| Foreign Capital | 12.911 | *** | 13.434 | *** | 13.999 | * |
| | (4.683) | | (4.344) | | (8.472) | |
| Finances | 0.056 | | 0.49 | | 0.481 | |
| | (0.818) | | (0.819) | | (0.795) | |
| Rural | 0.804 | *** | 0.552 | * | 0.548 | * |
| | (0.278) | | (0.304) | | (0.301) | |
| GDP pc (log) | 5.801 | | 3.717 | | 3.478 | |
| | (5.006) | | (5.136) | | (6.042) | |
| Service | – | | −0.645 | ** | −0.642 | *** |
| | | | (0.257) | | (0.247) | |
| Growth | – | | 0.061 | | 0.056 | |
| | | | (0.430) | | (0.431) | |
| Level | – | | 1.531 | | 1.459 | |
| | | | (4.656) | | (4.460) | |
| Intercept | – | | 35.539 | | 37.753 | |
| | | | (52.477) | | (61.003) | |
| N | 116 | | 104 | | 104 | |
| $R^2$ | 0.139 | | 0.240 | | 0.240 | |

P-values are based on two-tailed tests: *** p < 0.01; ** p < 0.05; * p < 0.10.
*Source:* Data set compiled by the author

TABLE A6.6 *First-Stage Regression Results Using County Data*

| Variable | Coefficient (Robust S.E.) | |
|---|---|---|
| Distance | −0.003 | ** |
| | (0.001) | |
| Migrant Population | 0.244 | ** |
| | (0.071) | |
| Finances | −0.061 | |
| | (0.205) | |
| Rural | −0.068 | |
| | (0.042) | |
| GDP per capita (log) | −1.325 | |
| | (1.083) | |
| Intercept | 16.918 | |
| | (10.398) | |
| N | 94 | |
| R² | 0.377 | |
| F(5,88) | 6.444 | |

*Note:* The dependent variable is Foreign Capital. P-values are based on two-tailed tests: *** $p < 0.01$; ** $p < 0.05$; * $p < 0.10$.

TABLE A6.7 *Foreign Capital and Government Corruption*

| | OLS | | 2SLS |
|---|---|---|---|
| Variable | Coefficient (Robust S.E.) | | Coefficient (Robust S.E.) |
| Foreign Capital | −0.633 | ** | −0.061 |
| | (0.282) | | (0.621) |
| Rural | −0.045 | | 0.006 |
| | (0.139) | | (0.151) |
| GDP pc (log) | 2.710 | | 2.372 |
| | (2.428) | | (2.425) |
| Intercept | −2.071 | | −1.803 |
| | (24.029) | | (24.376) |
| N | 94 | | 94 |
| R² | 0.056 | | 0.027 |
| F | 2.280 | | 0.580 |
| Durbin-Wu-Hausman χ² test | | | $\chi^2=0.989, p=0.320$ |

P-values are based on two-tailed tests: *** $p < 0.01$; ** $p < 0.05$; * $p < 0.10$.
*Source:* Data set compiled by the author

CHAPTER 7

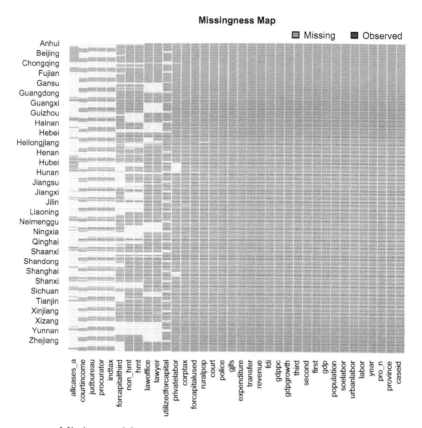

FIGURE A7.1 Missingness Map
*Source*: Data compiled by the author

PANEL DATA TO ANALYZE THE EFFECT OF FDI ON COURT
FUNDING

To test Hypotheses 7.1–7.4, an error correction model (ECM) is specified as
follows:[5]

$$\Delta \text{Court}_{i,t} = \alpha_0 + \alpha_1 \text{Court}_{i,t-1} + \beta_0 \Delta \text{China circle}_{i,t} + \beta_1 \text{China circle}_{i,t-1}$$
$$+ \beta_2 \Delta \text{foreign}_{i,t} + \beta_3 \text{foreign}_{i,t-1}$$
$$+ \beta_4 \Delta \text{private}_{i,t} + \beta_5 \text{private}_{i,t-1} + \beta_6 \Delta \text{SOE}_{i,t}$$
$$+ \beta_7 \text{SOE}_{i,t-1} + X\beta + \lambda_t + \gamma_i + \varepsilon_{i,t} \tag{A7.1}$$

---

[5] To follow the suggestions of De Boef and Keele (2008), the model is specified in a general way
that puts no restrictions on the dynamic components.

TABLE A7.1 *Effects of FDI on Court Funding across Chinese Provinces (1995–2006) (OLS with Panel-Corrected Standard Errors)*[a]

| Dependent Variable | | ΔCourt Funding per capita (*yuan*/person) | | ΔCourt Funding/Total Expenditure (%) | | |
|---|---|---|---|---|---|---|
| Variable | Expected Sign | Coefficient (P.C.S.E) | | Coefficient (P.C.S.E) | | Long-Run Effect[b] (S.E) |
| Court$_{i, t-1}$ | – | –0.619 | *** | –0.645 | *** | |
| | | (0.114) | | (0.089) | | |
| Δ China Circle$_{i, t}$ | – | –0.018 | ** | –0.012 | * | –0.019 * |
| | | (0.010) | | (0.007) | | 0.010 |
| China Circle$_{i, t-1}$ | – | –0.018 | | –0.012 | * | |
| | | (0.011) | | (0.006) | | |
| Δ Foreign$_{i, t}$ | + | 0.016 | * | 0.012 | * | 0.028 *** |
| | | (0.009) | | (0.006) | | 0.010 |
| Foreign$_{i, t-1}$ | + | 0.024 | ** | 0.018 | *** | |
| | | 0.009 | | (0.006) | | |
| Δ Private$_{i, t}$ | – | –0.003 | | –0.002 | | –0.005 *** |
| | | (0.002) | | (0.002) | | 0.002 |
| Private$_{i, t-1}$ | – | –0.004 | ** | –0.003 | *** | |
| | | (0.002) | | (0.001) | | |
| Δ SOE$_{i, t}$ | – | –0.003 | | –0.002 | | –0.002 |
| | | (0.002) | | (0.001) | | 0.002 |
| SOE$_{i, t-1}$ | – | –0.002 | | –0.001 | | |
| | | (0.001) | | (0.001) | | |
| Δ Total Spending pc$_{i, t}$ (log) | + | 0.905 | *** | –0.064 | | –0.107 |
| | | (0.056) | | (0.041) | | 0.085 |
| Total Spending pc$_{i, t-1}$ (log) | + | 0.520 | *** | –0.069 | | |
| | | (0.110) | | (0.056) | | |
| Δ GDP pc$_{i, t}$ (log) | | –0.075 | | –0.055 | | –0.195 * |
| | | (0.292) | | (0.196) | | 0.114 |
| GDP pc$_{i, t-1}$ (log) | | –0.165 | | –0.126 | | |
| | | (0.110) | | (0.077) | | |
| Δ Service$_{i, t}$ | | –0.002 | * | –0.002 | * | –0.006 |
| | | (0.001) | | (0.001) | | 0.005 |
| Service$_{i, t-1}$ | | –0.005 | | –0.004 | | |

Table A7.1 *(cont.)*

| Dependent Variable | | ΔCourt Funding per capita (*yuan*/person) | ΔCourt Funding/Total Expenditure (%) | |
| --- | --- | --- | --- | --- |
| Variable | Expected Sign | Coefficient (P.C.S.E) | Coefficient (P.C.S.E) | Long-Run Effect[b] (S.E) |
| | | (0.004) | (0.003) | |
| Δ GDP growth$_{i,t}$ | | 0.004 | 0.005 | 0.002 |
| | | (0.008) | (0.005) | 0.008 |
| GDP growth$_{i,t-1}$ | | −0.002 | 0.001 | |
| | | (0.006) | (0.005) | |
| Δ Rural pop$_{i,t}$ | | 0.004 | 0.003 | 0.002 |
| | | (0.003) | (0.002) | 0.003 |
| Rural pop$_{i,t-1}$ | | 0.001 | 0.001 | |
| | | (0.003) | (0.002) | |
| Δ Population$_{i,t}$ (log) | | −0.886 | −0.360 | −0.332 |
| | | (1.675) | (1.097) | 0.474 |
| Population$_{i,-1t}$ (log) | | −0.301 | −0.214 | |
| | | (0.459) | (0.307) | |
| Δ Cases$_{i,t}$ (log) | | 0.007 | −0.002 | −0.002 |
| | | (0.061) | (0.044) | 0.088 |
| Cases$_{i,t-1}$ (log) | | 0.017 | −0.001 | |
| | | (0.083) | (0.057) | |
| Δ Law Office$_{i,t}$ (log) | | 0.131 * | 0.085 | 0.256 ** |
| | | (0.077) | (0.054) | 0.118 |
| Law Office$_{i,t-1}$ (log) | | 0.248 ** | 0.165 ** | |
| | | (0.113) | (0.075) | |
| Δ Lawyers$_{i,t}$ (log) | | 0.001 | 0.012 | 0.042 |
| | | (0.054) | (0.039) | 0.064 |
| Lawyers$_{i,t-1}$ (log) | | 0.008 | 0.027 | |
| | | (0.056) | (0.041) | |
| Province Fixed Effects | | YES | YES | |
| Year Fixed Effects | | YES | YES | |

Table A7.1  *(cont.)*

| Dependent Variable | | ΔCourt Funding per capita (*yuan*/person) | ΔCourt Funding/Total Expenditure (%) | |
| --- | --- | --- | --- | --- |
| Variable | Expected Sign | Coefficient (P.C.S.E) | Coefficient (P.C.S.E) | Long-Run Effect[b] (S.E) |
| Intercept | | 0.370 (4.183) | 2.963 (2.803) | |
| N | | 340 | 341 | |

[a] The dependent variable (Δ $Court_{i,t}$) is measured in two ways: first-differenced per capita court funding and first-differenced court funding in the overall provincial budget. Parameter estimates are followed by panel-corrected standard errors in parenthesis. P-values are based on two-tailed tests: *** $p<0.01$; ** $p<0.05$; * $p<0.10$.

[b] Long-run effects and standard errors are calculated using De Boef and Keele's (2008, 971) formula. For example, the long-run effect of $\Delta ChinaCircle_{i,t} = \frac{\beta_1}{\alpha_1}$ and its standard error

$$= \sqrt{\left(\frac{1}{\alpha_1^2}\right)\mathrm{Var}(\beta_1) + \left(\frac{\beta_1^2}{\alpha_1^4}\right)\mathrm{Var}(\alpha_1) - 2\left(\frac{\beta_1}{\alpha_1^3}\right)\mathrm{Cov}(\beta_1, \alpha_1)}$$

*Source:* Data set compiled by the author

In Equation A7.1, $\Delta Court_{i,\,t}$ is the first-differenced dependent variable that measures the change in per capita court funding (log transformed) or the proportion of court funding in the overall government budget in province $i$ at time $t$ compared to province $i$ at time $t - 1$; $\alpha_0$ is the intercept; and $\alpha_1$ is the marginal effect of the lagged dependent variable. Lagged dependent variables are included to eliminate serial correlation of the errors. Another rationale of including the lag is that the budgeting process is incremental: this year's budget is based on last year's. $\beta_0$ is the marginal effect of the first-differenced China circle, which is measured by the change in weight of FDI from Hong Kong, Macao, and Taiwan in the overall provincial GDP from time $t - 1$ to $t$. $\beta_0$ measures the short-run effect of China circle. $\beta_0$ is expected to be negative because FDI from within the China circle should have a negative impact on court funding. The quantity $\beta_1 - \beta_0$ gives the short-run effect of China circle $_{i,\,t-1}$, which is the one-year lag of the independent variable. $\beta_2$ should be positive, because it estimates the marginal effects of the first-differenced FDI from outside the China circle. $\beta_4$ is the marginal effect of the first-differenced "private," which is the change in weight of private economy in the overall urban economy from time $t - 1$ to $t$. $\beta_6$ is the marginal effect of change in SOEs. Both $\beta_4$ and $\beta_6$ are expected to be negative. X is a vector of controls including *total expenditure per capita* (log transformed), *GDP per capita* (log transformed), *service, GDP growth, rural pop* (log transformed), *population*

TABLE A7.2 *2SLS Estimate of the Effect of Foreign Capital on Court Funding*

| Dependent Variable | Court Funding per capita i,t (*yuan*/person) | | Court Funding/Total Expenditure i, t (%) | |
|---|---|---|---|---|
| Variable | Coefficient (S.E) | | Coefficient (S.E) | |
| China Circle$_{i, t}$ | −2.897 | ** | −0.047 | * |
| | (1.280) | | (0.026) | |
| Foreign$_{i, t}$ (instrumented) | 5.084 | ** | 0.106 | ** |
| | (2.591) | | (0.053) | |
| Private$_{i, t}$ | 0.058 | | −0.006 | ** |
| | (0.126) | | (0.003) | |
| SOE$_{i, t}$ | −0.286 | ** | −0.003 | |
| | (0.115) | | (0.002) | |
| Total Spending pc$_{i, t}$ (log) | 8.649 | | −0.214 | |
| | (6.490) | | (0.133) | |
| GDP pc$_{i,t}$ (log) | 1.235 | | −0.624 | ** |
| | (12.362) | | (0.253) | |
| Service$_{i, t}$ | 0.071 | | 0.002 | |
| | (0.154) | | (0.003) | |
| GDP Growth$_{i, t}$ | 0.386 | | 0.014 | |
| | (0.596) | | (0.012) | |
| Rural pop$_{i, t}$ | −0.084 | | −0.005 | |
| | (0.184) | | (0.004) | |
| Population$_{i, t}$ (log) | 63.969 | ** | −0.047 | |
| | (26.527) | | (0.545) | |
| Province Fixed Effects | YES | | YES | |
| Year Fixed Effects | YES | | YES | |
| Intercept | −511.488 | * | 8.363 | |
| | (261.675) | | (5.372) | |
| N | 233 | | 233 | |
| R$^2$ | 0.776 | | 0.502 | |

P-values are based on two-tailed tests: *** $p<.01$; ** $p<.05$; * $p<.10$.
*Note:* This is the result of a 2SLS regression with foreign capital instrumented by the five-year lag of foreign tourists.
*Source:* Data set compiled by the author

(log transformed), *cases* (log transformed), *law offices* (log transformed), and *lawyers* (log transformed). $\lambda_t$ is the time fixed effect, which includes dummy variables for each year. The time fixed effects capture the remaining serial variation that is not explained by the independent variables, such as

TABLE A7.3 *Testing an Alternative Explanation: Foreign Capital in Tertiary Industry and Court Funding*

| Dependent Variable | Δ Court Funding per capita (*yuan*/person) | | Δ Court Funding/Total Expenditure (%) | |
|---|---|---|---|---|
| Variable | Coefficient (P.C.S.E) | | Coefficient (P.C.S.E) | |
| Court$_{i, t-1}$ | −0.603 | *** | −0.63 | *** |
| | (0.115) | | (0.089) | |
| Δ FDI in Tertiary$_{i, t}$ | 0.004 | | 0.003 | |
| | (0.007) | | (0.005) | |
| FDI in Tertiary$_{i, t-1}$ | 0.006 | | 0.004 | |
| | (0.011) | | (0.008) | |
| Δ Private$_{i, t}$ | −0.002 | | −0.002 | |
| | (0.002) | | (0.002) | |
| Private$_{i, t-1}$ | −0.003 | * | −0.003 | |
| | (0.002) | | (0.001) | |
| Δ SOE$_{i, t}$ | −0.002 | | −0.001 | |
| | (0.002) | | (0.002) | |
| SOE$_{i, t-1}$ | −0.001 | | −0.001 | |
| | (0.001) | | (0.001) | |
| Δ Total Spending pc$_{i, t}$ (log) | 0.885 | *** | −0.077 | |
| | (0.061) | | (0.044) | |
| Total Spending pc$_{i, t-1}$ (log) | 0.488 | *** | −0.078 | |
| | (0.115) | | (0.059) | |
| Δ GDP pc$_{i, t}$ (log) | −0.07 | | −0.056 | |
| | (0.289) | | (0.197) | |
| GDP pc$_{i, t-1}$ (log) | −0.120 | | −0.093 | |
| | (0.109) | | (0.077) | |
| Δ Service$_{i, t}$ | −0.002 | * | −0.002 | * |
| | (0.001) | | (0.001) | |
| Service$_{i, t-1}$ | 0.005 | | −0.004 | |
| | (0.003) | | (0.003) | |
| Δ GDP Growth$_{i, t}$ | 0.001 | | 0.003 | |
| | (0.007) | | (0.005) | |
| GDP Growth$_{i, t-1}$ | −0.005 | | −0.002 | |
| | (0.006) | | (0.004) | |
| Δ Rural pop$_{i, t}$ | 0.003 | | 0.002 | |
| | (0.003) | | (0.002) | |
| Rural pop$_{i, t-1}$ | 0.000 | | 0.000 | |
| | (0.002) | | (0.002) | |

Table A7.3 *(cont.)*

| Dependent Variable | Δ Court Funding per capita (*yuan*/person) | | Δ Court Funding/Total Expenditure (%) | |
|---|---|---|---|---|
| Variable | Coefficient (P.C.S.E) | | Coefficient (P.C.S.E) | |
| Δ Population$_{i,t}$ (log) | −0.915 | | −0.391 | |
| | (1.663) | | (1.089) | |
| Population$_{i,-1t}$ (log) | −0.237 | | −0.186 | |
| | (0.453) | | (0.301) | |
| Δ Cases$_{i,t}$ (log) | 0.032 | | 0.014 | |
| | (0.057) | | (0.041) | |
| Cases$_{i,t-1}$ (log) | 0.053 | | 0.021 | |
| | (0.070) | | (0.048) | |
| Δ Law Office$_{i,t}$ (log) | 0.135 | * | 0.087 | |
| | (0.081) | | (0.057) | |
| Law Office$_{i,t-1}$ (log) | 0.217 | * | 0.140 | * |
| | (0.109) | | (0.074) | |
| Δ Lawyers$_{i,t}$ (log) | 0.002 | | 0.015 | |
| | (0.056) | | (0.040) | |
| Lawyers$_{i,t-1}$ (log) | 0.021 | | 0.041 | |
| | (0.056) | | (0.041) | |
| Province Fixed Effects | YES | | YES | |
| Year Fixed Effects | YES | | YES | |
| Intercept | −0.705 | | 2.349 | |
| | (3.914) | | (2.703) | |
| N | 340 | | 340 | |

P-values are based on two-tailed tests: *** p<0.01; ** p<0.05; * p<0.10.
*Source:* Data set compiled by the author

national policy shift. Finally, $\gamma_i$ is the unit fixed effect, which consists of province dummy variables. These dummies take into account unexplained regional heterogeneity – for example, historical factors. $\varepsilon_{i,t}$ is the error term.

Pooled OLS regressions with panel-corrected standard errors are used to estimate Equation A7.1. An advantage of the ECM is that it makes calculations of both short- and long-term effects easier. While short-run effects can be directly estimated using ECM, long-term effects require more calculus.

# References

Achen, Christopher H. 2000. "Why Lagged Dependent Variables Can Suppress the Explanatory Power of Other Independent Variables." Paper presented at the Annual Meeting of the Political Methodology Section of the American Political Science Association, Los Angeles, CA, July, 20–22.

Apodaca, Clair. 2002. "The Globalization of Capital in East and Southeast Asia: Measuring the Impact on Human Rights Standards." *Asian Survey* 42 (6):883–905.

Arping, Stefan, and Zacharias Sautner. 2010. "Did the Sarbanes-Oxley Act of 2002 Make Firms Less Opaque? Evidence from Analyst Earnings Forecasts." Tinbergen Institute Discussion Papers, Tinbergen Institute,

Bardhan, Pranab. 1997. "Corruption and Development: A Review of Issues." *Journal of Economic Literature* 35 (3):1320–1346.

Barro, Robert J. 1997. *Determinants of Economic Growth: A Cross-Country Empirical Study*. Cambridge: MIT Press.

2000. "Rule of Law, Democracy, and Economic Performance." In *2000 Index of Economic Freedom*, edited by Kim R. Holmes, Melanie Kirkpatrick, and Gerald P. O'Driscoll, 31–49. Washington, DC: The Heritage Foundation.

Bates, Robert H., and Donald Da-Hsiang Lien. 1985. "A Note on Taxation, Development, and Representative Government." *Politics and Society* 14 (1):53–70.

Baum, Richard. 1994. *Burying Mao: Chinese Politics in the Age of Deng Xiaoping*. Princeton: Princeton University Press.

Borensztein, E., J. De Gregorio, and J.-W. Lee. 1998. "How Does Foreign Direct Investment Affect Economic Growth?" *Journal of International Economics* 45 (1):115–135.

Bueno de Mesquita, Bruce, Alastair Smith, Randolph M. Siverson, and James D. Morrow. 2003. *The Logic of Political Survival*. Cambridge: MIT Press.

Burns, John P. 1989. *The Chinese Communist Party's Nomenklatura System: A Documentary Study of Party Control of Leadership Selection, 1979–1984*. Armonk: M. E. Sharpe.

Cai, Hongbin, Hanming Fang, and Lixin Colin Xu. 2011. "Eat, Drink, Firms, Government: An Investigation of Corruption from the Entertainment and Travel Costs of Chinese Firms." *Journal of Law and Economics* 54 (1):55–78.

Cameron, A. Colin, and Pravin K. Trivedi. 1990. "The Information Matrix Test and Its Applied Alternative Hypotheses." Davis, CA: Institute of Governmental Affairs, University of California, Davis.

———. 2005. *Microeconometrics: Methods and Applications.* New York: Cambridge University Press.

Cao, Xun, and Aseem Prakash. 2010. "Trade Competition and Domestic Pollution: A Panel Study, 1980–2003." *International Organization* 64 (3):481–503.

Carmen, Rolando V. del. 1973. "Constitutionalism and the Supreme Court in a Changing Philippine Polity." *Asian Survey* 13 (11):1050–1061.

Carothers, Thomas. 1998. "The Rule of Law Revival." *Foreign Affairs* 77:95–106.

Chin, Ko-lin. 2003. *Heijin: Organized Crime, Business, and Politics in Taiwan.* London: M. E. Sharpe.

Cho, Young Nam. 2003. "Symbiotic Neighbour or Extra-Court Judge? The Supervision over Courts by Chinese Local People's Congresses." *China Quarterly* 176:1068–1083.

Clarke, Donald C. 2007. "Legislating for a Market Economy in China." *China Quarterly* 191:567–585.

Clarke, Donald C., Peter Murrell, and Susan H. Whiting. 2008. "The Role of Law in China's Economic Development." In *The Great Transformation: China's Economy since Reform*, edited by Loren Brandt and Thomas Rawski, 375–428. New York: Cambridge University Press.

Cook, R. Dennis. 1977. "Detection of Influential Observation in Linear Regression." *Technometrics* 19 (1):15–18.

De Boef, Suzanna, and Luke Keele. 2008. "Taking Time Seriously." *American Journal of Political Science* 52 (1):184–200.

de Soysa, Indra, and John R. Oneal. 1999. "Boon or Bane? Reassessing the Productivity of Foreign Direct Investment." *American Sociological Review* 64 (5):766–782.

Delios, Andrew, and Witold J. Henisz. 2003. "Political Hazards, Experience, and Sequential Entry Strategies: The International Expansion of Japanese Firms, 1980–1998." *Strategic Management Journal* 24 (11):1153–1164.

Desbordes, Rodolphe, and Vincent Vicard. 2009. "Foreign Direct Investment and Bilateral Investment Treaties: An International Political Perspective." *Journal of Comparative Economics* 37 (3):372–386.

Diamond, Alexis, and Jasjeet S. Sekhon. 2013. "Genetic Matching for Estimating Causal Effects: A General Multivariate Matching Method for Achieving Balance in Observational Studies." *Review of Economics and Statistics* 95 (3):932–945.

Dicey, Albert Venn. 1915. *Introduction to the Study of the Law of the Constitution.* London: Macmillan.

Dickson, Bruce J. 2003. *Red Capitalists in China: The Party, Private Entrepreneurs, and Prospects for Political Change.* New York: Cambridge University Press.

Elkins, Zachary, Andrew T. Guzman, and Beth A. Simmons. 2006. "Competing for Capital: The Diffusion of Bilateral Investment Treaties, 1960–2000." *International Organization* 60 (4):811–846.

Evans, Peter B. 1995. *Embedded Autonomy: States and Industrial Transformation.* Princeton: Princeton University Press.

Fei, Xiaotong. 1998. *Rural China, Family Institutions (Xiangtu Zhongguo, Shengyu Zhidu).* Beijing: Peking University Press (Beijing Daxue Chubanshe).

Feld, Lars P., and Stefan Voigt. 2003. "Economic Growth and Judicial Independence: Cross-Country Evidence Using a New Set of Indicators." *European Journal of Political Economy* 19 (3):497–527.

Ferejohn, John A., and Barry R. Weingast. 1992. "A Positive Theory of Statutory Interpretation." *International Review of Law and Economics* 12:263–279.

Finkel, Jodi S. 2008. *Judicial Reform as Political Insurance: Argentina, Peru, and Mexico in the 1990s.* Notre Dame: University of Notre Dame Press.

Freeman, John R. 1983. "Granger Causality and the Times Series Analysis of Political Relationships." *American Journal of Political Science* 27 (2):327–358.

Freeman, John R., John T. Williams, and T. Lin. 1989. "Vector Autoregression and the Study of Politics." *American Journal of Political Science* 33 (4):842–877.

Friedrich, Carl J., and Zbigniew Brzezinski. 1965. *Totalitarian Dictatorship and Autocracy.* Cambridge: Harvard University Press.

Frye, Timothy, and Ekaterina Zhuravskaya. 2000. "Rackets, Regulation, and the Rule of Law." *Journal of Law, Economics, and Organization* 16 (2):478–502.

Fu, Jun. 2000. *Institutions and Investments: Foreign Direct Investment in China during an Era of Reforms.* Ann Arbor: University of Michigan Press.

Gallagher, Mary E. 2002. "'Reform and Openness': Why China's Economic Reforms Have Delayed Democracy." *World Politics* 54 (3):338–372.

2005. *Contagious Capitalism: Globalization and the Politics of Labor in China.* Princeton: Princeton University Press.

2010. "Bottom-Up Enforcement: Legal Mobilization as Law Enforcement in the PRC." Paper presented at the Annual Meeting of the American Political Science Association, Washington, DC, September 2–5.

Gallagher, Mary E., and Yuhua Wang. 2011. "Users and Non-Users: Legal Experience and Its Effect on Legal Consciousness." In *Chinese Justice: Civil Dispute Resolution in Contemporary China*, edited by Margaret Woo and Mary E. Gallagher, 204–233. New York: Cambridge University Press.

Gambetta, Diego. 1993. *The Sicilian Mafia: The Business of Private Protection.* Cambridge: Harvard University Press.

Garrett, Geoffrey. 1998. *Partisan Politics in the Global Economy.* New York: Cambridge University Press.

Ginsburg, Tom. 2002. "Confucian Constitutionalism? The Emergence of Constitutional Review in Korea and Taiwan." *Law and Social Inquiry* 27 (4):763–799.

Ginsburg, Tom, and Tamir Moustafa. 2008. *Rule by Law: The Politics of Courts in Authoritarian Regimes.* New York: Cambridge University Press.

Gong, Ting. 2004. "Dependent Judiciary and Unaccountable Judges: Judicial Corruption in Contemporary China." *China Review* 4 (2):33–54.

Graber, Mark A. 1993. "The Nonmajoritarian Difficulty: Legislative Deference to the Judiciary." *Studies in American Political Development* 7 (1):35–73.

Grzymala-Busse, Anna. 2008. "Beyond Clientelism." *Comparative Political Studies* 41 (4–5):638–673.

Guo, Gang. 2009. "China's Local Political Budget Cycles." *American Journal of Political Science* 53 (3):621–632.

Guthrie, Doug. 1999. *Dragon in a Three-Piece Suit: The Emergence of Capitalism in China*. Princeton: Princeton University Press.

Haggard, Stephan. 1990. *Pathways from the Periphery: The Politics of Growth in the Newly Industrializing Countries*. Ithaca: Cornell University Press.

Hayek, Friedrich A. von. 1994. *The Road to Serfdom*. Chicago: University of Chicago Press.

He, Weifang. 1998. "Fuzhuan Junren Jin Fayuan" [Retired Military Officers Entering Courts]. *Nanfang Zhoumo [Southern Weekend]*, January 2.

He, Xin. 2008. "Zhongguo Fayuan de Caizheng Buzu yu Sifa Fubai" [Lack of Financial Resources and Judicial Corruption in Chinese Courts]. *Ershiyi Shiji [Twenty-First Century Review]* 105:12–23.

Hellman, Joel S. 1998. "Winners Take All: The Politics of Partial Reform in Postcommunist Transitions." *World Politics* 50 (2):203–234.

Helmke, Gretchen. 2002. "The Logic of Strategic Defection: Court-Executive Relations in Argentina under Dictatorship and Democracy." *American Political Science Review* 96 (2):291–303.

Helmke, Gretchen, and Frances Rosenbluth. 2009. "Regimes and the Rule of Law: Judicial Independence in Comparative Perspective." *Annual Review of Political Science* 12:345–366.

Hendley, Kathryn. 2001. "'Demand' for Law in Russia—A Mixed Picture." *East European Constitutional Review* 10 (4):73–78.

Henisz, Witold J. 2000. "The Institutional Environment for Multinational Investment." *Journal of Law, Economics, and Organization* 16 (2):334–364.

Hirschman, Albert O. 1970. *Exit, Voice, and Loyalty: Responses to Decline in Firms, Organizations, and States*. Cambridge: Harvard University Press.

Hoff, Karla, and Joseph E. Stiglitz. 2004. "The Transition from Communism: A Diagrammatic Exposition of Obstacles to the Demand for the Rule of Law." World Bank Working Paper, World Bank, Washington, DC.

Hsueh, Roselyn. 2011. *China's Regulatory State: A New Strategy for Globalization*. Ithaca: Cornell University Press.

Huang, Yasheng. 1998. *FDI in China: An Asian Perspective*. Hong Kong: Chinese University Press.

——— 2003. *Selling China: Foreign Direct Investment during the Reform Era*. New York: Cambridge University Press.

——— 2008. *Capitalism with Chinese Characteristics: Entrepreneurship and the State*. New York: Cambridge University Press.

Jensen, Michael C., and William H. Meckling. 1976. "Theory of the Firm: Managerial Behavior, Agency Costs and Ownership Structure." *Journal of Financial Economics* 3 (4):305–360.

Johnson, Chalmers A. 1982. *MITI and the Japanese Miracle: The Growth of Industrial Policy, 1925–1975*. Stanford: Stanford University Press.

Kang, David C. 2002. *Crony Capitalism: Corruption and Development in South Korea and the Philippines*. New York: Cambridge University Press.

Kaufman, Robert R., and Alex Segura-Ubiergo. 2001. "Globalization, Domestic Politics, and Social Spending in Latin America: A Time-Series Cross-Section Analysis, 1973–97." *World Politics* 53 (4):553–587.

Kaufmann, Daniel, Aart Kraay, and Massimo Mastruzzi. 2009. "Governance Matters VIII: Aggregate and Individual Governance Indicators, 1996–2008." World Bank Policy Research Working Paper No. 4978, World Bank, Washington, DC.

Keefer, Philip, and Stephen Knack. 1997. "Why Don't Poor Countries Catch Up? A Cross-National Test of an Institutional Explanation." *Economic Inquiry* 35 (3):590–602.

Keele, Luke. 2005. "Macro Measures and Mechanics of Social Capital." *Political Analysis* 13 (2):139–156.

Kennedy, Scott. 2009. "Comparing Formal and Informal Lobbying Practices in China." *China Information* 23 (2):195–222.

Kerner, Andrew. 2009. "Why Should I Believe You? The Costs and Consequences of Bilateral Investment Treaties." *International Studies Quarterly* 53 (1):73–102.

King, Gary, James Honaker, Anne Joseph, and Kenneth Scheve. 2001. "Analyzing Incomplete Political Science Data: An Alternative Algorithm for Multiple Imputation." *American Political Science Review* 95 (1):49–69.

Knack, Stephen 2006. "Measuring Corruption in Eastern Europe and Central Asia: A Critique of the Cross-Country Indicators." World Bank Policy Research Working Paper, World Bank, Washington DC.

Koehler, Mike. 2007. "The Unique FCPA Compliance Challenges of Doing Business in China." *Wisconsin International Law Journal* 25:397–438.

Kohli, Atul. 2004. *State-Directed Development: Political Power and Industrialization in the Global Periphery*. New York: Cambridge University Press.

Kornai, János. 2008. *From Socialism to Capitalism: Eight Essays*. New York: Central European University Press.

La Porta, Rafael, Florencio Lopez-De-Silanes, Andrei Shleifer, and Robert W. Vishny. 1997. "Legal Determinants of External Finance." *Journal of Finance* 52 (3):1131–1150.

1998. "Law and Finance." *Journal of Political Economy* 106 (6):1113–1155.

Landes, William M., and Richard A. Posner. 1975. "The Independent Judiciary in an Interest-Group Perspective." *Journal of Law and Economics* 18 (3):875–901.

Landry, Pierre F. 2008. *Decentralized Authoritarianism in China: The Communist Party's Control of Local Elites in the Post-Mao Era*. New York: Cambridge University Press.

2011. "The Impact of Nationalist and Maoist Legacies on Popular Trust in Legal Institutions." In *Chinese Justice: Civil Dispute Resolution in Contemporary China*, edited by Margaret Woo and Mary E. Gallagher, 139–168. New York: Cambridge University Press.

Landry, Pierre F., and Mingming Shen. 2005. "Reaching Migrants in Survey Research: The Use of the Global Positioning System to Reduce Coverage Bias in China." *Political Analysis* 13 (1):1–22.

Lau, Lawrence J., Yingyi Qian, and Gerard Roland. 2000. "Reform without Losers: An Interpretation of China's Dual-Track Approach to Transition." *Journal of Political Economy* 108 (1):120–143.

Leblang, David A. 1996. "Property Rights, Democracy and Economic Growth." *Political Research Quarterly* 49 (1):5–26.

Levi, Margaret. 1988. *Of Rule and Revenue*. Berkeley: University of California Press.

Li, Hongbin, Lingsheng Meng, Qian Wang, and Li-An Zhou. 2008. "Political Connections, Financing and Firm Performance: Evidence from Chinese Private Firms." *Journal of Development Economics* 87 (2):283–299.

Li, Lianjiang. 2004. "Political Trust in Rural China." *Modern China* 30 (2):228–258.

Li, Ling. 2010. "Corruption in China's Courts." In *Judicial Independence in China: Lessons for Global Rule of Law Promotion*, edited by Randall P. Peerenboom, 196–220. New York: Cambridge University Press.

2011. "Performing Bribery in China: Guanxi-Practice, Corruption with a Human Face." *Journal of Contemporary China* 20 (68):1–20.

Lieberthal, Kenneth. 2004. *Governing China: From Revolution through Reform*. New York: W. W. Norton.

Lindblom, Charles Edward. 1977. *Politics and Markets: The World's Political Economic Systems*. New York: Basic Books.

Lu, Susan Feng, and Yang Yao. 2009. "The Effectiveness of Law, Financial Development, and Economic Growth in an Economy of Financial Repression: Evidence from China." *World Development* 37 (4):763–777.

Malesky, Edmund J. 2008. "Straight Ahead on Red: How Foreign Direct Investment Empowers Subnational Leaders." *Journal of Politics* 70 (1):97–119.

Manion, Melanie. 1985. "The Cadre Management System, Post-Mao: The Appointment, Promotion, Transfer and Removal of Party and State Leaders." *China Quarterly* 102:203–233.

2004. *Corruption by Design: Building Clean Government in Mainland China and Hong Kong*. Cambridge: Harvard University Press.

Mann, Jim. 1989. *Beijing Jeep: The Short, Unhappy Romance of American Business in China*. New York: Simon and Schuster.

Marshall, Monty G., and Keith Jaggers. 2009. *Polity IV Project: Political Regime Characteristics and Transitions, 1800–2009*. College Park, MD: Center for International Development and Conflict Management, University of Maryland.

McCubbins, Mathew D., and Thomas Schwartz. 1984. "Congressional Oversight Overlooked: Police Patrols versus Fire Alarms." *American Journal of Political Science* 28 (1):165–179.

Merryman, John Henry. 1977. "Comparative Law and Social Change: On the Origins, Style, Decline and Revival of the Law and Development Movement." *American Journal of Comparative Law* 25 (3):457–491.

Michelson, Ethan, and Benjamin Read. 2011. "Public Attitudes toward Official Justice in Beijing and Rural China." In *Chinese Justice: Civil Dispute Resolution in Contemporary China*, edited by Margaret Woo and Mary E. Gallagher, 169–203. New York: Cambridge University Press.

Ministry of Finance of People's Republic of China. Various years. *Difang Caizheng Tongji Ziliao* [*Statistical Reports of Local Finance*]. Beijing: China Financial Economics Press (Zhongguo Cai Zheng Jingji Chubanshe).

Minzner, Carl F. 2011. "China's Turn against Law." *American Journal of Comparative Law* 59 (4):935–984.

Moran, Theodore H. 1978. "Multinational Corporations and Dependency: A Dialogue for Dependentistas and Non-Dependentistas." *International Organization* 32 (1):79–100.

Mosley, Layna, and Saika Uno. 2007. "Racing to the Bottom or Climbing to the Top? Economic Globalization and Collective Labor Rights." *Comparative Political Studies* 40 (8):923–948.

Moulton, Brent R. 1990. "An Illustration of a Pitfall in Estimating the Effects of Aggregate Variables on Micro Units." *Review of Economics and Statistics* 72 (2):334–338.

Moustafa, Tamir. 2007. *The Struggle for Constitutional Power: Law, Politics, and Economic Development in Egypt*. New York: Cambridge University Press.

National Bureau of Statistics of People's Republic of China. Various years. *Zhongguo Tongji Nianjian [Statistical Yearbooks of China]*. Beijing: China Statistics Press (Zhongguo Tongji Chubanshe).

Naughton, Barry. 2007. *The Chinese Economy: Transitions and Growth*. Cambridge: MIT Press.

Neumayer, Eric, and Indra de Soysa. 2006. "Globalization and the Right to Free Association and Collective Bargaining: An Empirical Analysis." *World Development* 34 (1):31–49.

Neumayer, Eric, and Laura Spess. 2005. "Do Bilateral Investment Treaties Increase Foreign Direct Investment to Developing Countries?" *World Development* 33 (10):1567–1585.

North, Douglass. 1981. *Structure and Change in Economic History*. New York: W. W. Norton.

   1990. *Institutions, Institutional Change, and Economic Performance*. New York: Cambridge University Press.

North, Douglass, and Robert Paul Thomas. 1973. *The Rise of the Western World: A New Economic History*. Cambridge: Cambridge University Press.

North, Douglass, and Barry R. Weingast. 1989. "Constitutions and Commitment: The Evolution of Institutions Governing Public Choice in Seventeenth-Century England." *Journal of Economic History* 49 (4):803–832.

O'Brien, Kevin, and Lianjiang Li. 1999. "Selective Policy Implementation in Rural China." *Comparative Politics* 31 (2):167–186.

Oi, Jean C. 1992. "Fiscal Reform and the Economic Foundations of Local State Corporatism in China." *World Politics* 45 (1):99–126.

Oliva, Maria-Angels, and Luis A. Rivera-Batiz. 2002. "Political Institutions, Capital Flows, and Developing Country Growth: An Empirical Investigation." *Review of Development Economics* 6 (2):248–262.

Olson, Mancur. 1965. *The Logic of Collective Action: Public Goods and the Theory of Groups*. Cambridge: Harvard University Press.

   2000. *Power and Prosperity: Outgrowing Communist and Capitalist Dictatorships*. New York: Basic Books.

Ostrom, Elinor. 1998. "A Behavioral Approach to the Rational Choice Theory of Collective Action: Presidential Address, American Political Science Association, 1997." *American Political Science Review* 92 (1):1–22.

Pearson, Margaret M. 1991. *Joint Ventures in the People's Republic of China: The Control of Foreign Direct Investment under Socialism*. Princeton: Princeton University Press.

Pedersen, Eric M. 2008. "Foreign Corrupt Practices Act and Its Application to U.S. Business Operations in China." *Journal of International Business and Law* 7 (13):13–48.

Peerenboom, Randall P. 2002. *China's Long March toward Rule of Law*. New York: Cambridge University Press.

———. 2007. *China Modernizes: Threat to the West or Model for the Rest?* New York: Oxford University Press.

Pei, Minxin. 2006. *China's Trapped Transition: The Limits of Developmental Autocracy*. Cambridge: Harvard University Press.

Pinheiro, Paulo Sergio. 1999. "The Rule of Law and the Underprivileged in Latin America." In *The (Un)Rule of Law and the Underprivileged in Latin America*, edited by Juan E. Mendez, Guillermo O'Donnell, and Paulo Sergio Pinheiro, 1–18. Notre Dame: University of Notre Dame Press.

Pinto, Pablo M., and Boliang Zhu. 2008. "Fortune or Evil? The Effect of Inward Foreign Direct Investment on Corruption." Paper presented at the Annual Conference of the American Political Science Association, Boston, MA, June 23.

Popova, Maria. 2010. "Political Competition as an Obstacle to Judicial Independence: Evidence from Russia and Ukraine." *Comparative Political Studies* 43 (10):1202–1229.

Qian, Yingyi. 2003. "How Reform Worked in China." In *Analytic Narratives on Economic Growth*, edited by Dani Rodrik, 297–333. Princeton: Princeton University Press.

Ramseyer, J. Mark, and Eric B. Rasmusen. 1997. "Judicial Independence in a Civil Law Regime: The Evidence from Japan." *Journal of Law, Economics, and Organization* 13 (2):259–286.

Rigobon, Roberto, and Dani Rodrik. 2005. "Rule of Law, Democracy, Openness, and Income." *Economics of Transition* 13 (3):533–564.

Rodrik, Dani. 1996. "Understanding Economic Policy Reform." *Journal of Economic Literature* 34 (1):9–41.

Roland, Gérard. 2000. *Transition and Economics: Politics, Markets, and Firms*. Cambridge: MIT Press.

Rosen, Daniel H. 1999. *Behind the Open Door: Foreign Enterprises in the Chinese Marketplace*. Washington, DC: Institute for International Economics.

Rudra, Nita. 2002. "Globalization and the Decline of the Welfare State in Less-Developed Countries." *International Organization* 56 (2):411–445.

———. 2005. "Globalization and the Strengthening of Democracy in the Developing World." *American Journal of Political Science* 49 (4):704–730.

Salzberger, Eli M. 1993. "A Positive Analysis of the Doctrine of Separation of Powers, or: Why Do We Have an Independent Judiciary?" *International Review of Law and Economics* 13 (4):349–379.

Sandholtz, Wayne, and Mark M. Gray. 2003. "International Integration and National Corruption." *International Organization* 57 (4):761–800.

Santoro, Michael A. 2000. *Profits and Principles: Global Capitalism and Human Rights in China*. Ithaca: Cornell University Press.

Schattschneider, E. E. 1960. *The Semisovereign People: A Realist's View of Democracy in America*. New York: Holt, Rinehart and Winston.

Scheve, Kenneth, and Matthew J. Slaughter. 2004. "Economic Insecurity and the Globalization of Production." *American Journal of Political Science* 48 (4):662–674.

Shen, Mingming, and Yuhua Wang. 2009. "Litigating Economic Disputes in Rural China." *China Review* 9 (1):97–122.

Sheng, Yumin. 2007. "Global Market Integration and Central Political Control: Foreign Trade and Intergovernmental Relations in China." *Comparative Political Studies* 40 (4):405–434.

Shih, Victor, Christopher Adolph, and Mingxing Liu. 2012. "Getting Ahead in the Communist Party: Explaining the Advancement of Central Committee Members in China." *American Political Science Review* 106 (1):166–187.

Shipan, Charles R. 1997. *Designing Judicial Review: Interest Groups, Congress, and Communications Policy*. Ann Arbor: University of Michigan Press.

Sonin, Konstantin. 2003. "Why the Rich May Favor Poor Protection of Property Rights." *Journal of Comparative Economics* 31 (4):715–731.

Steinfeld, Edward S. 1998. *Forging Reform in China: The Fate of State-Owned Industry*. New York: Cambridge University Press.

Su, Li. 2000. *Song Fa Xia Xiang: Zhongguo Jiceng Sifa Zhidu Yanjiu* [*Sending Law to the Countryside: A Study of Chinese Local Legal Institutions*]. Beijing: Chinese Political and Law University Press (Zhongguo Zhengfa Daxue Chubanshe).

Supreme People's Court. Research Department. 2000. *Quanguo Renmin Fayuan Sifa Tongji Lishi Ziliao Huibian (1949–1998)* [*Compiled Historical Materials of Legal Statistics on Nation-Wide People's Courts (1949–1998)*]. Beijing: People's Court Press (Renmin Fayuan Chubanshe).

Sutil, Jorge Correa. 1999. "Judicial Reforms in Latin America: Good News for the Underprivileged?" In *The (Un)Rule of Law and the Underprivileged in Latin America*, edited by Juan E. Mendez, Guillermo O'Donnell, and Paulo Sergio Pinheiro, 255–277. Notre Dame: University of Notre Dame Press.

Tamanaha, Brian Z. 2004. *On the Rule of Law: History, Politics, Theory*. New York: Cambridge University Press.

Tilly, Charles. 1990. *Coercion, Capital, and European States, AD 990–1990*. Cambridge: B. Blackwell.

Transparency International. 2007. *Global Corruption Report 2007: Corruption in Judicial Systems*. New York: Cambridge University Press.

Treisman, Daniel. 2007. "What Have We Learned about the Causes of Corruption from Ten Years of Cross-National Empirical Research?" *Annual Review of Political Science* 10:211–244.

Tsai, Kellee S. 2007a. *Capitalism without Democracy: The Private Sector in Contemporary China*. Ithaca: Cornell University Press.

Tsai, Lily L. 2007b. *Accountability without Democracy: Solidary Groups and Public Goods Provision in Rural China*. New York: Cambridge University Press.

Vernon, Raymond. 1971. *Sovereignty at Bay: The Multinational Spread of U.S. Enterprises*. London: Longman.

Voigt, Stepan. 1998. "Making Constitutions Work: Conditions for Maintaining The Rule of Law." *Cato Journal* 18 (2):191–208.

Volcansek, Mary L., Maria Elisabetta De Franciscis, and Jacqueline Lucienne Lafon. 1996. *Judicial Misconduct: A Cross-National Comparison*. Gainesville: University Press of Florida.

Walder, Andrew G. 1986. *Communist Neo-Traditionalism: Work and Authority in Chinese Industry*. Berkeley: University of California Press.

Wang, Qian, T. J. Wong, and Lijun Xia. 2008. "State Ownership, the Institutional Environment, and Auditor Choice: Evidence from China." *Journal of Accounting and Economics* 46 (1):112–134.

Wang, Yaxin. 2010. "Sifa Chengben yu Sifa Xiaolu" [Legal Costs and Legal Efficiency]. *Faxuejia [Legal Scholars]* 1(4):132–137.

Wang, Yuhua. 2013. "Court Funding and Judicial Corruption in China." *China Journal* 69:43–63.

Wank, David L. 1999. *Commodifying Communism: Business, Trust, and Politics in a Chinese City*. New York: Cambridge University Press.

Warin, Joseph F., Michael S. Diamant, and Jill M. Pfenning. 2010. "FCPA Compliance in China and the Gifts and Hospitality Challenge." *Virginia Law and Business Review* 5 (1):33–80.

Wedeman, Andrew Hall. 2003. *From Mao to Market: Rent Seeking, Local Protectionism, and Marketization in China*. New York: Cambridge University Press.

Weingast, Barry R. 1997. "The Political Foundations of Democracy and the Rule of Law." *American Political Science Review* 91 (2):245–263.

Whiting, Susan H. 2001. *Power and Wealth in Rural China: The Political Economy of Institutional Change*. New York: Cambridge University Press.

2004. "The Cadre Evaluation System at the Grassroots: The Paradox of Party Rule." In *Holding China Together: Diversity and National Integration in the Post-Deng Era*, edited by Barry Naughton and Yang Dali, 101–119. New York: Cambridge University Press.

Whittington, Keith E. 1999. *Constitutional Construction: Divided Powers and Constitutional Meaning*. Cambridge: Harvard University Press.

2009. *Political Foundations of Judicial Supremacy: The Presidency, the Supreme Court, and Constitutional Leadership in U. S. History*. Princeton: Princeton University Press.

Widner, Jennifer A. 2001. *Building the Rule of Law*. New York: W. W. Norton.

Wintrobe, Ronald. 2000. *The Political Economy of Dictatorship*. New York: Cambridge University Press.

Woo-Cumings, Meredith. 1999. *The Developmental State*. Ithaca: Cornell University Press.

World Bank. 2007. *Governance, Investment Climate, and Harmonious Society*. Washington DC: World Bank.

Wu, Jinglian. 2005. *Understanding and Interpreting Chinese Economic Reform*. Mason: Thomson/South-Western.

Yan, Jie, Pierre F. Landry, and Liying Ren. 2009. "GPS in China Social Surveys: Lessons from the ILRC Survey." *China Review* 9 (1):147–163.

Zeng, Ka, and Josh Eastin. 2007. "International Economic Integration and Environmental Protection: The Case of China." *International Studies Quarterly* 51 (4):971–995.

Zhu, Jiangnan, Jie Lu, and Tianjian Shi. 2013. "When Grapevine News Meets Mass Media: Different Information Sources and Perceptions of Government Corruption in Mainland China." *Comparative Political Studies* 46 (8):920–946.

Zhu, Jingwen. 2007. *Zhongguo Falv Fazhan Baogao: Shujuku He Zhibiao Tixi [Report on China Law Development: Database and Indicators]*. Beijing: Renmin University Press (Zhongguo Renmin Daxue Chubanshe).

Zhu, Rongji. 2011. *Zhu Rongji Jianghua Shilu [A Collection of Zhu Rongji's Speeches]*. Beijing: People Publishing House (Renmin Chubanshe).

# Index